D1234307

EDWARD VII
AND THE
ENTENTE CORDIALE

EDWARD VII
AND THE
ENTENTE CORDIALE

IAN DUNLOP

CONSTABLE • LONDON

Constable & Robinson Ltd
3 The Lanchesters
162 Fulham Palace Road
London W6 9ER
www.constablerobinson.com

First published in the UK by Constable,
an imprint of Constable & Robinson Ltd, 2004

A copy of the British Library Cataloguing in
Publication Data is available from the British Library

ISBN 1-84119-530-8

Printed and bound in the EU

To
DEIRDRE
With all my love

Contents

List of Illustrations	ix
Acknowledgements	xi
Preface	xiii
Louis-Philippe and the Failure of the First *Entente Cordiale*	1
The Young Prince of Wales	27
Napoleon III and the Franco-Prussian War	41
The Third Republic	61
Théophile Delcassé	85
Fashoda	119
Sir Thomas Barclay and the Death of Queen Victoria	143
King at Last	167
A Tour in Europe, May 1903	193
The Signing of the *Entente*	213
Morocco and the Fall of Delcassé	229
'Uncle of Europe'	257
The Death of King Edward	275
Epilogue: Europe Goes to War	293
Bibliography & Sources	303
Index	307

Illustrations

Plates

Louis Philippe with Queen Victoria and Prince Albert (*British Museum Photogaphs*)

Victoria arriving at the Château d'Eu (*The Royal Collection* © 2003, *Her Majesty Queen Elizabeth II*)

Henri, 8th Marquis de Breteuil (*Permission courtesy of 10th Marquis de Breteuil*)

Henry Petty-Fitzmaurice, 5th Marquess of Lansdowne (*Courtesy of Balliol College, Oxford*)

Sir James Reid (*Permission courtesy of Sir Alexander Reid*)

Henry Wickham Steed (*Times Newspapers Limited*)

Prince Edward and Princess Alexandra of Denmark, newly married (© *Getty images*)

Kaiser Wilhelm II by Max Koner (*Bildarchiv Preßischer Kulturbesitz*)

Spencer Cavendish, 8th Duke of Devonshire (*By courtesy of the National Portrait Gallery, London*)

Robert Cecil, 3rd Marquess of Salisbury (*By courtesy of the National Portrait Gallery, London*)

Algernon Freeman-Mitford, 1st Baron Redesdale (*By courtesy of the National Portrait Gallery, London*)

King Edward VII *(Private Collection)*
The Coronation of Edward VII *(By courtesy of the National Portrait Gallery, London)*
The reception of President Loubet *(The Royal Collection © 2003, Her Majesty Queen Elizabeth II)*

Cartoons
The end of Bismark's regime   100
The spirit of Fashoda   117
Un dîner en famille   132
Travelling third class   141
No changes   174
The *Entente Cordiale*   208
Friends   208
Links of friendship   272

Acknowledgements

I would like to express my gratitude to my wife Deirdre, to whom this book is dedicated, for her sound advice and accurate proof reading.

I would like also to thank M. Xavier North, former Conseiller Culturel at the French Embassy, who suggested my writing this book; his successor M. Nicolas Chapuis; Mme Chantal Morel at the Institut Français in London, for much help and advice; the marquis de Breteuil, grandson of one of King Edward's greatest friends, for his help and encouragement and for providing the photograph of his grandfather; the Lady Emma Tennant, great-granddaughter of Lord Redesdale, another close friend of Edward's, for her help with the illustrations; Mr Charles Noble LVO, Keeper of the Collections at Chatsworth; Sir Alexander Reid, grandson of Sir James Reid, who attended both Queen Victoria and King Edward on their deathbeds, for the photograph of his grandfather, and Lady Reid for permission to quote extensively from her biography entitled *Ask Sir James*.

I am most grateful also to the staff of the National Library of Scotland who have been unfailingly helpful and especially to Christopher Taylor, Curator responsible for the French and Italian division; to Christopher Sinclair-Stevenson, who has published most of my books and is now my literary agent; to Susan Owens, Assistant

Curator of the Royal Collection at Windsor; to Dr John Jones of Balliol College for providing the portrait of Lord Lansdowne; to Professor Muriel Chamberlain for permission to quote from her D. Phil thesis on Lord Aberdeen; to Dr Frank Sengpiel and Dr Jost Rebentisch for help with German illustrations; to Dr Jean-Marie Bertin, Lord Baker of Dorking and David Batterham for help and advice on French cartoons.

Finally I would like to thank Lieutenant-Colonel and Mrs Robert Reid for their unfailing hospitality in the Tower of London.

Preface

Comme quelqu'un pourrait dire de moi que j'ai seulement fait ici un amas de fleurs étrangères, n'ayant fourni du mien que le filet à les lier.

One might say of me that all I have done here is to make a bouquet of other men's flowers, and have provided of my own only the thread which binds them together.

Michel de Montaigne

I begin with this quotation because it does, to a large extent, describe my approach to this subject. The thread which ties my flowers together represents my attempt to arrange my material in a lucid and readable manner. But it is also in my selection of the material used that I offer my reader something of my own.

It has been for me a fascinating experience to do the research for this book. One of the things which has struck me most is the importance – the vital importance of personalities. It was not the political insights of Edward VII that enabled him to pave the way for the *Entente Cordiale*. It was his personality, his gift for listening, his skill as a speaker, together with his perfect command of French, his ability, which was almost a charisma, to get across to a wide range of people, that made him so effective. After his three-day visit to President Loubet in Paris in 1903, the crowds – initially hostile – were shouting '*Vive notre roi!*'

Edward's nephew and opposite number, Kaiser Wilhelm II, described by the Countess of Athlone as 'always blowing hot and cold', treated the *Entente* with France and the alliance with Russia as a deliberately hostile 'encirclement of Germany' – an attitude which paved the way to the First World War. The culmination of the *Entente* was the spectacle, rare in the annals of history, of England and France fighting on the same side.

The personalities of the Foreign Secretary, Lord Lansdowne, of his opposite number, Théophile Delcassé, of the French Ambassador, Paul Cambon, and the way in which they related to each other, also played an important part in the drama.

This idea of drama has led me to deal with the events as essentially narratives, and narratives in which the players have, for the most part, been allowed to speak for themselves. All of them have left letters, diaries, speeches and recorded conversations, and it is from these that I have gathered my 'flowers'.

One of the difficulties with which I was faced was deciding where to start. In history one thing leads to another; each period needs to be seen against the background of the preceding one. There is a story, no doubt apocryphal, of a professor in one of our universities who was invited to do a one-year course on the causes of the French Revolution. At the end of the first term he had got as far as the building of the Pyramids.

I have elected to start this book with the first conscious effort to draw Great Britain and France into a relationship of mutual understanding and appreciation. Throughout our history the two countries had usually been on opposite sides on the battlegrounds of Europe. But war, in those days, often only meant the confrontation of two armies, leading to a treaty favourable to the winning side.

Like Philip II and Louis XIV, Napoleon offered a real threat to Britain – the threat of invasion. France became 'the enemy' in a new and more sinister sense. Even on the one occasion, during the Crimean War, when the two countries were on the same side, the British Commander-in-Chief, Lord Raglan, habitually referred to enemy as 'the French'.

It was Louis-Philippe and the young Victoria, assisted by their ministers, Lord Aberdeen and François Guizot, who took the first positive step towards mutual good will, and the term *Entente Cordiale* was first used to describe this. It ended in failure. By the end of the nineteenth century the two countries had gone to the opposite extreme. Their relationship could hardly have been worse.

Queen Victoria was understandably germanic in her outlook. Somewhat unpredictably, her son showed an early appreciation of the French way of life. Three times in the latter part of the century the French mounted an International Exhibition in Paris. Three times Prince Edward was invited to chair the English sector. He saw that it was through the mutual love of the Arts of Peace that the cause of unity could sometimes best be furthered. It is in our mutual appreciation of the literature, the architecture and the visual arts that we are often first able to bridge the gap.

In April 1938 I was taken on a cycling tour of the châteaux of the Loire. The tour concluded with a visit to Chartres Cathedral and finally to Versailles. By the end of it I was completely under the spell of the architecture of France. In 1954 I had the luck to be appointed *assistant anglais* at the Lycée Hoche at Versailles. This gave me the opportunity to write my first book – perhaps predictably – about the great palace at the end of the road. In this and my subsequent books I have tried to share with my compatriots my own delight in the beauties of French architecture, from the little Romanesque churches of Burgundy, in which holiness and homeliness have met together, to the great cathedrals of the Gothic north – from the châteaux of the Loire to the royal palaces of the Ile de France. If I have helped British visitors to share my enthusiasm I hope that I may have made my own contribution, however modest, towards the *Entente Cordiale*.

1

Louis-Philippe and the Failure of the First
Entente Cordiale

On 30 July 1830 Charles X, the younger brother of Louis XVI, abandoned the throne of France. He renounced his own claim and that of his son the duc d'Angoulême, but not that of his grandson the duc de Bordeaux, later known to history as the comte de Chambord. On the following day those who were in control of events offered the crown to the First Prince of the Blood, Louis-Philippe, duc d'Orléans, son of the self-named Philippe Egalité, who had supported the Revolution and voted for the death of his cousin the King.

Louis-Philippe himself had spent most of his exile at Twickenham and had established a real friendship with the Duke of Kent, the father of Queen Victoria. In a letter to the Bishop of Llandaff, written on 28 July 1804, he makes it clear how much he had come to appreciate England and the English. He had apparently just heard of the judicial murder of his cousin the duc d'Enghien by order of Napoleon. Louis-Antoine-Henri de Bourbon, duc d'Enghien, a grandson of the Prince de Condé, had been a childhood friend and companion to Louis-Philippe

You can imagine that this event was a terrible blow to me . . . I feel today more than ever the happiness of the generous protection and support which has been accorded us by the magnanimity of your country . . . I can say with perfect sincerity that I am attached to England, not only by gratitude but also by taste and familiarity.

But he saw further than his own personal position.

It is not only on account of my own feelings that I take an interest in the welfare, prosperity and success of England; it is also for the benefit of humanity. The safety of Europe, of the whole world, the future happiness and independence of the human race depends on the preservation of England, and there you see the main cause of the rage of Bonaparte and that of his partisans against you. May you confound his wicked plans and preserve this country in its present prosperity! That is the sincere desire of my heart and my most ardent prayer.

Louis-Philippe at this time had no immediate prospect of sitting on the throne of France. When he found himself in that position he remembered his debt to England.

One of the first urgent necessities confronting the new regime was to establish its credibility in the eyes of Europe. Most of the countries of Europe were governed by kings and emperors who were firm believers in the divine right of the principle of legitimacy. France, in appointing Louis-Philippe by a more or less democratic process to be King, had bypassed the senior branch of the House of Bourbon and placed the head of the cadet branch at the helm. How was France to gain acceptance by the upholders of primogeniture? The Tsar Nicholas I refused to address Louis-Philippe as '*Monsieur mon frère*' and thus recognize him as a fellow sovereign.

The single but notable exception to this belief in the right of primogeniture was Great Britain which, with its Glorious Revolution and its constitution of Crown and Parliament, seemed to offer the *Monarchie de Juillet* a fitting ally. By rejecting the Stuarts and accepting the

Hanoverians, and by finding their authority for this act in the Houses of Parliament, Britain provided a role model for the government of Louis-Philippe. It was at once obvious that France's relationship with the British government was a matter of the first importance. It followed that the first and most important appointment to be made was that of Ambassador to the Court of Saint James's.

'There was needed a man,' writes Duff Cooper, 'of great political experience, of consummate diplomatic skill, who should have had some previous acquaintance with the prominent people in English public life, and who should, if possible, combine liberal opinion with aristocratic manners, for an Ambassador who was not a Gentleman would be equally at a disadvantage in London whether Tories or Whigs were in office or whether the Duke of Wellington or Lord Grey were Prime Minister.'

There was one man – perhaps only one man – outstandingly qualified on all these counts of character, capability and experience: Charles-Maurice de Talleyrand–Périgord, Prince de Talleyrand and former Bishop of Autun.

There were, however, certain difficulties. Charles Greville, author of the famous Diary, admitted that 'no name was once in greater detestation in England than that of Talleyrand . . . a debauched Abbé and Bishop, one of the champions and then one of the victims of the Revolution', who had accepted office under the Consulate and 'was looked upon all over Europe as a man of consummate ability, but totally destitute of principle in public or in private life'. But whatever Talleyrand was, he was not a fool.

Talleyrand had already been to London. He had come as an exile. A German officer, Ferdinand von Funck, wrote of him: 'Talleyrand liked the English nation. He regarded Pitt's policy as the most astute and at the same time the most logical a statesman had ever pursued.' Years later, on 22 January 1833, Greville writes: 'dined with Talleyrand the day before yesterday. After dinner he told me about his first residence in England and his acquaintance with Fox and Pitt.'

On 1 September 1830 Talleyrand returned to London as Ambassador.

Listening to the resounding volleys of the fortress cannons which announced the arrival of the French Ambassador, I could not help remembering that, thirty-six years previously I had quitted these shores, exiled from my country and turned away from the soil of Britain by the intrigues of the *émigrés*; I now returned animated by the hope, but above all by the desire, to establish the alliance between France and England which I had always regarded as the most solid guarantee of the welfare of these two countries and the peace of the world . . . These were the reflections that occupied my mind as I travelled through beautiful England, so rich and so peaceful.

One of the first problems to confront the new Ambassador at the Court of Saint James's was caused by rioting in Brussels. Belgium had been incorporated into France by Napoleon who saw that Antwerp was 'a pistol pointed at the head of England'. The Congress of Vienna had decided to join Belgium and Holland under the rule of the House of Orange. It was not a wise course of action. The two countries did not even speak the same language; Holland was strongly Protestant, Belgium loyally Catholic. In August 1830 the dominating attitude of Holland led to the riots in Brussels. It might have been expected that Protestant England, with its connection with the House of Orange, would have sided with Holland. It was morally certain that France would support Belgium. To one committed to improving relationships between France and England this presented a delicate diplomatic problem.

The first step was to set up Belgium as a kingdom on its own. The Belgians offered the throne to Louis-Philippe's second son, the duc de Nemours. On the advice of Talleyrand the offer was refused. The throne was next offered to Leopold of Saxe-Coburg. Leopold was the widower of George IV's daughter, Princess Charlotte. He was Victoria's uncle. All that was now needed was a French connection. Talleyrand wanted a marriage between Leopold and Louis-Philippe's daughter, the Princesse Louise. Duff Cooper tells of the skill with which he put this across.

'In conversation with Palmerston on this subject he so manoeuvred that it was Palmerston who first mentioned the name of Leopold. "I showed some astonishment," wrote Talleyrand, "as though the idea had never occurred to me, but my astonishment had slightly the air of a happy discovery." The more Palmerston believed the idea to be his own, the more he liked it. Finally it proved to be the proposal that prevailed and Leopold in due course, with Talleyrand's full approval, became the first King of the Belgians and Louise d'Orléans the first Queen.' On 10 February 1840 Victoria married Albert of Saxe-Coburg-Gotha. Leopold was uncle to both. There was now a strong dynastic alliance between the three countries – England, France and Belgium.

In November 1830 Lord Palmerston had been appointed Foreign Secretary. He was a colourful and controversial character. Prince Paul Esterhazy, the Austrian Ambassador, said, according to Greville, that 'for a long time past the affairs of Europe had been extensively influenced by personal feelings and individual interests. Palmerston,' continues Greville, 'appears to exercise an absolute despotism at the Foreign Office, and deals with all our vast and complicated questions of diplomacy according to his own views and opinions, without the slightest control, and scarcely any interference on the part of his colleagues.' On the rare occasions when he was called to account, 'which he always meets with consummate impudence and, it must be allowed, skill and resolution which always carry him through . . . His motto seems to be that of Danton: *de l'audace, encore de l'audace et toujours de l'audace*. But there is a flippancy in his tone, an undoubting self-sufficiency and a levity in discussing interests of such tremendous magnitude, which satisfies me that he is a very dangerous man to be entrusted with the uncontrolled management of our foreign relations.'

Palmerston is described by E. L. Woodward as 'the personification of England, his patriotism, his prejudices, his language summarized the opinions of the ordinary man.' He distrusted both France and Russia; he described Austria as an 'old woman' and considered that 'all foreigners, at some time or other, might benefit by English advice and English examples.' Roger Bullen describes Palmerston as 'an optimist who maintained an undimmed confidence in the power and strength of England. It was his country's special vocation, he admitted, "to throw her moral weight into the scale of any people who are spontaneously striving for freedom, by which I mean rational government, and to extend as far and as fast as possible civilization all over the world."'

This somewhat insular over-confidence in himself and in the high destiny of his country made him all that the French dislike most about the English. The duc de Broglie, after six months as French Ambassador, returned to Paris in 1837 because he was unable to work with Palmerston.

To Sir Frederick Lamb, Ambassador in Vienna, Palmerston made his position clear. 'My doctrine is that we should reckon upon ourselves; pursue a policy of our own and act upon principles; use other Governments as we can, when we want them and find them willing to serve us; but never place ourselves in the wake of any of them. Lead when and where we can, but follow never.'

As Count Metternich warned Louis-Philippe: 'your alliance with England is that of the rider and the horse; only you must not be the horse.' Palmerston was quite prepared to negotiate with France, but always provided that he was the rider. As Roger Bullen puts it: 'in 1832 Palmerston began to speak publicly of the advantages of "a good understanding between England and France . . ." For Palmerston, however, it was also a means whereby England could contain France, forcing her to accept a secondary role, particularly in western Europe.'

Palmerston was becoming afraid of a Russian/Austrian pact to divide the Ottoman Empire between themselves. By the end of 1833 he felt that this could lead to war. 'The danger is best guarded against,' he concluded, 'by a friendly union with France.'

He used the word 'friendly', but the forming of a pact with another country in the face of a common threat is not the same as an *Entente Cordiale*. Palmerston was merely using France as a diplomatic counterbalance against the kingdoms of eastern Europe – Prussia, Austria and Russia – 'the triple league of despotic governments.' The idea of a quadruple league of constitutional monarchies was in many ways attractive to Palmerston, but on 10 April 1834 he told Lord Granville, British Ambassador in Paris: 'England and France stand in different situations in this matter. England is bound by treaties to Portugal . . . France has not the same motive for being a party concerned, and I think it would be more agreeable to many parties that the treaty be confined to Spain, England and Portugal.'

Anyone more sensitive to French feelings would not have acted in this way. He called on Talleyrand at the French Embassy and informed him, without having consulted him, of the terms of the proposed triple alliance. Talleyrand, predictably, replied that this proposal was an insult to the dignity of France. France could accept no lower status than that of equal partner.

Palmerston admitted that he believed that 'all Frenchmen want to encroach and extend their territorial possessions at the expense of other nations, their vanity prompts them to be the first nation in the world . . . It is a misfortune to Europe that the national character of a great and powerful people, placed in the centre [sic] of Europe, should be such as it is.'

Much the same might have been said of Great Britain. It was, in fact, exactly the reproach that Guizot was to make against the British: 'the ambitious pride, the constant and passionate preoccupation with themselves, the ardent and exclusive need in everything to take their part and their place, the greatest place possible, at no matter what cost, by what means, and to whom.' Guizot was, in fact, an anglophile, but he was a realist first. His appreciation of England was largely based on his admiration for her constitution of Crown and Parliament. Lord Aberdeen, writing to Princess Lieven on 30 November 1837, acclaimed him as 'the only foreigner who has read our history like an Englishman.'

But, sadly, the relations between the governments of Britain and France were deteriorating. The two sovereigns were anxious for an alliance: the two governments were not. There were several minor issues which gave rise to trivial and needless antagonisms. One of these concerned the details in the process of abolishing slavery. It was known as the *droit de visite*.

In 1807 the abolition of slave trading by British subjects or by ships flying the British flag had made a start. During the next ten years France, Portugal and Spain followed suit. But slavery continued to exist, notably in America, and smuggling took the place of open trading. The abolition of slave trading required an international agreement; it required that the Atlantic should be patrolled by warships and for this to be effective a right of examination or *droit de visite* had to be established. In practice this only applied to the ships of Britain and France. A convention agreed in 1831 and revised in 1841 granted to British and French cruisers the right to search commercial vessels off the coast of Africa. But since the number of British cruisers was considerably greater than those of the French this was taken by the Chambre Française to be 'prejudicial to the interests and honour of France.' In a letter of 19 November 1842 writes Professor Muriel Chamberlain (in her thesis for a D. Phil): 'Guizot drew the attention of Lord Aberdeen to article 3, which provided that the number of cruisers to be employed must be fixed again each year and the number employed by one Power must not be more than double that of the other, that the exercise of the right of search must be applied with great prudence and that there must be prompt payment of compensation in cases of error.' The convention was abolished in 1845.

The Queen of the Belgians regarded Palmerston as being largely to blame for this state of affairs on account of 'his blindness and infatuation'. Leopold described him as 'too irritable and too violent'. Victoria urged Palmerston not to push France to extremities. She would have liked a meeting with the French King, but for the time being a meeting between the two sovereigns seemed impossible. On 23 August 1839 Victoria had to write to Leopold admitting that 'now that the moment is approaching, I see great difficulties for an interview being managed this year'. On 2 October 1840 Leopold wrote to Victoria, enclosing a copy of a letter from Louis-Philippe.

> All our people, wrote the King, are persuaded that England wants to reduce France to the status of a Secondary Power, and you know what is the national pride and the vanity of all peoples. I therefore think that there is an urgent need for the present crisis to be terminated soon and peacefully. The more I believe that the union between England and France is basic to the peace of the world, the more I regret seeing such irritation between the two countries.

In 1841, with the fall of Lord Grey's government, Palmerston was replaced by Lord Aberdeen. He and his opposite number, François-Pierre-Guillaume Guizot, created an immediate *détente*. George Hamilton Gordon, 4th Earl of Aberdeen, was a minister after the Queen's heart. If ever a man was 'safe', he was. Instead of enraging the French, he set out to deal tactfully with them – *les ménager*.

> Aberdeen came to the Foreign Office [writes Muriel Chamberlain] in 1841 with a long experience of diplomacy, stretching back to a mission in Austria in 1813. He quickly came to be regarded as the protagonist of the opposite principles of foreign policy to those professed by Lord Palmerston. Aberdeen himself denied the validity of this distinction. In their aims the two men differed little. Both wanted peace, stability and the maintenance of the balance of power in Europe and freedom of commerce. It was in their methods that they differed. Aberdeen was cosmopolitan in outlook and his

strong sense of justice and complete freedom from jingoism often made him approach problems more in the spirit of a mediator than a national spokesman, even when British interests were at stake.

He was very much a man of his time, sensitive when questions of national 'honour' were involved, ready to use British strength to coerce weaker nations, and well hardened to all the subterfuges of international diplomacy. Although a Conservative he was even prepared to welcome a Revolution, as, for example, in Greece in 1843, when he thought it beneficial. The real contrast between Aberdeen and Palmerston lay in their personalities. Lord Aberdeen entirely lacked Palmerston's energy and flair for publicity. Outside a small circle his policy was neither known nor understood. His diplomacy was always of a very personal kind and he relied heavily on his personal friendship with foreign politicians and diplomats, such as Guizot, Metternich and the comte de Jarnac [*chargé d'affaires* in London].

Guizot was a scholar and a statesman who had done much to pave the way for state-aided popular education. Serious-minded and middle-class, he seemed made to be a minister to the 'Bourgeois King' and he directed the policy of France during the last eight years of Louis-Philippe's reign. John Stuart Mill, however, wrote of his administration that it was 'wholly without the spirit of improvement and that it wrought almost exclusively through the meaner and more selfish impulses of mankind.'

It was the Princess Lieven who got Aberdeen and Guizot together. She was one of the most forceful and colourful personalities of her time. Her husband was the Russian Ambassador in London. 'She almost immediately took her place,' writes Greville, 'in the cream of English Society, forming close intimacies with the most conspicuous women in it and assiduously cultivating relations with the most remarkable men of all parties . . . It was her duty as well as her inclination to cultivate the members of all the successive Cabinets which passed before her.' Business and pleasure were closely combined in her way of life. 'She had an insatiable curiosity for political information and a not unnatural desire to make herself useful and agreeable to her own Court by imparting to her Imperial masters and mistresses all the information she acquired and anecdotes she had picked up.'

In 1836 Guizot became Minister of Public Instruction. Princess Lieven described him as 'a man respected for his great abilities and of a probity rare in *les hommes nouveaux.*' Lord Aberdeen was lavish in his praise. He admitted to the Princess that, if ever he were in office again, Guizot was someone 'with whom I would like to act, because he is a man who inspires confidence and whom I could truly respect.'

In 1840 Guizot was appointed Ambassador in London. Aberdeen was delighted with the opportunity to make a deeper acquaintance. 'It is not the talents and reputation of M. Guizot,' he wrote to their mutual friend, 'but the respect which is due to his character. Although an Ambassador, the features of his character which are most impressed upon me are honesty and rectitude. You know that I am not a passion-ate lover of France, or of a French alliance, but I can willingly honour and esteem a Frenchman.' Lord Aberdeen was a person who fully real-ized the primacy of personal relationships rather than policies. 'I regard the mutual esteem entertained by Peel and M. Guizot as worth fifty alliances.' In this he was the direct opposite of Palmerston. On 22 January 1842 Palmerston attacked Aberdeen's policy of trust and understanding as 'merely a means of dragging down England to the position of acting in subserviency to the views of France.'

But, if relations between the respective governments were often strained, the dynastic link was being forged which was to provide a per-sonal connection between the two ruling families. As early as 19 April 1837 Victoria had written to Leopold: 'As regards France I have no need to remind you, dear Uncle, how much we desire to be on the best and most friendly terms possible and to co-operate with her.' Two months later, on 28 June – the anniversary of the battle of Waterloo – Victoria became Queen. She was now in a position to realize some of her desires.

On 19 October that year Leopold was staying at Trianon and could write: 'My very dear Victoria, there is a very great disposition here to be on the best possible terms with England . . . I greatly hope that you may tell your ministers to respond to dispositions so friendly as these with candour and alacrity. It is the desire of the King here that the matters should be treated by the diplomatic representatives of the two countries acting in concert.'

Leopold was in many ways the architect of the first *Entente Cordiale*. He was determined to bring about a meeting between the two sovereigns. On 9 August 1839 he wrote to Victoria to suggest such a meeting. The answer was eagerly awaited. Ten days later Louise, Queen of the Belgians, wrote to her mother, the Queen of the French: 'At last Leopold has received Victoria's answer. She will be delighted to receive *le Père* and all his family at Brighton.' The meeting, however, did not take place. 'The year 1843,' writes Muriel Chamberlain, 'was a very peaceful year in international affairs. Guizot's position was stronger and in March he had, for the first time, dared to speak in public of his desire to cultivate "most friendly relations with Britain".'

In July 1843, Queen Louise was in London visiting her niece. On the 10th of the month she wrote from Buckingham Palace to her mother: 'I will tell you, under the seal of the greatest secrecy, that Victoria hopes to make excursions in her yacht along the coast of England and that she even intends, and indeed desires, to pass on to Eu and see the Father and all of us.'

The Château d'Eu, just outside Le Tréport, had belonged to the duc d'Orléans – Philippe Egalité. It was Louis-Philippe's favourite summer residence and he had spent a lot on improving it and filling the rooms with appropriate portraits of previous owners and his own royal ancestory.

On 3 August Queen Louise wrote to her mother: 'It is, I dare say, more the *Père de Famille* than the King whom Victoria wishes to see. You will appreciate the *nuance*. The excellent Father must therefore be natural, paternal, patriarchal, straightforward as he always is. Above all he must keep off politics, though Albert and the King might do so.' Once again the key note of the *Entente Cordiale* was struck. It was to be a personal relationship, not a political agreement. Guizot, Peel and Aberdeen, however, were to be present.

On the morning of Saturday, 2 September the royal yacht was sighted from Cherbourg and the Prince de Joinville, Louis-Philippe's third son, came on board. At 5 that evening they were at Le Tréport. Louis-Philippe, with a brilliant cortège of coaches, landaus and *calèches* descended 'in a cloud of dust' down to the quayside. Here he embarked in a former whaler, suitably embellished and rowed by twenty-four oarsmen, to await the Queen's arrival.

Victoria describes the day in her Journal. 'The morning was superb and the sea like a mirror . . . At half past six I was on deck, where I found Joinville in uniform, who greeted us in the most civil and engaging manner. We continued our journey following the coast of France, which is charming. For me it was like a dream to find myself so soon in France . . . As we approached Le Tréport I became more and more agitated.' This agitation was somewhat increased by the sight of the King's whaler approaching. 'The good King was standing up and so impatient to come on board that it was with some difficulty that they made him wait until his ship's boat was near enough. He came on board as swiftly as possible and embraced me tenderly. It was a very touching scene and I shall never forget the emotion that I felt.' Victoria was the first Sovereign of England to set foot on French soil since 31 May 1520, when Henry VIII had landed at Calais, which he still possessed, for the Field of the Cloth of Gold. When the two Kings, both highly suspicious of a trap, finally embraced each other, wine and hippocras were served and the toast was 'English and French – good friends'.

A local chronicler named Désiré Le Boeuf has left an ecstatic account of the Queen's landing at Le Tréport. 'This old King! This young Queen! No, we will never forget such a day. On arrival at the

Château d'Eu, the King conducted the Queen on to the balcony, where she listened to more acclamations.' Le Boeuf then made an interesting comment on the effect of the visit on French morale. 'During these days of national pride, seeing the young Queen next to the Old King, who seemed to be her father, we felt that France could again rank as Mistress of the Nations.'

On 3 September Sir Robert Peel wrote to Lord Aberdeen: 'The French papers seem disconcerted by the visit of the Queen to the Château d'Eu. Some of them are afraid that the Queen will come back with a commercial treaty in her pocket. What asses the writers of these articles are!' Lord Aberdeen replied: 'So far as the English papers are concerned none of them seem to have criticized the visit . . . The visit goes on, very pleasant for the Royal family and there have been great echoes in France. She has appealed to the emotions of the French and has aroused their sense of chivalry to its highest degree. I really believe that if the Queen showed herself in Paris, she would be received with the greatest enthusiasm.'

On Sunday, 3 September, Victoria and Albert recited the Divine Office together, after which they joined the King's family circle. 'The whole family is so good, so united, that it does the heart good to be here,' wrote Victoria. 'I feel completely at ease, just as if I were one of the family.' At 10.30 they went down to lunch – 'except for poor Hélène'.

'Poor Hélène', the duchesse d'Orléans, was still in mourning for her husband. The duc d'Orléans had been the strongest hope of the dynasty. 'Witty and talented and deeply versed in a wide variety of subjects,' wrote the comtesse de Boigne, 'he was of a charming appearance, liberal, generous, magnificent . . . he was loved by all for his good grace and desire to give pleasure. But where he was absolutely adored was by the army.' If he gave promise of being perhaps the best King to sit on the throne of France since Henri IV, his wife, Princess Helen of Mecklenburg-Schwerin, would certainly have been the best Queen. She had a majesty that was natural and could therefore be worn lightly.

It was not to be. On 13 July 1842 the duc d'Orléans set out from the Tuileries to visit his mother at Neuilly. He went in a light phaeton drawn by two fiery young horses. At the porte de Maillot they took a wrong turning. The Duke stood up to direct the postillion and fell backwards onto the road, fracturing his skull. He was carried into the back room of a greengrocer's shop where he died. The greatest hope for an Orléans dynasty had disappeared.

After her return Victoria reflected in her Journal on the events of the last two days.

> It seems that our visit has done a lot of good and has been the cause of great satisfaction among the French. I have even been told that I would have been received very well in Paris. I hope that the *haine pour les perfides Anglais* will cease . . . On several occasions he told me how greatly he desired an even closer *rapprochement* with the English, adding that it was the most certain means of preventing war in Europe, and that his love for the English *était dans le sang*.

On the same day she wrote to her uncle Leopold: 'I write to you from this dear place where we are living in the middle of an admirable and truly lovable family, where we feel ourselves completely at home.' Victoria was delighted to find herself 'in a family circle of persons of my own rank with whom I could be on terms of equality and familiarity'.

On 7 September the royal family returned to England. The Prince de Joinville accompanied them and they had a most interesting conversation.

> He gave great praise to Lord Aberdeen [wrote Victoria, adding] that the King could not endure Lord Palmerston, and I must say with some reason. I then said to Joinville that he was accused of not liking the English. He smiled and after a moment he replied: 'I have no dislike but, to speak frankly, I have no great affection for the

English, for, if we look back, we see that at all times the two nations have been opposed to each other and that it is moreover humiliating to the French to feel, on so many counts, inferior to the English' and that, for himself, he would like to be at least on the level of equality. All this was said so frankly and naturally that one could not take offence.

On arrival at Brighton Victoria admitted in her Journal: 'I could not help feeling a little sad at the end of this charming and happy visit.'

On 10 September Prince Albert wrote to Stockmar in praise of Joinville. 'I have seen a young man who pleased me so much. His views are particularly sound. He is upright, honourable, of great ability and lovable, but very deaf.' He added: 'Lord Brougham wrote to me yesterday to congratulate Victoria and myself on the good effect produced in France by our visit, and that there could be, in this wise approach, something capable of giving birth to good feelings between the two countries.'

On 17 October Victoria wrote to Louis-Philippe, addressing him as '*Sire et mon très cher frère*'. She thanked him for his two recent letters. 'The expressions of kindness and friendship which you address to me as well as to my dear Albert have touched us deeply; I need not tell you again how greatly we desire to see confirmed more and more this *entente cordiale* between our two countries, which exists so happily between us personally.'

Reactions to the royal visit at official levels were predictably varied, but on the whole they were favourable. The French Ambassador in Berlin, the comte de Bresson, wrote to Guizot: 'It is a long time since I have received such welcome news as that of the Queen of England's visit to Eu.' He ended on a personal note. 'You need to have lived and breathed, like me, for long years surrounded by such narrow prejudices and petty, but passionate emotions, to be able to appreciate fully the service which you have rendered . . . The meeting at Eu is in itself an important occasion.'

The coverage of the occasion by the French press ranges between the extremes of cautious approval and sarcasm and contempt. The *Journal des Débats* for 2 September is of the former nature.

The meeting of the first two crowned heads in the world should not be seen as an empty ceremony. It is more. It is a great deed; it is a blessing because it is a new pledge given to the security of the world . . . France and England will no doubt continue to pursue their diverse fortunes, often as rivals . . . but it will always mean a lot to know that above all these hazards presides the goodwill of the two Governments and the mutual sympathies of the great majority of the two peoples.

The *Révue des Deux Mondes* for the month of September took a broad view.

Strictly speaking it was doubtless completely outside politics, but this act is none the less for us an auspicious sign; it makes us hope that the two constitutional Governments will return to the path from which, in their own interests of course, they never should have diverged and that they may be able to arrive at a solution at once pacific and worthy of the great issues which still hang over Europe.

One significant result of the new *Entente Cordiale* was that, at the end of the year 1843, Victoria declined to receive the duc de Bordeaux at Windsor. On 7 December, Greville noted in his Diary, 'there has been a great botheration whether the Queen should receive him or not' since he had come 'without any political object or pretension'. He was the grandson of Charles X. His claim to the throne of France had not been renounced and he represented the legitimist line. His father, the duc de Berry, had been assassinated in 1820. The duchesse de Berry was two months pregnant at the time. Seven months later she gave birth to a son. He was at once hailed as *'l'enfant du miracle'*.

At the opening of Parliament on 1 February 1844 the Queen made reference in her speech to 'the good understanding happily established between England and France.' Sir Robert Peel, went further. 'It is important,' he said, 'not only to the interests of England, but also to the interests of Peace, that we should maintain a friendly understanding with France.'

Guizot, in his Memoirs, records that 'on this side of the Channel the English are not loved. During our wars with England Le Tréport was burnt two or three times and pillaged. Nothing would be easier here than to excite popular passion which would be extremely embarrassing to us, but they are saying and repeating: "the Queen of England has shown a politeness to our King: we must be polite to her." They shouted, and will go on shouting, "Long live the Queen!" with all their hearts.'

Guizot then becomes more serious politically. 'Lord Aberdeen had just had a long tête-à-tête with the King, with which he was content and much struck; content with the views and political intentions which the King had unfolded to him, especially on the question of Spain; struck with the abundance of his ideas and his memories, by the rectitude and the independence of his judgement and by the natural and gay vivacity of his talk. He told me that "the King had talked with him profoundly and very seriously."'

In October 1844 Louis-Philippe made a return visit to England. He was the first King of France ever to cross the Channel. Louis-Philippe arrived on 8 October. He was accompanied by his youngest son, the duc de Montpensier, now aged twenty-one. The little Prince of Wales took to him immediately. Victoria noted that the young Duke 'is very fond of children and plays with them as if he were their age.'

The French King was accorded a hearty welcome by the people of Windsor, who greeted him with shouts of '*Vive le Roi!*' uttered, noted Victoria, 'with an accent more English than it would be possible to imagine.'

On Friday, 11 October Louis-Philippe was admitted to the Order of the Garter and on the next day the Lord Mayor and Aldermen of London came down to Windsor for an audience. Speeches were exchanged in the course of which Louis-Philippe said: 'I am convinced, like yourselves, that peace and friendly relations between France and England are, for two countries which were made to esteem and honour one another, the source of mutual equality and innumerable advantages. The maintenance of this good understanding is, at the same time, the pledge of the peace of the world and the progress of civilization.'

Guizot was even more enthusiastic. 'Between France and England,' he commented in his Memoirs after the King's visit, 'peaceful and friendly relations were fully re-established; the questions of Egypt, of Tahiti, of Morocco were settled; that of the *droit de visite* near to being so. Everywhere in Europe the regard for the King's government and its influence have visibly increased.'

The situation was not as rosy as Guizot paints it. There was already on the horizon a dark cloud which was to become a storm which, when it broke, brought to the surface the underlying enmity between England and France and put an end to the first *Entente Cordiale*. It was the problem of the Spanish Marriage.

In September 1833 King Ferdinand VII of Spain had died. He had no son. His brother, Don Carlos, would have succeeded had not Ferdinand abolished the Salic Law. This made his daughter Isabella, a child of three, heiress to the throne. She had a younger sister, the Infanta Luisa-Fernanda who now became heiress apparent.

In Spain the position of the throne was of paramount importance. When Queen Isabella reached the age of sixteen the question of marriage was beginning to loom large. Sir Henry Bulwer, British Ambassador in Madrid, wrote to Lord Aberdeen on 8 July 1846: 'Everything in Spain has depended upon the character of the Sovereign . . . It is not to be forgotten that on the throne of Spain sits the destiny of Spain.' His opposite number, the comte de Bresson, wrote at the same time to Guizot: '*aucun ministère, aucun homme ne peut se soutenir ici contre ou malgré la Cour.*' As Roger Bullen, in his detailed study of the subject, emphasizes: 'On one thing we are all agreed: the role of the Queen's husband would be crucial; his influence would be second to none.' Bulwer, in the same letter, wrote: 'If superstition, ignorance and imbecility are to occupy the Palace, all the rest will be of no avail.'

The choice of likely candidates, however, did not give much ground for encouragement. It was agreed that the young Queen should take a husband from the descendants of Philip V, Louis XIV's second grandson who became King of Spain. Unfortunately this restriction, while ruling out the sons of Louis-Philippe, left the two cousins of Isabella as the obvious candidates.

The elder of these, Don Francisco de Assis, Duke of Cadiz, was not unacceptable to the Queen Regent, but was repulsive in the eyes of the young Queen. There were doubts, wrote Bresson, with extreme delicacy, whether he was '*en état de remplir toutes les obligations du mariage*'. The younger cousin, Don Enrique, Duke of Seville, was unacceptable. The Queen Regent regarded him as 'evil, perverted and utterly unprincipled'. Her sense of maternal responsibility obliged her to exclude him.

Spain was divided politically into two main parties – the Moderados, conservative and aristocratic and favoured by the Queen Regent, and the Progresistas who were strongly liberal. France and England came out on opposite sides. France supported the Moderados and England, especially when represented by Palmerston, the Progresistas. Both countries wanted to increase their influence in Spain. As Roger Bullen says, 'Louis-Philippe concealed from Queen Victoria his determination at all costs to marry his son the duc de Montpensier to the Infanta Luisa-Fernanda; Queen Victoria was equally reticent about her wish to effect a marriage between Prince Leopold of Coburg and Queen Isabella.'

The question had been discussed between Lord Aberdeen and Guizot during the visit to Eu. Guizot promised not to support an

Orléanist prince: Aberdeen promised not to support a Coburg. The condition was then suggested not only that the marriage of the Queen should precede that of her younger sister, but that the marriage of Montpensier to the Infanta could not take place before the Queen had had some children. Aberdeen was ready to agree to this.

But in August 1845 there was a great family reunion in Coburg, at which, of course, the presence of both Victoria and Albert was indispensable. At a banquet in Bonn the future Kaiser Wilhelm I proposed a toast in the course of which he admitted to being 'the open enemy of France and of the Orléans family'. He stressed the strong ties of friendship between Prussia and England. He recalled the days, thirty years back, when, on the heights above Waterloo, Prussia and Britain had shared 'the glorious triumph of our brothers in arms. Victoire! Victoria! Gentlemen, fill up your glasses and drink to the health of Her Majesty Queen Victoria and to that of her august Consort.' Victoria embraced him with tears in her eyes.

This was a heavy blow for Louis-Philippe. The *Entente Cordiale* seemed to be in danger. He sought above all a new meeting between the sovereigns of France and England that would give proof to all Europe that the relations between the two countries had not altered. He wrote to his daughter that 'tempers had risen to such an extent as the result of this incident that he had begun to fear for his throne and his dynasty if Victoria left the continent without seeing him'. He begged Victoria to call on him on the way back from Coburg. She came. Since her last visit the Château d'Eu had been enlarged with a new picture gallery – the Galerie Victoria – filled with paintings, mostly by Eugène Lami and Winterhalter, of their previous visits to each other. It was an obvious compliment. Victoria's first priority was to pay a call on the Queen 'for whom I have almost the love of a daughter.' It had been a radiantly beautiful day and it ended in that mixture of beauty and sadness of a lovely sunset.

The King and Guizot opened the subject of Spain. Lord Aberdeen wrote to Peel. 'As regards the Infanta, they both say in the most positive and explicit manner that, until the Queen is married and has had children, they regarded the marriage of her sister with a French Prince as being quite out of the question.' All seemed to be well.

On 28 December the King wrote to Victoria: 'I was happy to pronounce yesterday, when opening the session of our Chambers, the expression of my feelings for your Majesty and for this *entente cordiale* which continues so happily between our two governments.' His words were received with an enthusiasm 'which is wisely forbidden in England, but which the difference between our national characters has consecrated here.'

It was a situation, however, which needed the most tactful handling. But in June 1846 Peel went out of office, and with him Aberdeen. Lord Palmerston was back at the Foreign Office. Lord Palmerston was not exactly noted for his tact. On 9 July he sent a dispatch to Sir Henry Bulwer, British Ambassador in Madrid, which made no reference to the conversations between Guizot and Aberdeen, which brought back the Coburg candidature and excluded any French candidate.

Greville, discussing the character of Lord Palmerston, recalled a conversation with Melbourne on the subject.

He talked to me about Palmerston, of the aversion he had inspired, not only in France, but in all Germany, and said that his notion had been that everything was to be done by violence; that by never giving way or making any concession, and an obstinate insistence, every point was sure to be gained. This was *à propos* the French refusal to ratify the Slave treaty [the *droit de visite*] and Guizot having delayed to sign it, because he would have nothing to do with Palmerston.

Such was the man chosen to take over these delicate negotiations. On 18 July, when Palmerston had been back in the Foreign Office for only a fortnight, the Duke of Bedford told Greville that 'many disagreeable things are occurring . . . Palmerston had already begun to disturb the harmony that subsisted in Aberdeen's time.' It was too much for Guizot. 'In early September,' writes Greville, 'the news came like a thunderclap that both marriages were settled and declared.' This was in direct contravention of the terms agreed by Aberdeen and Guizot at Eu.

On 6 September Palmerston wrote to the comte de Jarnac, in London: 'I will no longer talk to you of the *Entente Cordiale* because it has been only too clear to us that in Paris they no longer want either cordiality or understanding.' He also told Alexandre Dumont, Guizot's special envoy to London, that this was 'the first time that a King of France has not been true to his word'. Victoria, Greville reported, 'is outraged by the conduct of Louis-Philippe. It is all up with the *Entente Cordiale* and God knows when it will come back.' Victoria herself, writing to Queen Louise, stated that 'this behaviour on the part of the French Government is absolutely incompatible with the *Entente Cordiale*.' But she admitted in a letter to King Leopold, written on 21 September, 'It is so sad for dear Louise to whom one cannot say that her father has behaved dishonestly.'

The end of the *Entente* seems to have been the prelude to the end of the reign. The King's government was beginning to lose its appeal to the people of France. As André Maurois observes: 'Louis-Philippe had afforded France some of the happiest years in her history, but the French do not live on happiness. The French thirst for glory, and the Bourgeois King had not provided it.' Lamartine summed up the verdict of the people with the ominous phrase, '*la France s'ennuie!*'

In February 1848 matters came to a head. It all happened rather suddenly and ended quickly. On Wednesday 23rd the architect Horace Vernet was working with the King, whom he described as 'very calm'. Outside the Tuileries the mob was shouting 'A bas Guizot! A bas les Ministres!' Vernet tried to enlighten the King about the riots, but he was brushed aside. 'Set your mind at rest, my dear Horace; it is just a flash in the pan. It will put itself out.'

At midnight the comtesse de Boigne went to bed. '*Le calme et le silence régnaient.*' She records, as an eye witness, the last days of the Orléans dynasty. On Thursday, 24th she awoke to the news of a general uprising. 'I learnt successively of the invasion of the Tuileries, the departure of the King and the expulsion of the duchesse d'Orléans from the Chambre des Députés.' About the departure of the King she was able to fill in some of the details. 'In the middle of all this agony I had one real satisfaction. All the accounts show the Queen as being as noble and as great as I could have desired.' Louis-Philippe, however, had lost his calm. Seeing the columns of the people led by the National Guard, he cried out, 'All is lost!'

It was the end. The King, the Queen, the duchesse de Nemours and her children and the duc de Montpensier left by way of the garden. 'They all crammed into two small vehicles which had been summoned to the Place Louis XV.' The Bourgeois King and his wife adopted the unassuming names of Mr and Mrs William Smith. It was in England that they sought asylum. Here they had the most generous reception from Victoria.

The Bourgeois King is sometimes underestimated. At least he had a vivid sense of his country's great days. On 7 June 1837 he had re-opened the Château de Versailles as a museum dedicated *A Toutes les Gloires de la France*. The great Galerie des Batailles records many of Napoleon's victories and the Salle du Sacre contains Louis David's monumental depiction of his coronation.

Louis-Philippe had been prepared to recognize the position of Napoleon, no longer regarded as the Corsican Usurper, in the history of France. He even consented to the return of Napoleon's remains to a special mausoleum in Les Invalides. Thiers sent a dispatch to Palmerston with the words: 'The King has given his consent to the transporting of the remains of Napoleon from Sainte-Hélène to Les Invalides. He is as keen about this as I am. The consent of the English Cabinet is needed for this . . . England cannot say to the world that she wishes to keep a corpse a prisoner.'

England had no such desire. The response was made in the following terms: 'The Government hopes that the promptitude of this reply will be regarded in France as proof of its desire to obliterate all trace of those national animosities which, during the life of the Emperor, armed the English nation and the French nation one against the other. Her Majesty's Government is convinced that if such sentiments still survive, they will be interred in the tomb in which the remains of the Emperor will be laid.'

Fifteen years later Queen Victoria, on a visit to Paris, made her eldest son kneel before the tomb of Napoleon. The Prince of Wales was thirteen and a half at the time. Nearly fifty years later he was to play the leading role in the achievement of the second *Entente Cordiale*.

2

The Young Prince of Wales

Born on 9 November 1841 Queen Victoria's first son was christened Albert Edward. His mother insisted on the name Albert coming first. 'O how happy, how grateful did I feel,' she wrote in her Journal, 'to that Almighty Providence who had blessed me so particularly.' The newspaper cutting recording his baptism was pasted into her Journal by Victoria. Above it she wrote: 'we prayed that our little boy might become a true and virtuous Christian and *I* pray that he may be the image of his beloved father.'

That second prayer was not to be granted. Although he had scarcely a drop of English blood in his veins, Edward was to become the most English of our sovereigns since the Tudors. We have to go right back to George I's grandmother Elizabeth, daughter of Charles I, who married Frederick, Elector Palatine, to find the last of his forebears who was not German. His father, the Prince Consort, Albert of Saxe-Coburg, was not only German but thoroughly germanic. In marrying Queen Victoria he had no intention of adapting himself to his new country. Rather, he set out, with the help of Baron Stockmar, to convert England to the serious-mindedness of his native land.

An important part of this process would be the training of the heir to the crown to become *ein treuer, fester Coburger*. Leopold I of Belgium,

27

who was uncle to both Victoria and Albert, reinforced this attitude. 'What luck to have Stockmar with you,' he wrote; 'he will make your son worthy of your throne and of the virtues of his father and will counteract the disturbing tendencies of the family.' The previous generation of the royal family, the sons of George III, had given, it must be admitted, little grounds for confidence.

Thus the forces of heredity and environment united powerfully to orientate the young prince towards a teutonic attitude to life. It did not work out that way. What Albert and Stockmar seemed incapable of appreciating was the force of counterproductivity.

Charles Greville records some interesting details about the upbringing of the royal children. In August 1853 he was staying at Althorp and talked at length with Lady Lyttleton, their governess. She said that the Queen was very fond of her children 'but severe in her manner and a strict disciplinarian in her family'. She described the Prince of Wales (aged twelve) as 'extremely shy and timid, with very good principles and particularly an exact observer of truth.'

Three years later Greville was discussing the same subject with Lord Clarendon, who had been talking about it to the Prince Consort. 'I have six children,' Clarendon said, 'and after all our children are much like Royal children, and require the same treatment. Now we have never used severity in any shape or way, never in their lives had occasion to punish any of them, and we have found this mode of upbringing entirely successful.' Albert told Clarendon 'that he had always been embarrassed by the alarm he felt lest the Queen's mind should be excited by any opposition to her will, and that with regard to the children the disagreeable office of punishment always devolved upon him . . . He told me that the Prince himself, in spite of his natural good sense, had been very injudicious in his way of treating his children and that the Prince of Wales resented very much the severity which he had experienced.'

Albert was essentially an intellectual, and the ruling class of England, though not unappreciative of true scholarship, distrusted those who were merely academic. Lord Melbourne, a perfect representative of the English position, who had for so long been Victoria's mentor, warned her not to overdo the academic regime. 'Be not over solicitous about education,' he wrote, 'it may be able to do much but it does not do so much as is expected from it.' But Victoria no longer listened to Melbourne. She listened only to Albert.

Albert believed in a policy of unrelenting supervision. Only thus could the undesirable tendencies of adolescence be counteracted. His policy required that the pupil should have as little contact with his contemporaries as possible. 'A boy or two,' Lord Redesdale records in his Memoirs, 'carefully selected, were sent up to Windsor from Eton, to stand about in hopeless shyness in the presence of tutors, or even under The EYE.' The first time Redesdale saw the Prince of Wales 'was when his father brought him to Eton, as a little boy of twelve, to hear the 'speeches' on the Fourth of June. What a diversion for a child of his age, to listen to us sixth form boys spouting Demosthenes, Aeschylus, Cicero! I can see his poor, bored little face now. It was pitiful.'

Another of these selected Etonians was Charles Carrington, later Marquess of Lincolnshire. He relates how Edward and his brother Alfred 'were strictly treated and brought up – Prince Alfred was the favourite, but I always liked the Prince of Wales far the best. He had such an open, generous disposition and the kindest heart imaginable. He was a very plucky boy and always ready for fun, which often got him into scrapes. He was afraid of his father, who seemed a proud, shy, stand-offish sort of man not calculated to make friends with children . . . I was frightened to death of him.'

These contacts with acceptable young Etonians did, however, sometimes lead to lasting friendships. One of these was William Henry Gladstone, eldest son of the future Prime Minister. The connection here was with Edward's governess, Lady Lyttleton, but the important fact is that it led to a life-long friendship. William Henry died in July 1891. Edward wrote immediately from Windsor to the stricken father: 'Never can I forget the days of my boyhood when your son came to see me here when he was at Eton – then the happy days we spent on the Rhine in the summer of '57 [when they were both sixteen] and our Oxford days. I shall always deeply regret him from the kindliness and simplicity of his nature.' In later days Edward was to enjoy a warm friendship with the Prime Minister which was not shared by his mother.

Albert and Stockmar, however, were agreed that the heir to the throne must be surrounded 'by persons morally good, intelligent, well informed and experienced and who fully enjoyed parental confidence'. But the young prince, always known as 'Bertie' to his family, showed an early resistance to such measures. When he was still only four, Lady Lyttleton described him as 'uncommonly averse to learning', and showing instead 'a marked taste for violent exercise and enjoyment of life.' The greatest mistake made by Albert and Stockmar was that they paid little or no attention to the boy's real gifts and abilities. One of these gifts was a most attractive personality. As Louis Blanc, a French observer, noted: '*le petit bonhomme est vraiment charmant. Il a un je ne sais quoi qui plaît.*' This attractiveness opened the door to easy and meaningful relationships with others.

One of the first of such relationships was with his tutor Henry Birch, an Eton master in his early thirties. Bertie was then seven. Birch found his royal pupil 'extremely disobedient, impertinent to his tutors and unwilling to submit to discipline'. Albert, disturbed by these reports, consulted a phrenologist, Sir George Coombe, the fashionable theorist of the time, who examined the boy's cranium and 'pointed out the peculiarities of his temperament and brain.' Albert was puzzled. 'I wonder whence that Anglo-Saxon brain of his has come . . . it must have descended from the Stuarts, for the family has been purely germanic since that day.'

At a less intellectual level, Henry Birch was more successful. He and Bertie soon established a relationship of mutual esteem and affection. 'I saw numerous traits of a very amiable and affectionate disposition,' he admitted; 'he always evinced a most forgiving disposition after I had occasion to complain of him to his parents or to punish him. He has a very keen perception of right and wrong, a very good memory and very singular powers of observation.' Birch went so far as to predict that Bertie would turn out a good 'and in my humble opinion a *great* man'.

Birch was convinced that the policy of keeping the Prince so strictly isolated from other boys was one of the reasons for his tiresome behaviour. He expressed his opinion that many of the boy's peculiarities arose from the effects of this policy. He spoke from experience. 'I have always found that boys' characters at Eton were formed as much by contact with others as by the precepts of their tutors . . . The Prince has no standards by which to measure his own powers, and nothing that a tutor, or even a parent can say has such influence as intercourse with sensible boys of the same age or a little older, unconsciously teaching by example.' Even when Bertie's younger brother Alfred shared a lesson with him there was 'a marked improvement in his temper, disposition and behaviour . . . far less selfish, far less excitable, and in every way more amiable and teachable'.

Lord Esher, in his *Influence of King Edward*, makes the same observation. 'Without the stimulus of competition . . . deprived of the freer companionship of boys of his own age, it is not surprising that the Prince of Wales, although he never rebelled, passively resisted the high pressure of his father's system of education.'

The happy relationship between Birch and the Prince was not, however, shared by his parents. The breach came over their differing attitudes to the Catechism. On 10 October 1851 Disraeli wrote to Lady Londonderry:

You know, or have heard of Mr Birch, the model tutor of the Prince of Wales and hitherto at the Château a prime favourite. It seems that Albert, who has imbibed the Lutheran (alias Infidel) doctrines and holds that all churches (reformed) are alike . . . and that ecclesiastical formularies of all kinds ought to be discouraged, signified the other day that he did not approve of the Prince of Wales being taught the catechism, His Royal Highness not approving of creeds and all

that. Conceive the astonishment and horror of Birch, a very orthodox if not a very High Church man, at this virtual abnegation of all
priestly authority! He informed His Royal Highness that he must
resign his post.

Apparently it had not occurred to Albert that his son would one day
be the 'Supreme Governor' of the Church of England of whose catechism he was disapproving.

Birch had to leave the royal household. Lady Canning records that
the young prince 'has done no end of touching things since he heard
he was to lose him. He is such an affectionate, dear little fellow.' Thus,
at the age of nine, Bertie was deprived of a fruitful human relationship
in the interests of bigotry.

Relations between Bertie and his parents were not, on the whole,
good. During the autumn of 1855 Victoria was at Balmoral. She wrote
to the Empress of Prussia: 'Even here, when Albert is away all day long,
I find no special pleasure in the company of my elder children ... only
very occasionally do I find the rather intimate intercourse with them
easy or agreeable.' When they were naughty, writes Christopher
Hibbert, 'she found them intolerable, and was insistent that they
should be punished even more severely than their father would have
approved.'

Victoria's chief interest was that her children should adulate their
father, rather than love him. 'None of you can ever be proud enough of
being the child of such a father, who has not his equal in this world – so
great, so good, so faultless.' Of course, she insisted, none of them could
possibly equal his standard, but she urged them 'try, therefore, to be like
him in some points and you will have acquired a great deal.'

When he had reached the appropriate age it was decided that Bertie
should go first to Edinburgh University and then to Oxford and finally
to Cambridge. Edinburgh did not have colleges and the prince lived at
Holyrood. But when, in the autumn of 1859, he went to Oxford, his
father tried to insist that Bertie should be a member of the University

without owing allegiance to any particular college. But he had to yield to the University authorities and the young man was duly admitted to Christ Church, but on a strict understanding that he was to lodge 'in an entirely separate establishment', under the ever watchful eye of his governor, Colonel Robert Bruce. 'The more I think of it,' wrote Albert to Dean Liddell, 'the more I see the difficulties of the Prince being thrown together with other young men and having to make his own selection of acquaintances . . . The only use for Oxford,' he added, 'is that it is a place for study.' Oxford has a lot more to offer its students than erudition, but Albert was incapable of seeing this. In a letter from his parents the Prince was solemnly reminded that 'life is composed of duties, and that in the due, punctual and cheerful performance of them the true Christian, the true soldier and the true gentleman is recognized.'

At Oxford Bertie was lodged at Frewin Hall, a gloomy house off Cornmarket Street. Bruce was to be 'entirely master of the choice of society which he might encounter.' Colonel the Honourable Robert Bruce, a brother of Lord Elgin, was a rather dull, grim and strict person, always worried and deeply suspicious of any form of recreation. Albert had impressed on him his own anxiety that 'time was being wasted in pleasure'; recreations, especially hunting, were 'encroaching too much on time which ought to be devoted to study.' Albert even sought an ally in the Prince's elder sister Vicky, now Crown Princess of Prussia, confiding in her about Bertie's 'indescribable laziness'. In November 1858 Bertie went out to stay with her. Albert begged her 'not to miss any opportunity of urging him to hard work.' It was important for him to have some 'mental occupation' while he was at Potsdam.

Naturally Bertie saw a lot of the Dean of Christ Church, who quickly warmed to him. 'The nicest fellow possible,' he said; 'so simple, so naif, ingenuous and modest and moreover with extremely good wits; possessing also the royal faculty of never forgetting a face.'

In autumn 1860 Bertie was sent on a visit to Canada and the USA. He was to go to Canada officially as heir to the throne with authority to confer knighthoods. The tour was organized by the Duke of Newcastle, Secretary of State for the Colonies in Palmerston's ministry. In Quebec Bertie had his first experience of a rift between the English and the French, which was somewhat eased by his presence. He threw himself into the receptions with gusto. It was recorded that at the Mayor's ball he took the floor for every one of the twenty-two dances. One regrettable incident was reported at the French University at Laval. Roman Catholics were shocked to hear the Prince of Wales address their Bishops as 'Gentlemen'. The Orangemen were outraged at the Duke of Newcastle's apology for this discourtesy and the visit was disrupted by their shouting their slogans and waving their placards along the Prince's route.

In the United States he was to travel incognito with the title of Lord Renfrew. Of course everybody knew who he was, but this enabled him to approach the Americans on terms more like equality. In this dual role he was well placed to match the ambivalent attitude of the citizens for, beneath an ardent republicanism, many had retained a sentimental attachment to royalty. They turned out in their thousands to welcome the prince. The actress Fanny Kemble wrote: 'the whole land was alive with excitement and interest.' At least Bruce was able to give praise where praise was due. He told Sir Charles Phipps, Keeper of the Privy Purse, that 'it would be quite impossible to exaggerate the enthusiasm of the Prince's reception in New York . . . With the exception of the Orange difficulty, the affair has been one continual triumph.'

Victoria was delighted. 'He was immensely popular,' she wrote to her daughter Vicky, 'and he really deserves the highest praise.' Albert's praise was more grudgingly bestowed. The regular reports which the young Prince had been obliged to write were disappointingly trivial. Bruce complained of his lack of conversation and 'growing sense of his own importance . . . and longing for independence from control.' Nothing, however, could have been more natural.

It was in the American visit that Bertie made his first important contribution to international relations and discovered in himself the special gift which was to underlie his role as – in Brook Shepherd's phrase – 'the uncle of Europe'. He had a flair for getting across to people.

After the excitements of the transatlantic tour the prospect of returning to the boredom and restraints of university life, this time Cambridge, caused him to beseech his parents to let him begin a military career. Bruce opposed the idea on the predictable grounds of the dangers which such a course could present in the form of the 'temptation and unprofitable companionship of military life'. Bertie was to be protected against temptation – not taught to face up to it.

He was admitted to Trinity College with the same proviso as at Oxford that he should lodge entirely outside it. He lived at Madingley Hall, some four miles out of town. His tutor, Charles Kingsley, was more famous as a social reformer and writer of fiction than as a historian, but Bertie responded to his infectious enthusiasm. Kingsley himself was nervous about his royal pupil. He confessed to having been 'reduced to fear and trembling' by a letter from the Prince Consort which stated the exact way in which the Prince of Wales was to be taught and the period of history which was to be covered. With deeper experience Kingsley could say that he was 'much pleased with his attention to lectures and that he asked very intelligent questions.' He ended: 'I tremble at my responsibility, but I have made up my mind to speak plain truth as far as I know it.'

In January 1861 the poet Munby recorded that the Prince's stature was 'manly and well made, and his frank, intelligent face (with a good deal of fun and animal vigour in it too) has a pure, rich sunbrown tint, which his golden hair and large blue eyes make all the more artistic . . . and his hands suggestive of healthy outdoor use.'

During the summer that year it was decided that Bertie should spend ten weeks with the Grenadier Guards at the Curragh, near Dublin. It was not a great success. The training was too much for him and the Commander-in-Chief, the Duke of Cambridge, did not consider that he had the makings of a soldier.

The ten weeks at the Curragh, however, were to have a very significant effect on his life. Frederick Stanley, one of those 'suitable' Etonians who had been occasionally entertained at Windsor Castle, introduced the Prince to the young officers in the Mess. 'After a rather noisy and drunken party,' writes Christopher Hibbert, 'some of these persuaded a young actress to creep into his quarters and wait for him in his bed.' Her name was Nellie Clifden, a 'vivacious, cheerfully promiscuous and amusing girl who was also unfortunately most indiscreet.' They continued seeing each other.

During the time when Bertie was having his first experience of sex, his parents were beginning to look seriously for someone for him to marry. Tradition required that his future bride should be of royal blood: the law of the land required that she should be a Protestant. The field was not likely to be a large one. By far the most attractive proposition was the Princess Alexandra of Schleswig-Holstein-Sonderburg-Glücksburg, usually known for short as Alexandra of Denmark. Vicky described her as having 'a lovely figure but very thin, a complexion as beautiful as possible . . . She is as simple and natural and unaffected as possible, and seems exceedingly well brought up.'

In September 1861 the Prince of Wales, chaperoned by Robert Bruce (now a General), went to Strelitz to meet the young lady. On 24 September they met each other. Vicky gave an account of the occasion. 'At first I think he was disappointed about her beauty and did not think her as pretty as he had expected . . . But as her beauty consists more in her sweetness of expression, grace of manner and extreme refinement of appearance, she grows upon one the more one sees her.' Bertie was perfectly frank with his sister. 'He said he had never seen a young lady who pleased him so much.' He found, however that 'her nose was too long and her forehead too low'. Vicky concludes: 'I see that she has made an impression on him, though in his own funny and undemonstrative way.'

To his parents Bertie admitted that 'he thought her charming and very pretty', but he begged them to wait until he saw them next. When he rejoined his parents he seemed nervous about making any decision.

'As for being in love,' Victoria wrote to Vicky, 'I don't think he can be, or that he is capable of enthusiasm about anything in the world. Poor boy – he does mean well – but he is so different from darling Affie' (his younger brother Prince Alfred, Duke of Edinburgh). Vicky tried to defend her brother. She wrote back: 'Only one thing pains me and that is the relation between you and Bertie. His heart is very capable of affection, of warmth of feeling.' Then she added tactfully: 'I admire dear Papa's patience and kindness and gentleness to him so much that I can only hope and pray there may never be an estrangement between you.'

Vicky, however, was disappointed. 'It gives me a feeling of great sadness when I think of the sweet, lovely flower [Alexandra], young and beautiful – that even makes my heart beat when I look at her – which would make most men fire and flames – not even producing an impression enough to last from Baden to England.'

During the year 1861 both Victoria and Albert suffered serious bereavements. On 16 March, Victoria's mother, the Duchess of Kent, died. In spite of earlier disagreements they had ended up on very good terms. The Duchess, in Elizabeth Longford's words, still added 'an extra dimension to family life'. Now there was a gap. 'I feel as if we were no longer cared for,' wrote Victoria to Uncle Leopold.

On 12 November Albert lost his cousin King Pedro of Portugal, a young man whom he claimed to love 'like a son'. Pedro had died of typhoid. His death greatly increased Albert's melancholy. 'We did not need this fresh loss,' wrote Victoria, 'in this sad year, this sad winter, already so different to what we have ever known.'

On the same day as the arrival of the news of Pedro's death there came a letter from Baron Stockmar. It referred to the news of Bertie's amorous affair with Nellie Clifden. He was wondering whether this might not compromise the arrangements for Bertie's marriage.

One can hardly imagine a greater shock for both Victoria and Albert. It was four days before Albert was able to write to his son. Finally he wrote 'with a heavy heart upon a subject which had caused me the greatest pain I have ever felt in my life.' The letter was long and at times histrionic, underlining the enormity of the sin and enlarging upon the possible and dreadful consequences. 'If you were to try and deny it, she can drag you into a Court of Law and force you to own it, and there with you, the Prince of Wales, in the witness box, she will be able to give before a greedy multitude disgusting details of your profligacy for the sake of convincing the jury; yourself cross examined by a railing, indecent attorney and hooted and yelled at by a Lawless Mob!! Oh! horrible prospect, which this person has in her power, any day, to realize! and to break your poor parents' hearts.' The Prince, he commanded, was to confess everything, 'even the most trifling circumstance', to General Bruce. Bertie did make a most abject apology.

Rightly or wrongly, this crisis was used as an argument for accelerating the procedure for Bertie's marriage. Without that he would be lost – 'he *must* not, *dare* not be lost. The consequences for this country and for the world would be too dreadful.'

Two days later Albert went to inspect the new buildings at Sandhurst. The weather was bad and he came back with a heavy cold. 'I am at a very low ebb,' he wrote to Vicky, 'much worry and great sorrow (about which I beg you not to ask questions) have robbed me of sleep during the last fortnight. In this shattered state I had a very heavy catarrh and pains in my limbs which may develop into rheumatism.' In fact they were developing into typhoid. Elizabeth Longford calculates that the ten days which separated the death of Pedro from the Prince's unfortunate liaison coincided with the incubation period of the typhoid germ.

Friday, 22 November was the likely date – the day of Albert's visit to Sandhurst. On Monday, 25 November he felt it his solemn duty to go to Cambridge to remonstrate once more with Bertie. His condition became increasingly alarming. On Saturday, 14 December he died. Victoria's feelings are better imagined than described. Bertie had been at the foot of his father's bed at the moment of his death. He tried to comfort his mother. 'Indeed, Mama, I will be all I can to you.' She answered: 'I am sure, my dear boy, you will.'

One of the possible results of bereavement is anger – anger at having been so badly hurt. Sometimes it can be anger against God; sometimes even anger against the deceased person. It is as if there were a need to put the blame on someone. Somewhat illogically Victoria put the blame on Edward.

A fortnight later, in a letter to her daughter Vicky about Bertie, Victoria wrote: 'I never can or shall look at him without a shudder.' Vicky tried to defend her brother, but Victoria answered: 'All you say about poor Bertie is right and affectionate in you, but if you had seen what I saw, if you had seen Fritz [Vicky's husband] struck down, day by day get worse and finally die, I doubt if you could bear the sight of the one who caused it.' *The one who caused it:* Victoria had found an outlet for her anger.

During Albert's life Victoria had regarded the supervision of Bertie's upbringing as being his father's concern. 'I wish,' she stated, 'that he should grow up entirely under *his father's eye* and every step be guided by him'. Now that Albert was dead she was determined not to deviate a single inch from the course which Albert had laid down for her son. 'No human power,' she wrote to her uncle, King Leopold, 'will make me swerve from what *he* decided and wished.' In so far as it is humanly possible, the spirit of Albert lived on in his widow. Albert dead was sometimes more intransigent than Albert living.

Victoria was averse to the Prince of Wales having any public responsibilities, but she felt herself unequal to the task of receiving foreign sovereigns or their representatives. Her son, however, made private contacts with many of them. *The Times* boldly suggested that he should be officially authorized. 'We feel sure that His Royal Highness, who has won golden opinions as the guest of foreign sovereigns, will also know how to greet the friends of England in his own country.' Victoria turned a deaf ear to all such advice.

On coming of age, the Prince of Wales acquired by hereditary right the Duchy of Cornwall, together with its not inconsiderable revenues. This conferred upon him a financial independence which could not be subject to parental control. Parliament had already agreed to assign Marlborough House as his London residence. Sandringham was bought and enlarged out of the revenues of the Duchy. Bertie was now a wealthy landowner. There were certain dangers in that position, but he was now free to visit France unofficially. He was to form a great affection for Paris, an affection which was to play an important part in the creation of the *Entente Cordiale*.

3

Napoleon III and the Franco-Prussian War

The return of Napoleon's ashes to Les Invalides and the consequent revival of interest in the idea of an Empire had played into the hands of his nephew, Louis-Napoleon. In 1848 he was living in some poverty in London, but he was biding his time. In February he learnt that there was an uprising against the Bourgeois King. By the end of the month the Republic had been proclaimed. He returned to France.

By the autumn of 1851, Louis-Napoleon, already 'Prince-President', had all prepared for a *coup d'état*. In December his claim to the imperial throne was confirmed by a plebiscite. Seven million, four hundred thousand votes were in favour: six hundred and fifty thousand against. With tactful regard for the claims of his uncle's son, the late duc de Reichstadt, the Prince-President took the title of Emperor Napoleon III.

Some twelve years previously, in February 1839, Charles Greville had found himself co-guest with Prince Louis-Napoleon. 'He is a short, thickish, vulgar looking man,' he wrote, 'without the slightest resemblance to his imperial uncle, or any intelligence in his countenance.'

On 20 December 1848, writing from Bowood, he revised his opinion. 'Van der Weyer, who is here, says he has long known him and well, that he is generally underrated here and is really a man of considerable

41

ability. The result of the French election for President,' he noted, 'has astonished the whole world. Everybody thought Louis-Napoleon would be elected, but nobody dreamt of such a majority. The ex-ministers and Legitimists, who were hot for his election, considering him merely as a bridge over which the Bourbons might return to power, begin to think the success greater than is agreeable, and that such a unanimous expression of public opinion may lead to the restoration of the Bonapartes instead of that of the Bourbons.'

On 2 December 1851 the new President became Emperor. The next day Greville recorded that 'at 12 o'clock yesterday morning the wonderful [new] electric telegraph brought us word that, two hours before, the President had accomplished his *coup d'état* in Paris with success.' Two days later, the Foreign Secretary, Lord Palmerston, without asking the opinion of the Cabinet, told the French Ambassador of his 'entire approval' of the act.

This cost Palmerston his post at the Foreign Office. Lord Clarendon was offered and refused the position. Lord Granville accepted it. Clarendon had reservations about the exact constitutional position of the Crown in foreign affairs. He believed that both Victoria and Albert 'laboured under the curious mistake that the Foreign Office is their own peculiar department and that they have a right to control, if not to direct the foreign policy of England.'

On 19 February 1853 Greville noted that 'the Queen seems to be intensely curious about the Court of France and all details connected with it, and, on the other hand Louis-Napoleon has been equally curious about the etiquette observed in the English Court and desirous of assimilating his to ours, which in great measure he appears to have done.' He also made an immediate impact on Victoria herself. As Lytton Strachey noted: 'from behind the vast solidity of her respectability, her conventionality, her established happiness, she peeped out with delicious pleasure at that unfamiliar, darkly glittering foreign object, moving so meteorically before her.' It was not long before Queen Victoria's relationship with Louis-Napoleon became distinctly cordial.

The new Emperor made it clear that what would help him most was an alliance with Great Britain.

Both Britain and France were, at that moment, drifting into a state of war with Russia. The Crimean War, 'a contest,' according to H.A.L. Fisher, 'entered into without necessity, conducted without foresight, and deserving to be reckoned from its archaic arrangements and tragic mismanagement rather among medieval than modern campaigns', at least afforded the unfamiliar spectacle of British and French soldiers fighting on the same side.

A long period of peace, although greatly beneficial to a country, can be disastrous to the armed forces. They tend to be neglected. The commanders of the British forces in 1852 had mostly had no experience beyond the parade ground for forty years. They were still living in the age of the Peninsular War. This was only too true of the man appointed Commander-in-Chief, Lord Raglan. During the Crimean campaign he habitually referred to the enemy as 'the French'.

In 1855 a State Visit was arranged and on 17 April the Emperor and his newly wedded wife Eugénie de Montijo arrived in London. She was, according to Princess Essling, '*de caractère à monter avec dignité sur l'échafaud.*' It was a new angle from which to assess a royal bride, Greville describes their reception by the Londoners.

> Yesterday I went out 'with all the gazing town' to see not the least curious events I have lived to witness, the entry of the Emperor and Empress of France into London. The day was magnificent, the crowd prodigious, the reception not very clamorous but cordial and respectful. A fine sight for them to see such vast multitudes, so orderly and so prosperous, and without a single soldier except their own escort . . . The fineness of the weather brought out the whole population of London, as usual kept in excellent order by a few policemen.

Three days later he completed his account.

The visit of the Emperor has been one continual ovation, and the success is complete. None of the sovereigns who have been received here before have ever been received with such magnificence by the Court or by such curiosity and delight by the people. Wherever and whenever they have appeared, they have been greeted by enormous multitudes and prodigious acclamations.

Cries of '*Vive le Hemperor!*' were recorded in the royal carriage.

On Saturday, 18 August Victoria and Albert, accompanied by the Prince of Wales and his sister Vicky, made a return visit to Paris. It provided one of the more productive aspects of Bertie's upbringing – the influence of foreign travel. Victoria's excitement and enthusiasm for everything about Paris and France must have been infectious, especially to a boy at the impressionable age of thirteen and a half. 'Here,' writes Brook Shepherd, 'was a Court which managed to be splendid without being stuffy and a throne occupied by somebody who actually seemed to enjoy this earnest business of ruling.' The comtesse d'Armaillé noted in her diary that 'whereas Prince Albert followed [the Queen] bashfully, very bald for his age and looking very tired . . . his little boy, on the contrary kept looking all round him as though anxious to lose nothing of these last moments in Paris.'

Bertie took at once, however, to Louis-Napoleon and Eugénie, begging the latter to let him and his sister stay on in Paris. Eugénie suggested that their parents could not do without them, to which Bertie replied: 'there are six more of us at home, and they don't want us.' Driving once in Paris with the Emperor, Bertie said: 'I should like to be your son.'

'The Queen, as usual, has had magnificent weather for her Paris visit,' wrote Greville, 'and all has gone well there.' On 5 September he reported again, this time with information obtained from Lord Clarendon, who had been put in charge of the young Prince, and who assured him that 'the Queen was delighted with everything and especially with the Emperor himself, who, with perfect knowledge of women, had taken the surest way to ingratiate himself with her by making love to her . . . As his attentions tickled her vanity without shocking or alarming her modesty, and the novelty of it (for she never had any love made to her before), made it very pleasant and his success was complete.'

Victoria was the first reigning sovereign of England to enter Paris since Henry VI. She was, as always, superlative in her enthusiasm.

Indeed no description can give an idea of the splendour of the whole scene. Paris is the most beautiful and gayest of cities, with its high, handsome houses, in every one of which there is a shop. Imagine all these decorated in the most tasteful manner possible, with banners, flags, arches, flowers, inscriptions and finally illuminations; the windows full of people up to the tops of the houses, which tower storey upon storey, the streets lined with troops and everybody most enthusiastic, and yet you will have but a faint notion of this triumph as it was.'

Victoria left her own description of the French Court. 'Everything magnificent, but much more quiet, very different from things in the poor King's time – much more royal.' But the Court of the Second Empire was not only magnificent and royal: it was enjoyable. It is impossible to read the memoirs of the period and not to feel the breath of fresh air. In the long chronicles of Court life, it seems that only Joséphine and Eugénie had the capacity for being royal without in some way ceasing to be human. Significantly, neither of them was born to the role. Eugénie was a hostess without equal. 'Only a woman of the world who had become an Empress,' wrote Princess Metternich, 'could have managed to create such a company . . . it required a worldly *savoir faire* as well as the authority of the throne.'

The Château de Saint-Cloud had been appointed for the reception of the royal family; it was the Emperor's summer palace. One of Eugénie's ladies, Mme Carette, described it as the most agreeable residence of the Court. 'Although large and sumptuous,' she wrote, 'this palace did not have the immense proportions of Fontainebleau, the solemnity of the Tuileries, the severe and somewhat monotonous lines of Compiègne. Here, more than anywhere, one felt the atmosphere of a *home*.'

Set in a garden of cascades and fountains and perched on the high ground across the river from the Bois de Boulogne, Saint-Cloud enjoyed the combined advantages of rural seclusion and proximity to the capital. It was after dark when the carriages arrived at the foot of the long oblique slope which formed the drive, but they did not want for artificial illumination. 'In all this blaze of light from lamps and torches,' wrote Victoria, 'we reached the palace. The dear Empress and Princess Mathilde received us at the door and took us up a beautiful staircase.'

Once again a good relationship was established between the two Sovereigns. This time it was followed by a mutual understanding at a different level. In 1860 Richard Cobden brought off a commercial treaty with France which was intended to promote friendship as well as trade. 'The people of these two nations,' he wrote, 'must be brought into mutual dependence by the supply of each other's wants. It is God's own method of producing an *entente cordiale*.'

Bertie's next visit to the continent, in August 1857, was to Germany. He stayed at Königswinter, just across the Rhine from Bonn. The high point of his visit was a meeting with the aged Prince Metternich at Schloss Johannisberg. The Prince remarked that he looked 'embarrassed and very sad'.

Napoleon III managed to remain in power for eighteen years, but his popularity was waning. At the election in 1869 the opposition polled nearly half the votes. Something was urgently needed to restore public confidence in the Empire. The Premier, Emile Ollivier, stated that two things were needed to re-establish the prestige of the Empire – a war and a plebiscite. An impressive victory somewhere by the French army would be the surest way, but the rise of the Liberal Party under Ollivier gave hopes of a peaceful solution. In January 1870, he submitted a programme of reforms to a plebiscite. He obtained a majority of some six million votes. The Republican Gambetta remarked sadly that 'the Empire is stronger than ever.' Napoleon had been criticized for remaining neutral in the war between Prussia and Austria, but after the Prussian victory at Sadowa he hoped that his mediation in the ensuing peace talks would win him some credit. He did not succeed.

If Napoleon could not restore his popularity by diplomatic success, the alternative, as suggested by Ollivier, was by military success. In January 1867 the Emperor had confronted his legislative body with a demand to increase their defence forces and 'to organize ourselves so as to be invulnerable'. On 21 June the Minister for War, the Maréchal Niel, presented the Chambre des Députés with a detailed project. It met with heavy opposition, in the face of which he reduced his estimates, but he was still asking for an armed force of four hundred thousand men, supported by an equal number of territorials. This received the support of a majority. But any permanent army was opposed in principle by the Republicans; all were opposed to compulsory military service; all insisted on further reduction of costs. The result was that when war did break out between France and Prussia the French forces were lamentably inferior to those of the enemy. And yet Ollivier could claim that 'on whichever side we look there is an absence of troublesome questions; at no moment has the maintenance of peace in Europe been better secured.' He reckoned without Bismarck.

Otto von Bismarck was born in 1815 at Schönhausen, in the old Mark of Brandenburg, into a typical Junker family – a class somewhat like the country gentlemen of England, but often living closer to the soil. At the age of forty-seven he became Prime Minister and Foreign Secretary of Prussia. His biographer, A. J. P. Taylor, describes him as 'a solitary figure, following a line of his own devising. He had no colleagues, only subordinates. The Prussian Council of Ministers rarely debated policy . . . Bismarck conducted foreign policy in autocratic isolation, easily aroused to anger if some Ambassador tried to influence him. Opposition infuriated him. Bismarck never respected an opponent or listened to his argument.'

On 21 November 1876, Lord Salisbury describes a meeting with Bismarck in Berlin. 'He lectured me for more than an hour.' Lady Maud Cecil wrote to her sister: 'Papa looks quite small beside him. His face is very ugly, the features all put on anyhow; they look more as if they had been caused by a volcanic eruption, like granite mountains.' His appetite was in proportion to his stature. Lady Salisbury recorded in her diary that 'he ate more enormously than I ever imagined a man could eat.'

Surprisingly, according to Taylor, Bismarck had 'great personal charm when he cared to use it. He bewitched the Tsar Alexander II, Napoleon III and Queen Victoria. In April 1888 Victoria visited the old Emperor Frederick, whose ninety-nine-day reign had just begun. On 22 April she gave Bismarck an interview. He left the room mopping his brow and exclaiming, 'That was a woman! One could do business with her.' She confessed surprise to find that 'the horrid monster was so amiable and gentle.'

Bismarck needed the unifying influence of a war in order to draw together the northern and southern halves of Germany. 'The abyss which has deepened in the course of history between the north and the south of the Fatherland,' he said, 'the divergence of sentiment, of race, of dynasty and difference in the way of life could not have been more happily filled in than by a national war against a neighbouring country which was our age-old aggressor.' Some people had not forgotten Iena. Years afterwards, in July, 1892, Bismarck declared: 'We could not have set up the German Reich in the middle of Europe without having defeated France.'

On the eve of France's declaration of war against Prussia, Lavalette was expressing his confidence that France could count upon the support of Austria and possibly Bavaria. The Minister for Bavaria, however, speaking in Berlin, said that 'it only had to be stated that it was France who had declared war to arouse enthusiasm for German solidarity.' In the event Austria remained neutral. Bismarck had been wanting war and preparing for war for three years, but he wanted the war to be started by France.

It was trouble in Spain which gave him his opportunity. A new revolution had left the throne vacant. In October 1868 Edward wrote to his mother: 'The Spanish Revolution is, as you say, a sad thing, but I think for the last two years everyone could have foretold it sooner or later. I am only surprised they allowed the Queen [Isabella] to remain in Spain as long as she did, as, besides being one of the worst sovereigns in Europe, her character is, I fear, very indifferent. The whole country, too, is in a state of poverty and disaffection and priest-ridden and rotten to the core.'

Two of the major powers in Europe had their eyes on the throne of Spain – France and Germany. France still had two of Louis-Philippe's sons to provide for, the Dukes of Montpensier and Aumale. 'What an excellent thing', wrote Edward, 'the duc d'Aumale's election would be. But the Emperor would never stand it.'

Germany also had put up a candidate. At Bismarck's recommendation the name of Prince Leopold von Hohenzollern-Sigmaringen was nominated. On 4 July he accepted nomination. To France this looked like encirclement. It looked like a reinstating of the old Habsburg Empire of Charles V.

Leopold and Edward were good friends, but Edward saw the hand of Bismarck behind the move and opposed it. In the same month Lord Granville, a childhood friend of the Prince, had become Foreign Secretary. He got off to a good start. On 10 July he was able to announce that the Hohenzollern candidate had been withdrawn. The Prince wrote to him: 'hearty congratulations to you and the country on the excellent news you have been kind enough to send me. Let us trust that the clouds which have overshadowed Europe may be dispersed without their bursting over our heads.'

It could have meant peace, but the duc de Gramont, the Foreign Minister, tried to push his luck a little further. He required an assurance from Prussia that the candidature would not be renewed. Napoleon sent his Ambassador Benedetti to meet the King of Prussia at Ems. William's reply was polite but firm: he could give no such guarantee. He sent a telegram to Bismarck, who was dining with the two great military leaders Moltke and Roon, informing him of his reply. Bismarck immediately saw that, with certain careful omissions, it could be construed as being insulting and peremptory. He sent the altered text to the press.

On the morning of the historic date of 14 July Gramont burst into Ollivier's room with a copy of the *North German Gazette* and exclaimed excitedly, 'They wish to force us into war!' – which was true. At midnight on 14 July war was declared by France. The news caused an outburst of joy in Paris. People were shouting, 'A Berlin! Vive la Guerre!' As André Maurois states: 'Never has an international cataclysm been set in motion on a flimsier excuse.'

The war, however, had started. There could have been only one possible outcome. The Prussian troops were highly trained and very well equipped. They knew exactly what they were going to do. The French had no idea what they were doing. That did not prevent the Maréchal Leboeuf from boasting: 'We are ready, more than ready . . . Were the war to last for a year we would not have to buy so much as a button for a pair of leggings.'

He met his Waterloo immediately. The Germans, over the last three years, had been preparing with meticulous care for the campaign on which they now embarked, up-to-date with the latest technology of artillery and field telegraphy. The French were unprepared, untrained and under-equipped. Louis-Napoleon had put himself in supreme command. On 18 July he gave a dinner at the Château de Saint-Cloud for the officers of the Guards Light Infantry. The dinner was in the Galerie d'Apollon, '*splendidement illuminée*'. When the dessert was served, the Emperor gave the order *sotto voce* to the band to strike up the *Marseillaise*. 'He knew well,' wrote the comte de Fleury, the historian of the Château de Saint-Cloud, 'that it would stir up patriotic vibrations in the hearts of the officers.' They rose to their feet, raised their glasses to the Emperor and shouted '*Vive la France! Vive l'Empereur! A Berlin!*'

The following day the Prince Imperial, now aged fourteen, dressed in an Eton collar and a top hat, '*comme un jeune anglais*', went to see Maréchal Baillehache. 'Suddenly he turned towards the Marshal, his eyes dancing with excitement. "Vous savez, Maréchal, que je pars aussi, moi!" He stressed the word *moi* with youthful satisfaction and the Maréchal, deeply moved, replied: "I do know, Monsieur, and the whole army is proud of it."'

The next day the Emperor and the Prince left for the front from the little private railway station in the park at Saint-Cloud known as the Gare de l'Empereur. Eugénie was of course there to see them off. '*Fais ton devoir Louis*,' were her last words to her son as the train pulled out of the station. Shaken with sobs, she returned to the bleak emptiness of the palace.

The campaign was an immediate and total disaster. On 6 August, two days after crossing the frontier, the Crown Prince, Edward's brother-in-law, had defeated the French Army of the Rhine, commanded by the Maréchal MacMahon, at Wörth. 'This defeat,' Edward wrote to Lord Granville, 'will be a terrible blow to the Emperor, and the feeling in Paris is easier imagined than described.' Six days later the Maréchal Bazaine's army was almost completely surrounded and destroyed at Metz.

The next day the comte de Cossé-Brissac brought Eugénie a telegram from the Emperor. '*L'armée est en déroute*,' read the message; '*il faut élever notre courage à hauteur des circonstances*.' Considering the circumstances the imperial family were lucky to find themselves before the end of the year safe in England. Lord Lyons, the British Ambassador in Paris, reported back to the Queen: 'There will, I suppose, be a battle at Châlons, and if the French are beaten again, which seems inevitable, the war must come to an end.'

Of all this the Prince of Wales was the agonized spectator. It was the

sense of his own helplessness, as much as sympathy for the sufferings of
the French, which stimulated him to write to his mother:

> If only something could be done to stop this terrible war. Could not
> England, backed by the other neutral Powers, now step in and try
> and induce the belligerents to come to terms, as it might yet save the
> lives of some thousands of fellows . . . I cannot bear sitting here and
> doing nothing whilst all this bloodshed is going on. How I wish you
> could send me with letters to the Emperor and King of Prussia, with
> friendly advice, even if it ultimately failed. I would gladly go any dis-
> tance, as I cannot help feeling restless when so many one knows and
> likes are exposed to such dangers.

Victoria, while commending his anxiety as highly creditable, replied
that his position 'would make it impossible, even if he were personally
fitted for such a difficult task.' It is quite possible that she was wrong
about him. Edward had the instincts of the peacemaker, and his first
experience of war 'on his doorstep' had given him a profound distaste
for it.

As it was, he had to content himself with one or two acts of individual kindness. Eugénie had managed to escape from Paris and found at
Deauville Sir John Burgogne who took her across the Channel in his
yacht. Edward immediately wrote to her with an offer of accommodation. 'The Princess and I, imagining that a residence close to London
would be acceptable to you, venture to offer to your Majesty our
country house at Chiswick which is entirely at your disposition.'
Chiswick House had been lent to Edward by its owner, the Duke of
Devonshire. Victoria disapproved of this offer, but Eugénie saved the
situation by declining it, renouncing the palladian perfection of Lord
Burlington's villa for the more homely comforts of Campden Place,
Chiselhurst.

It was the measure of Bismarck's genius that not only did the Ems
telegram cause France herself to declare the war for which he was

preparing, but he convinced Victoria that Germany was the injured party. Germany in her eyes stood for 'civilization, liberty, order and unity', whereas France represented 'despotism, corruption, immorality and aggression'. One can almost hear the voice of Albert at her elbow urging 'the necessity that this vainglorious and immoral people should be put down'. As for Germany, she wrote on 9 September: 'A powerful Germany can never be dangerous to England, but the very reverse, and our great object should therefore be to have her friendly and cordial towards us.' Events were to prove how mistaken Queen Victoria was.

On 19 September the German armies surrounded Paris. Victoria had learnt two days previously of Bismarck's determination that the cession of Alsace and part of Lorraine must be an essential condition for peace. The French provisional government replied that they would not cede 'one inch of territory nor one stone of their fortresses'. They were in no position to make any conditions. Queen Victoria complained of France's unrealistic posturing and warned Edward not to do or say anything that might alienate the German government 'who resent our neutrality'.

'At the outset of the war,' wrote Lady Gwendolen Cecil – Lord Salisbury's daughter and biographer – 'the feeling in England, as a whole, was in favour of Germany – until shocked into condemnation by the horrors of the siege of Paris and the severity of the terms exacted from the defeated country. But Lord Salisbury was a partisan on the side of France from the first. There was an intimacy to start with, both actual and intellectual. Diplomatically he was destined to be often in opposition to her; politically his essentially British temperament distrusted her faith in impractical logic, while her later policy towards Religion was necessarily repellent to him. But with her culture and her civilization his sympathies were very close.'

This put him sometimes in an awkward situation. Bismarck had managed to persuade the English, including Queen Victoria, that France had been the aggressor. But Salisbury did not accept this. In an article in the *Quarterly Review* (October 1870) he argued that 'there are calamities which transcend all ordinary rules, and to the authors of these we are bound to speak . . . Rebuffs suffered in such a cause would not be dishonourable; they would at least save us from any moral complicity with acts which we abhor, and from the danger of being estopped by a seeming acquiescence at this time from the chances of action which future contingencies might offer.' The Ems telegram makes Bismarck's responsibility for the declaration of war quite clear.

Salisbury continues in a sarcastic vein. 'At the head of six hundred thousand men, Count Bismarck has the courage to pretend that peaceful, idyllic Germany needs to be protected against her formidable and turbulent neighbour. Other Nations will be disposed to think that there is more to fear from the intoxication of German triumph than from distracted and revolutionized France . . . There is nothing in history to justify such a pretension.'

Lord Salisbury's daughter-in-law, Viscountess Milner, who spent much of her life in France and became a close friend of Georges Clemenceau, wrote of him: 'As a young man, as Mayor of Montmartre, he had helped Paris to resist Germany. He had then seen his country dismembered and occupied . . . I am always proud to remember that of the three Englishmen who made a public protest in 1871, when Alsace and Lorraine were torn from France, my father was one. The thought of Alsace and Lorraine was always present with M. Clemenceau, though he was essentially a man of peace, and would never have provoked a war to recover a lost province. Still, from time to time, the wound bled.' Clemenceau did, however, say: 'If I could live to see England and France march together against Germany, I think I should die from pure joy.' Lady Milner continues: 'England and France *did* march together to save civilization from Germanism. Clemenceau *did* live to see Alsace and Lorraine re-united with France.'

The Prince of Wales was profoundly disturbed by the situation. He had strong personal ties with individuals on both sides, but he was known for his predilection for the French way of life. Edward tried to secure the repatriation of one his French friends, the marquis de

Gallifet, through an exchange of prisoners. Gallifet had greatly distinguished himself at Sedan by a charge of the light cavalry, but he had ended up a prisoner of war in Coblenz. He was repatriated in 1871. During his detention he managed to meet Napoleon III, who was interned at Wilhelmshöhe. Napoleon had hoped for an early peace, but he had 'no belief in the generosity of Prussia and was confident that if Alsace and Lorraine had to be abandoned to Germany, France, in due course, would seek to reverse the defeat and the annexation.' Although he had lost his throne, he had not lost his political foresight.

On 18 January 1871, in the Grande Galerie at Versailles, King William I of Prussia was proclaimed Emperor of a united Germany. The term 'Kaiser' became part of the vocabulary of Europe. The event was a triumph for Bismarck and, by the choice of its setting, the final humiliation of France. On 1 March the German army staged a triumphal march down the Champs Elysées. A new star had been set in the firmament of Europe.

A new star also appeared in the firmament of French politics – Léon Gambetta. As a young lawyer he had gained a reputation as a distinguished orator and an 'irreconcilable' Republican. On 7 October he made a dramatic escape from Paris in a balloon. This enabled him to provide the necessary leadership to a resistance group in Tours. 'This man,' wrote Delcassé, 'with his imperturbable faith in the destiny of the country, alone stood upright during the terrible hour when everything was sinking and when, as well as the enemy, black despair was invading France. By his ardent speech he had everywhere disseminated courage and strength for resistance . . . His genius improvised armies which, though they could not throw back the invaders, at least saved the honour of *la Patrie*, the only thing that France had left to lose.'

The German Empire was a new threat to the balance of power. Both Britain and Russia had made a mistake in allowing the triumph of Prussia and the crippling of France to proceed unopposed. Russia was the first to realize it.

In the following year the Tsar, Alexander II, and the Emperor of

Austria, Franz-Joseph, were invited to Berlin. The French Ambassador, M. de Gontaut-Biron, had no doubts that Bismarck was trying to enlist the Eastern Powers of Europe in the isolation of France. The Tsar, however, in a private conversation with Gontaut-Biron, assured him that: 'I have the greatest respect for M. Thiers; please give him my assurance that he has nothing to apprehend from what has happened here; France could know for certain that I would have had no share in anything that could have been attempted here against her.' The way was open for a Franco-Russian alliance.

The duc de Broglie, who followed Thiers as Prime Minister, relates that Gortchakoff, the Chancellor of Russia, had put the point thus: 'We have an interest and a sympathy for France; *il faut que la France soit forte et sage.*' The historian Lanessan interprets the term *sage*, at that time and in that context, as meaning, if not an actual return to monarchy, at least an abstention from revolutionary tendencies. The recent horrors of the Commune in Paris had revived memories of the September massacres in 1792.

Gontaut-Biron reported back to his government that: 'Russia and Austria want a strong France and Germany would like to keep France weak. There you have the essential difference between the policies of the three Powers, and of which Germany, whatever she does, will have to take note.'

But while the governments were hoping to see a return of the monarchy to France, Bismarck was not. On 20 December 1872 he wrote to von Arnim, his Ambassador in Paris: 'We have certainly no duty to make France strong by consolidating her internal situation, and, by re-establishing the monarchy in power, to enable the country to make alliances with the Powers who have up till now been on terms of friendship with us . . . That is my conviction and it prevents me from advising His Majesty to uphold the rights of monarchy in France.' There is in this an implicit contempt for the efficiency of a republic.

The legitimist pretender to the throne of France, the comte de Chambord, was first and foremost an ultramontane Catholic. This, had he come to the throne, would have put him at enmity with the Italian government. A common hostility to the Vatican was the basis of the understanding between Germany and Italy expressed in the Triple Alliance.

Gambetta seemed to be the man of the future. 'No other man,' wrote Christopher Andrew, 'was a greater inspiration to his contemporaries.' Clemenceau stated that: 'all who met him felt the impact of his dominant personality, and I use that word in its noblest sense.'

In their own very different ways Gambetta and the Prince of Wales were both working towards the same end – friendly relations between France and England. It was not long before the two met. On 6 May 1878, the French Foreign Secretary, W. H. Waddington, who, as his name implies, was of English extraction, gave a dinner at the Quai d'Orsay in the course of which the British Ambassador, Lord Lyons, presented Gambetta to the Prince of Wales, with whom he had a long conversation. Gambetta was the most notable figure in France and Edward had recently heard him speak in the Chambre des Députés and had been fascinated by his eloquence. As Sidney Lee puts it: 'at their first meeting at M. Waddington's table he fell completely under M. Gambetta's spell.'

'The Prince's confidence in the fair prospects of Anglo-French amity,' writes Sidney Lee, 'was fostered by his continued intercourse with M. Gambetta, the most potent force in France, whose Anglophile sympathies were never in doubt . . . Sir Charles Dilke was the illustrious Frenchman's friend of long standing, and the Prince's intimacy with Sir Charles increased his opportunities of association with Gambetta.'

Gambetta fully reciprocated the Prince's interest. 'The politics of Europe and the world,' he wrote to his friend and political disciple, Mme Edmond Adam, 'interest him as much as they interest us. It is no waste of time to talk with him over a merry supper at the Café Anglais. He loves France *gaîment et sérieusement*, and his dream of the future is an *entente* with us.' It was most remarkable. Two men, whom birth and social context could hardly have set further apart, the one destined to a crown, the other the Apostle of republicanism, had found, in their common devotion to improving relations between their two countries, mutual appreciation and mutual respect. Seldom can so great a gap have been so quickly and so easily bridged. Both were in agreement also with their distrust of Bismarck's policy and in 'their strong dislike of the doctrine that nations having large armies at their command might upset all treaties in defiance of those concerned and contrary to public law'. In the words of Gambetta: '*Le Prussianisme – voilà l'ennemi!*'

A year and a half before he died, Gambetta had another important meeting with the Prince of Wales. This had been arranged by one of the Prince's particular friends in France, Henri-Charles, marquis de Breteuil. He records the event in his memoirs. The Prince of Wales had approached him. '*Mon cher Breteuil*,' he said, 'you would give me great pleasure in having me to dinner or luncheon one of these days with Gambetta . . . I know that you are on friendly terms with him, and your home is the one place where I could meet him without anyone knowing. I promise to keep it a secret, but please convey my desire to him when you have a chance.'

The luncheon was arranged and Gambetta arrived punctually at midday. 'I must admit,' continues Breteuil, 'that this short, heavily built man, with a red, shiny face and single eye, his long hair, his heavy and vulgar bearing, jarred with my wife's elegant salons like an oil stain on a piece of satin.' He had just shaken hands with the other guests when the Prince arrived: 'I introduced Gambetta who was delighted by the warm handshake and the friendly word.' Breteuil noted elsewhere that Gambetta, 'like many republicans . . . is flattered at the thought of finding himself in the presence of a Royal Highness.'

The luncheon began somewhat awkwardly, 'everyone looking at his own plate. But with the cutlets the ice broke. Gambetta, who had set his heart on pleasing His Royal Highness and my friends . . . uttered a few friendly words directed to each of us and soon he was doing all the talking . . . Everyone was captivated by him and we all felt perfectly at ease.' This was one of Gambetta's greatest accomplishments. 'I was amused to notice once again,' continued Breteuil, 'how quickly Gambetta could make those who met him forget their first impressions which are always unfavourable.'

Cigars and brandy completed what luncheon had begun and Gambetta once more monopolized the conversation. He knew well that he had captured the interest of the Prince. 'He affirmed that, so far as he was concerned, the alliance with England should be the pivot around which the present policies of France should turn.' With Gambetta in power an *Entente* could have become a reality. At three o' clock the Prince of Wales took his leave. 'He was delighted with the luncheon,' claimed Breteuil, 'and in the best humour in the world, he told us that he counted upon our discretion and parted with Gambetta on the best of terms.'

After the 1881 elections, President Grévy invited Gambetta to form a cabinet, but on 31 December 1882 Gambetta died at the age of forty-four. It was a serious setback for Franco-British relations.

On 18 July Gambetta had made what turned out to be his last speech to the Chambre des Députés which was punctuated by loud applause. 'I have the right to say that both before and after the 1870 war I have had no concern more constant or superior, both to personal interests and to those of the Party, than the security of my country [profound emotion] and I should detest myself, I would forbid myself the honour of speaking to my country, if I were capable of putting anything in the balance against its future and its greatness [prolonged applause].' Although he could not have known that it was to be his last speech, there was something in it of an *apologia pro vita sua*.

At the end of it he advised the deputies 'I have seen enough of affairs to say this to you: never break the alliance with the English, even at the cost of the greatest sacrifices.' But he added: 'I am certainly a well-informed and sincere friend of the English, but not to the extent of sacrificing the interests of France to them.' England and France could only meet on equal terms.

An important aspect of Gambetta's dedication to the *relèvement* of

France was his insistence on colonialisation. His aims were twofold. One was concerned with economics – the increase of the country's wealth. The other was concerned with morale – the restoration of the country's self-respect by a succession of colonial victories. The acquisition of Tunis in 1882 provided both these advantages. Northern Africa was the obvious area for France's colonialisation owing to its proximity to France and its coastline on the Mediterranean. In due course this was to focus itself on Morocco.

'Dignity and firmness' were the keynotes of foreign policy demanded by Gambetta. 'He favoured an *entente cordiale* with England,' writes Porter, 'and thought of the Franco-Russian alliance as an *alliance de guerre*, because although France and Russia had "no interests in common", they might well have the same enemies.'

In 1875 Gambetta had written:

the political ambitions of Russia will be impeded by Austria, who is already assuming a hostile attitude. She is exerting every pressure upon Rumania. Do you see, as a consequence, Austria allying herself with Rumania and Turkey against Russia? What a conflict! The Prince of Wales, however foresees it. He does not share the hostility of a section of the English nation against Russia. With all his young authority he fights against measures which may be prejudicial to Russia. I see in him the making of a great statesman.

4

The Third Republic

With the fall of Louis-Napoleon the Second Empire had been replaced by the Third Republic. This change of political outlook in France coincided with – if it did not actually stimulate – a similar change of political mood in England. At the end of the year 1871 the outlook for the British monarchy in general and for Edward in particular was far from encouraging. Charles Dilke, the Member of Parliament for Chelsea, launched an attack on the prodigious cost – in his eyes not just waste but mischief – of maintaining the royal family. How many of the positions in the royal household were expensive sinecures? In the course of a speech in Manchester Dilke referred to the existence of a Court Undertaker. A voice from the audience shouted that it was a pity there was not more work for him. Charles Bradlaugh, in his pamphlet *Letter from a Freemason*, openly expressed the hope that the Prince of Wales 'would never dishonour his country by becoming its King.'

Another radical, who was to play an important role in Edward's life, was Joseph Chamberlain, a brilliant young Mayor of Birmingham. He had been brought up a cobbler at a time when cobblers were notoriously radicals. In November 1874 Edward made an official visit to Birmingham. To many it looked as if he was deliberately putting his head into the lion's mouth. But Chamberlain, who, as Mayor had to propose the toast, did so with great tact, stating that 'here in England the throne is recognized and respected as the symbol of all constituted authority and settled government.' The cartoonist Sir John Tenniel could not resist depicting the occasion in *Punch*. On 14 November there appeared a cartoon with the title 'A Brummagen Lion'. It showed Chamberlain, writes Sidney Lee, as a lion 'gently kneeling before the Prince and Princess of Wales,' who is clipping his 'red republican claws and comporting himself as a gentleman.'

One of Edward's greatest virtues was to set out to make friends of his enemies. With Joseph Chamberlain he was entirely successful. In 1884, when the publication of the *Bitter Cry of Outcast London* had resulted in the setting up of the Royal Commission on Housing, Chamberlain had made an attack on the aristocracy, comparing them to 'the lilies of the field; they toil not neither do they spin,' and said that 'although there were no Royals present they would not be missed.' In due course he became a frequent guest at Chatsworth, Marlborough House and, of course, Windsor Castle.

On 29 September 1871 an article in the highly respectable *Pall Mall Gazette* claimed that 'republicanism of a very revolutionary form was flooding in.'

At what might have been a critical moment for royalty Fate intervened. At the end of October Edward was staying with Lord and Lady Londesborough in Yorkshire. One of his fellow guests was Lord Chesterfield. Edward returned to Sandringham to celebrate his thirtieth birthday on 9 November. Soon afterwards he was taken ill. So was Lord Chesterfield and so was the Prince's groom Blegge. Both of these died. The disease was diagnosed as typhoid, the same that had killed Edward's father. On 7 December Lady Macclesfield wrote to her husband that the situation was becoming 'worse and worse. The doctors say that if he does not rally within the next hour, a very few more must see the end.' On 12 December the leading article in *The Times* reported: 'The Prince still lives and we may therefore hope; but the strength of the patient is terribly diminished and all who watch his bedside as, indeed, all England watches, must acknowledge that their minds are heavy with apprehension.'

On 14 December, the tenth anniversary of his father's death, there were signs of improvement. The 8 a.m. bulletin announced that the physicians had perceived 'some abatement in the gravity of the symptoms.' From that moment on progress was steady. On 21 December it was declared that danger was past. A series of telegrams reported a continued, if gradual improvement. Mr Gladstone admitted that 'it was impossible to repress the cheerful feelings which they inspire.' Why he should have wanted to repress them is not clear.

Queen Victoria took the unprecedented step of addressing a letter to her people.

> The Queen is very anxious [it read] to express her deep sense of the touching sympathy of the whole nation on the occasion of the alarming illness of her dear son, the Prince of Wales. The universal feeling shown by her people during those painful, terrible days . . . as well as the general joy at the improvement of the Prince of Wales' health have made a deep and lasting impression on her heart which can never be effaced.

It was indeed nothing new to her, for the Queen had met with the same sympathy when, just ten years ago a similar illness removed from her side the mainstay of her life, the best, wisest and kindest of husbands.

'This outburst of popular sympathy,' writes Sidney Lee, 'which the Prince's illness evoked was vastly to strengthen throughout the country the monarchical sentiment.' Lee quotes some interesting sources. The Baron Brunnow, the Russian Ambassador in London, wrote to Prince Gortschakov, the Chancellor of the Russian Empire: 'Incontestably this crisis has produced in England a happy reaction in favour of the monarchical institutions which govern this great land.' The Duke of Cambridge wrote to his mother : 'The republicans say their chances are up. Thank God for this! Heaven has sent this dispensation to save us.'

On 19 March 1872, Dilke moved in the House of Commons for a full inquiry into the Queen's expenditure. The motion was ignominiously defeated and Gladstone made, amid loud applause, a speech affirming his faith in the monarchy. Lord Henry Lennox wrote to Disraeli: 'what a sell for Dilke this illness has been!' Sir Richard Jebb, a professor at Cambridge, felt that Providence had given the Prince 'the chance, if he knows how to use it, of becoming the most popular man in England . . . the prolongation of his life means the indefinite prolongation of the life of the monarchy.'

There was a chance also that Edward might respond to these manifestations of affection by taking a more serious attitude to life. His *rendez-vous manqué* with death was the turning point in his life. It was in the affairs of France that he was to find an opening. But it was no longer the royal or imperial France to which Edward had been accustomed. It was the Third Republic.

Not surprisingly the beginnings of the new Republic had been a period of confusion. Its leaders had little experience to guide their steps. There was, of course, the noble precedent of Ancient Rome and the more recent example of the Dutch Republic. They claimed the principle of 'moral order', but it was neither particularly moral nor necessarily conducive to order.

The outstanding character of the new regime was its instability. Lord Salisbury was to complain of the impossibility of forming an alliance with a government which changed every six months. During the period between 1870 and 1905 France changed its Prime Minister twenty-nine times. In England the corresponding figure was nine. It was the same with the Foreign Ministers. During the same period there were twenty-three French names, of which Théophile Delcassé had a record run of six. In England there were only seven names, that of Lord Salisbury occurring four times.

Robert Gascoyne-Cecil, third Marquess of Salisbury, was to play the leading role in British politics during the latter part of the reign of Queen Victoria. On Monday, 22 June 1885, she asked him to form a cabinet. It was an interesting choice. Randall Davidson, Dean of Windsor and later Archbishop of Canterbury, who was one of the men closest to the Queen, had made the observation that she only respected people who showed themselves capable of standing up to her. Lord Salisbury certainly belonged to that category. Shortly before her death she named him her favourite Prime Minister, superior even to her beloved Disraeli. 'Salisbury,' writes Andrew Roberts, 'had emerged as the man best placed to save her from the ultimate political nightmare – five more years of William Ewart Gladstone.'

Salisbury does not lend himself easily as a subject for a potted biography, but anecdotes about him abound and many shed an interesting light on his character and personality. Andrew Roberts describes him as 'the most un-Victorian Victorian statesman, who in certain things was almost a left-over from the reign of George IV.' He quotes in evidence the Liberal politician G. W. E. Russell who insisted on the 'utter freedom from pomposity, formality and self assertion and the agreeable clash of genuine cynicism which modifies, but does not mask, the flame of his fun.' Victorian high politics, Roberts reminds us, 'are not automatically associated with fun.'

Salisbury could even be cynical about the Conservative Party. 'It is a party shackled by tradition,' he told Sir Alfred Milner, 'all the cautious, all the timid, all the unimaginative, belong to it. It stumbles slowly and painfully from precedent to precedent with its eyes fixed on the ground. Yet the Conservative party is the Imperial party. I must work with it – who, indeed am just such a one myself, but you must work with it if you are to achieve even a part of your object.'

Salisbury had the sort of mind that could master every detail of a complex situation, but he had more than that: he was a brilliant communicator. He was undoubtedly one of the greatest public speakers of his time. His daughter and biographer, Lady Gwendolen Cecil, devotes considerable space to this subject. She makes the interesting connection between his style of speaking and his style of writing. 'What he supremely dreaded was any excess of fluency – the use of language divorced from thought he always treated as an unforgivable sin in oratory . . . At the same time he deliberately refused to prepare the wording of his speeches beforehand – a resolve presumably due to a conviction of the greater effectiveness of purely extempore speaking.'

It was a practice which he shared with King Edward. It presupposes a complete command of one's subject. 'He compelled himself,' continues Lady Gwendolen, 'at the moment of utterance, to concentrate his thought upon the substance of his speech. It was an art understood by the Romans and summed up in the neat little epigram "*Rem tene; verba sequuntur*" . . . "hold to the matter and the words will follow."'

It is this which provides the connection between the spoken and the written word. Salisbury often expressed, in after years, the opinion that 'excellence in speaking could only be achieved by practice in writing. He was fastidious in composition with his pen – never content till he had achieved the precise shade of meaning or suggestion of which he was in search. He thus acquired at his desk both a facility of expression with the subtleties of the language, which enabled him ultimately to achieve spontaneity in speech without sacrifice of literary form.'

Another factor contributing to Salisbury's command of language was his appreciation of French. 'He used to declare,' wrote Lady Gwendoline, 'that clear thinking in the world would be greatly benefited if it could be forbidden to publish any metaphysical philosophy except in French: a Frenchman *could not* write obscurely however hard he might try – just as mistiness was inseparable from the "intolerable" German language. The clarity, the subtlety, the perfect finish of the French mentality attracted him; the quickness of its apprehension, the audacity of its humour, the fineness of its wit, were a constant satisfaction.' On one occasion he was himself the butt of a French witticism. A man in his position naturally picked up various honours, such as Chancellor of the University of Oxford. Another was the position of Elder Brother of Trinity House. When a Frenchman asked him what the uniform was which he was wearing he replied: '*Frère Aîné de la Trinité.*' He got the reply: '*Mon Dieu, quelle distinction!*'

He was particularly interested in the French Revolution and had collected a large number of books and pamphlets which were frequently quoted in his writings and speeches. 'Its lessons,' writes Andrew Roberts, 'infused his political beliefs.' In particular this applies to his insistence on the need for strength in government. 'The witness of History,' he wrote in 1860, 'is uniform to this; that Nemesis may spare the sagacious criminal, but never fails to overtake the weak, the undecided and the over-charitable fool.'

Before the Third Republic was firmly established, there was one last attempt to restore the Bourbon monarchy. The throne was offered to the legitimist heir, '*l'Enfant du Miracle*', the duc de Bordeaux, now known as the comte de Chambord, grandson of Charles X. The comte de Calonne had managed to raise enough money to purchase and restore the Château de Chambord and to present it to this providential Prince. He was offered the throne of France with the title of Henri V. Thiers, however, had insisted on the formula of 1830: 'The Princes must be good enough to recognize the fact that the Monarchy is fundamentally a Republic with a hereditary President.' But the Comte de Chambord shared his grandfather's rigid belief in Divine Right. It was not for any government to offer him the throne. It was not theirs to offer. He retreated to the château from which he took his title and from there issued his manifesto, dated 5 July 1871.

The actual issue over which the negotiations broke down was the French flag. The Prince could not accept the tricolor flag of the Revolution. The white flag of the monarchy was sacrosanct. 'On the subject of this flag,' he wrote, 'conditions have been talked of to which I cannot and must not submit. I am ready to do anything to help my country to rise from its ruins and take up once more its rank in the world. The only sacrifice which I cannot make is that of my honour.' He ends on a somewhat sentimental note: '*Il a flotté sur mon berceau; je veux qu'il ombrage ma tombe . . . Henri V ne peut abandonner le drapeau d'Henri IV!*' (It floated over my cradle; I want it to shade my tomb. Henri V cannot abandon the flag of Henri IV). The Bishop of Orléans, who had been with a deputation of anxious Royalists to dissuade the Prince from his folly, declared that 'never has such absolute moral blindness been witnessed.' Thiers, more sarcastic, suggested that the Prince should be called 'the French Washington', for he had founded the Republic.

On 12 February 1871 the British government had officially recognized the French Republic. The first President elected was Louis-Adolphe Thiers. Described by Maurois as 'a learned, ambitious little man from the South,' he had, with the help of Talleyrand, founded the Opposition newspaper, the *National*. (It is noteworthy how often at this period journalism provided the formation for a political career.) At the beginning of February 1871, after the defeat of France by Germany, Thiers had been appointed Chief Executive of the Provisional Government of the French Republic. He was immediately faced with a civil war – the Commune took control of Paris. The Provisional Government retreated to Versailles. The Commune had, in fact, no single creed and, after much bloodshed, was stamped out by Thiers and his government. France, however, was in a sorry state of disarray.

On 11 March 1872 the Foreign Secretary, Lord Granville, asked Edward to pay a formal visit to President Thiers. The Prince admitted that it went 'very much against the grain' – but he undertook to do so. The meeting went off well. When Bismarck heard of the visit, he took it for the sign of a new and unwelcome understanding between France and Great Britain.

Edward was now faced with a new situation. Hitherto he had always been dealing with crowned sovereigns. Now it was beginning to look as if the Republic had come to stay. It took Edward some time to digest and to manage to adjust to it. But he succeeded in doing so. He was, however, still hopeful of the return of a royal or an imperial regime. In spite of his contact with the French Republic, he continued to maintain friendly relations with both the Orléanist and the Bonapartist parties. He made frequent visits to the duc d'Aumale, Louis-Philippe's youngest son, at his newly resurrected Château de Chantilly where he was amassing his magnificent collection of works of art.

On the whole, however, Edward favoured a return of the Napoleonic dynasty. He had high hopes for the Prince Imperial. 'I had always entertained for him feelings of the greatest affection and always looked towards the day when he might be called upon to rule the destinies of that great, friendly power, France . . . I believe that he would have proved an admirable sovereign and that he, like his father, would have been a true and great ally of this country.' He was to be disappointed.

In exile, the Prince Imperial had joined the British army and in the spring of 1878 took part in the war against the Zulus. On 19 June while making a reconnaissance in enemy territory, his party was ambushed and he was killed. Edward was dumbfounded. 'I look upon his loss,' he wrote to the Duke of Cambridge, 'as a national one to his country.' To Victoria he wrote: 'I cannot get the poor little Prince Imperial out of my thoughts, and look upon his untimely and horrible death as a most dreadful catastrophe . . . The poor, poor Empress, what has she to live for? Nothing . . . my heart bleeds for her, especially as one can offer no consolation.'

There was, however, the slight consolation of a funeral appropriate to his birth. A British man-of-war was sent to collect the coffin, Edward acted as pall-bearer at the funeral and Victoria sat with Eugénie throughout the ceremony. On 12 July Disraeli, who had opposed the whole idea of a royal style funeral, wrote: 'I hope the French Government will be as joyful. In my mind nothing could be more injudicious than the whole affair.'

With the death of the Prince Imperial Edward somewhat reluctantly accepted that republicanism might have come to stay in France. His visit to Thiers in March had been a success largely due to the warmth of the reception by his host and hostess. He was the only person of royal rank to make this gesture. But his acceptance of the Republic did not cause him to sever his connections with the remaining princes of the House of Orléans.

There are several interesting passages on the subject of royalty in the

Journal Secret of Henri, marquis de Breteuil. He was one of Edward's closest friends and a man who moved with ease in Europe's highest society – the guest of kings and emperors, the confidant of statesmen and diplomats and an acute observer of political events. On 2 July 1886, shortly after the Orléanist princes had, for the second time, been exiled from France and had, for the second time, found a welcome in England, the marquis de Breteuil was spending a night in London and notified Edward of his presence. He was immediately summoned to Marlborough House. At ten o'clock the next morning he found Edward still dressing. *'Il était de la plus belle humeur du monde.'*

Since the marriage of Edward's brother-in-law, Prince Waldemar of Denmark, and since the death of the Prince Imperial, Edward had become a firm supporter of the Orléanist cause. 'Never,' continues Breteuil, 'has he opened his heart so completely with regard to this subject.'

'France is lost,' stated Edward, 'if she does not understand – and fairly soon – that the monarchy of the comte de Paris is alone capable of saving her and restoring her to the position in Europe which should be hers. Your country has become a hotbed for every subversive idea and every revolutionary doctrine. The time has come for kings and emperors to protect themselves from you. I know well that M. de Bismarck, who has a hatred of France, and whom the spectre of a France morally restored haunts like a nightmare, is the all-powerful protector of your Republic, and, by the same token, the irreconcilable enemy of your Princes.' Bismarck needed a weak France.

What made matters worse was that the future Kaiser Wilhelm II was 'a profound admirer of the Chancellor. I wish your party to know,' concluded Edward, 'of my personal sympathies and of those of my family. France ought to be the ally of England: the comte de Paris ought to know that he has no greater friend than myself.'

On 17 September 1887 the comte de Paris (senior grandson of Louis-Philippe and Pretender to the throne of France) issued a manifesto. 'At first sight,' commented the marquis de Breteuil, 'these instructions

seemed a little long, but not a phrase in it is redundant. It is a real programme: it is a Charter.'

Earlier that summer, on the occasion of Victoria's Golden Jubilee,
Breteuil had made a visit to London as the guest of Lord and Lady
Randolph Churchill. On 21 June he witnessed the Queen's ceremonial
drive through London.

She was seated alone on the back seat of the open barouche; facing
her were placed the Princess of Wales and the future Empress of
Germany [Vicky]: she was dressed with her customary simplicity, refusing to wear a crown or diadem, and with the benevolent gestures which
she made to right and left, her good, broad countenance and the generous proportions of her figure, she seemed not to be the Queen of
England or the Empress of India, but the mother of her people, and her
people certainly seemed to welcome her as such.

The occasion made a deep impression on Breteuil.

I do not think it would be possible to have been present at a demonstration more national, more sincere or more imposing. The Country
finds its personification in the ceremonial of the Monarchy and cel-
ebrates its own jubilee: it congratulates itself on a long period of
wisdom, prosperity and glory.

Those who think that, for free countries, a republic is the last word
in progress could reflect usefully on yesterday's spectacle: the most
free country in the world displayed its joy in having lived happily for
half a century and proved that an indisputable principle, even when
represented by a woman, is necessary to the functioning of a regime
that is truly constitutional and truly liberal, that it is no obstacle to
progress and that it is necessary to defend the interests of a nation in
the affairs of the world.

In October the same year Breteuil had a long and interesting discussion with Edward on the comte de Paris' charter. Edward began by
expressing his disapproval and claimed that most of the ruling families

of Europe agreed with him. Breteuil insisted that their opinions would have no effect on the domestic policies of France.

> You approve the restoration of monarchy, but you will not advance that cause by one minute. The comte de Paris has to reckon here with a new and ineradicable force: Democracy. That is what he has to reckon with, and, if he manages to prove that hereditary Monarchy can come to terms with it, he will have simplified the task of other crowned heads . . . The Prince believes that universal suffrage cannot be withdrawn from the French, and this necessarily imposes certain particular duties. In the history of European monarchies, has not that of Great Britain during the last two centuries, Monseigneur, set the example to others of its suppleness and demonstrated that the institution of monarchy both can and should submit to the modifications necessitated by progress?

On the French side it is noticeable that the new government continued to appoint prominent members of the aristocracy to their Embassy in London. First, in February 1871, was the duc de Broglie who was succeeded a year later by the comte Bernard d'Harcourt. He remained at the Court of St James's for an unusually long time – nearly four years. This enabled him to establish a good relationship with Edward. They worked together to further an understanding between the two countries. In autumn 1873 a more distinguished diplomat, the duc Decazes, held the post for two months before being recalled to become Foreign Secretary. Once at the Quai d'Orsay, Decazes insisted that their objective should be an *entente* and not an alliance.

Decazes began to make overtures towards a better understanding between France and Britain. Victoria approved up to a point. On 17 August 1874 Sir Henry Ponsonby, her Private Secretary, wrote to Lord Derby, the recently appointed Foreign Secretary, 'A new and intimate *alliance* with France, especially with Republican France, the Queen would strongly deprecate. Germany, Austria and even Russia [the three most autocratic States in Europe] are far more useful, natural and good allies for England; but we should always be on *good and friendly terms* with France.'

The first Ambassador to be appointed by Decazes was the duc de La Rochefoucauld-Bisaccia who held the post until the summer of 1874. Back in France he entertained the Prince of Wales in truly royal style at his Château d'Esclimont, near Chartres. 'Esclimont,' wrote the comte Ernest de Ganay in 1919, 'remains in France one of the very rare châteaux where a charming welcome, where genuine high standards, where old-fashioned courtesy transmitted by a noble tradition, still preserve the image of the once legendary *douceur de vivre* of the 18th century.' Edward made a regular progress round the private palaces of France. It was like a conducted tour of the *Ancien Régime*. He stayed with the duc de La Tremoïlle at Serrant, on the Loire, the duc de Mouchy at Mouchy-le-Châtel, the prince de Sagan at the Château de Mello, and with the duchesse de Luynes at Dampierre.

Edward's contacts with France were not approved of either by his mother or by Disraeli, who wrote on 3 October 1874 to say that 'a visit to France at this moment' was of doubtful prudence, but insisting that, if he did go to Paris, he should pay 'some marked respect to the Chief of the French State'. The Chief of the French State at the time was the Maréchal MacMahon, an old friend of Edward's. Edward did go to Paris and did make a ceremonial call on the President who invited him and Lord Lytton, an attaché at the British Embassy, to a stag hunt in the Forêt de Marly. MacMahon favoured a return of the monarchy and the new constitution was drawn up with this in mind.

In the summer of 1875 Franco-German relations began to deteriorate. As so often, the actual *causa belli* was a trivial matter – a rumour that France was importing German horses in large numbers, which Bismarck instantly forbade. In the end Queen Victoria intervened. She wrote a personal letter to Kaiser Wilhelm I. At Bismarck's request the Kaiser informed the Queen that she was mistaken. On 8 June she wrote to her daughter, the Crown Princess: 'Bismarck is a terrible man, and he makes Germany greatly disliked – indeed *no-one* will stand the over-bearing, insolent way in which he acts and treats other nations – Belgium, for instance. You know that the Prussians are not popular unfortunately, and *no-one* will tolerate any Power wishing to dictate to all Europe. This country, with the greatest wish to go hand in hand with Germany, *cannot* and *will not stand it*.'

On 27 January 1859 there had occurred in Berlin an event which was to alter the history of Europe: Prince Frederick William Victor Albert, later to be Kaiser Wilhelm II, was born. He was the son of Frederick III, Crown Prince of Prussia. Frederick was married to Edward's sister Victoria, the Princess Royal, always known as Vicky. Brother and sister enjoyed a close relationship and she was one of his main sources of information about Germany. She exercised considerable influence over her husband who became an outspoken liberal. Had his father died earlier, the reign of Frederick might have altered the course of history.

It had been a difficult childbirth and it was not until the next day that Mrs Innocent, the midwife, drew the doctor's attention to the fact that 'there was something wrong' with the baby's left arm. It fitted loosely into its socket. It soon became apparent that the sometimes drastic attempts to remedy this defect were of no avail. William was permanently crippled. He learned to live with it, however, and even became a good shot and an accomplished horseman. Whether this disability had any psychological effect is difficult to establish. His education may have exercised a creative influence as much or more decisive. Dr Georg Hinzpeter was appointed his tutor. A 'spartan idealist' and a strict Calvinist, he was devoid of any sense of humour, incapable of praise, even when praise was due, and insisted upon a regime of twelve hours a day of study and physical exercise. As Wilhelm himself puts it in his Memoirs: 'the strain on a boy of seven was severe.' His coming of age, on 27 January 1877 was marked by Queen Victoria sending him the Order of the Garter.

During the intervening years – usually the most formative – Wilhelm had been subjected to the opposite influences of his father and his

grandfather. There was a great gulf fixed between their political positions. There were two main parties in Germany, described by
Christopher Clark, in his biography of Wilhelm, as 'the western-
orientated conservative liberal party and the pro-Russian arch-
conservatives. The Crown Princess was particularly hostile to the
Russian set . . . Narrowly orthodox or evangelical in religion, reactionary
in domestic politics, they represented the cultural and political antipode
of the Crown Prince couple and their entourage.' Frederick and Vicky
were 'theologically liberal, politically progressive and their views on
foreign policy were British orientated and marked by distrust of Russia.'

In July 1862 Vicky wrote to her mother: 'The reactionary party gets
stronger every day and have the King now completely in their power.'
By the summer of that year father and son had drifted so far apart that
rational communication was virtually impossible. 'The slightest allusion to political matters,' wrote Vicky, 'drives him [Frederick] into a
frenzy and excites all the opposition in his nature, so that it impossible
to argue or reason with him . . . The feeling of humiliation is the hardest
to bear. Nothing remains but silence as passive witnesses of the lamentable mistakes made by those we love and reverence.' Among these was
her son.

It is not unusual, especially in royal families, for sons to be opposed
to their fathers and this was certainly the case with the young Wilhelm.
There was no love lost between him and his father. He was much more
attracted by his grandfather. 'The awkward division of power between
parent and grandparent,' writes Clark, 'was the single most important
fact in Wilhelm's early life.' According to Herbert von Bismarck, the
Chancellor's son, Wilhelm had told him that the 'unprecedented
circumstances of there being three generations of the ruling family
made things difficult for his father. In every case, in ruling and in other
families, the father had the authority and the son was financially
dependent upon him, but he [Prince Wilhelm] was not under his
father's authority . . . since everything derived from the head of the
family, he was independent of his father.'

Wilhelm's preference for his grandfather had brought him under the influence of the great Bismarck. When Bismarck had suggested that Wilhelm should be initiated into the workings of the Foreign Office, his father objected that 'his lack of maturity and experience, together with his tendency towards arrogance and exaggeration, would make such a move premature'. He was making the same mistake that Victoria made with Edward. Bismarck disagreed and pointed out that Wilhelm was now twenty-seven years old. He went on to remind the Crown Prince that in the royal family the authority of the father is subsumed in that of the monarch. The episode led to an outburst of anger by the Crown Prince.

Michael Balfour, in his biography of Wilhelm, explains his dualism in terms of his heredity. 'He was the product of two cultures, not of one. He had two ideals held out in front of him: that of the Prussian Junker and that of the Liberal English Gentleman . . . But the desire to be the English Gentleman was alternating all the time with the desire to be the Prussian Prince – and each conspiring to frustrate the other. The tension between the two, superimposed on his physical disablity and upon the tensions already endemic in Prussian society, is the ultimate key to his character: taut, restless, lacking in the self-confidence which comes with integration.' Christopher Clark sums up the position. 'It is plausible to suppose that the pervasive irresolution of William's upbringing, its oscillation between two opposed lifeworlds, its lack of a unifying theme, militated against the crystallization of a coherent outlook or stable code of conduct.'

Alice, Countess of Athlone is another interesting source of information. A first cousin of Wilhelm's, she spent much time in Germany while her brother, the Duke of Albany, was training at the Military Cadet School, and she had many occasions to observe her cousin. She described him as 'a strange man who always blew hot and cold.' This made him 'temperamentally unstable'. She found him 'shy-making and one who enjoyed being formidable', but she added: 'William was the last person to want war.'

In the natural course of events Frederick III would have been expected to succeed to the throne and to govern Germany for a number of years. In this case Wilhelm I nearly outlived his son. The year 1888 was called in Germany 'the Year of the Three Kaisers'. Everyone's eyes were centred on the Emperor's palace on Unter den Linden, where the old soldier was slowly dying, and on the Villa Zirio at San Remo where his son was equally stricken. Many eyes were also on Prince Wilhelm's Berlin palace. His grandfather died on 9 March. His father only occupied the throne for ninety-six days and he was already at death's door.

The poignancy of this situation is pin-pointed by Breteuil in his *Secret Journal*. On 10 March he wrote of Frederick:

The dying man, who has no illusions, speaks a noble and patriotic language. The counsels he gives, the policy that he indicates, seem to be his last testament in advance; one who expresses himself thus seems already not to belong to this world.

The state of things in Europe would take on a new aspect and an era of peace would certainly open up if this Prince could reign and hold on. What sad reflections do not come to one in the face of such caprice of fortune! If only he could live for long enough to leave the imprint on the politics of his country of a lasting orientation. If he could exercise his power for long enough to make the benefits of it understood, the memory of him would outlive him and his son might, perhaps, respect his last wishes. Unfortunately this is not likely.

A week later Breteuil was able to discuss the situation with England's ablest statesman. He was staying with Lord Randolph Churchill who told him that Lord Salisbury was anxious to meet him. Naturally he accepted and they had a long talk together.

He is a large, bulky man [Breteuil noted] with a vulgar appearance. He looks more like a Norman stock-breeder than an English Lord, but after five minutes conversation this first impression is effaced and one is captivated by the *finesse* of his language, his charming manners and his great knowledge of all things . . .

Lord Salisbury did not conceal from me his sympathy for the Royalist Party; as the true leader of the Tory Party, he has a thorough detestation for the radicals in all countries. 'Besides', he said to me, 'you are not ready for parliamentary rule in France. Parliamentary government is an Anglo-Saxon combination for the use of northerners; leave it with us and have no regrets.'

He went on to discuss the imminent death of Frederick III.

He made no secret, as well of his personal regrets, of how much he deplored his disappearance from the point of view of England: he said enough for me to understand the hopes which Great Britain had the right to base on the politics of this Prince and the fears which are inspired by those of his successor.

Frederick died on 15 June. The young Wilhelm was now Kaiser, but in many ways the real ruler of Germany was Bismarck.

Wilhelm has left, in his Memoirs, his own account of his relations with Bismarck. 'While I was still Prince of Prussia I often thought to myself: "I hope that the great Chancellor will live for many years yet, for if I could govern with him I should be safe."' This did not prevent him, however, from disagreements with his Chancellor.

I could not wage the open war against the Social Democrats which the Prince [Bismarck] desired. Nevertheless this quarrel concerning political measures cannot lessen my admiration for the greatness of Bismarck as a statesman. He remains the creator of the German Empire and, surely, no *one* man need have done more for his country than that.

Wilhelm shows himself as being quite perceptive about his own position.

> The tragic element for me in the matter of Bismarck lay in the fact that I became the successor of my grandfather. In other words . . . I skipped a generation. That is a serious thing. In such a case one is constantly forced to deal with deserving old men who live more in the past than in the present and cannot look to the future. When a grandson succeeds his grandfather and finds revered but ancient statesmen of the calibre of Bismarck, it is not a matter of good luck for him, as one might suppose, and as, in fact, I did suppose. As for me personally I have the satisfaction of recalling that Bismarck entrusted me in 1886 with the very delicate Brest mission and said of me: 'Some day that man will be his own Chancellor.'

If the Countess of Athlone was right in saying that Wilhelm did not want war, at least he delighted in military magnificence. The Baron von Eckardstein tells an anecdote about the marquis de Gallifet. He had been lunching with Count Münster at the German Embassy, where he had been shown the latest portrait of the Kaiser by Lolo Handke. There, 'in his best War Lord mien', in his military uniform and the mantle of the Order of the Garter, his Field Marshal's baton held assertively in his right hand and the hilt of his sword in his crippled left hand, and looking confidently towards Heaven, stood Wilhelm. 'When I asked Gallifet what he thought of it,' continues Eckardstein, 'he said: 'To tell you the truth . . . that portrait is a declaration of war.'

Edward was the exact opposite. He had a natural, as opposed to an assumed, dignity and a presence, which is the sign of an integrated character. It was not likely that the two would agree with one another.

In April 1876 Lord Lyons, the British Ambassador in Paris, reported that the French would like the Prince of Wales to be President of the British Section of the Paris International Exhibition. There was, however, a definite political slant to the exhibition. In the minds of the original promoters it was seen as 'a celebration of the Republicans' triumph over their monarchist rivals'. Edward, nevertheless, willingly agreed. It was evidence of his readiness to accept, perhaps a little reluctantly, republicanism in France and to salute the Republic as the expression of the Nation's will. In this he showed a marked difference from the more important crowned heads in Europe, none of whom came but who were all represented by their ambassadors, with the exception of Germany who sent none.

Although the Prince valued the Exhibition as a demonstration of the progress in industry and art, he saw it as an outward and visible sign of France's renewed vigour and prosperity, as well as her leadership in the arts of peace. On 1 March 1878 he wrote to his mother: 'I find I shall have a great deal to do with the Exhibition.' He took considerable trouble over the Gallery of English Art, persuading owners of important pictures to loan them. The success of the British section was universally attributed to Edward's energy.

On one occasion a group of Deputies cried '*Vive la République!*' as they passed him. He accepted their greeting with a laugh. On 3 May he made a public declaration that he still believed in the *Entente Cordiale* and at the same time in the victory of the Republic. At a dinner given by Lord Granville it was Edward who proposed the toast of 'Le Président de la République Française'.

He then went on to deliver a notable speech, half in English and half in French. 'I am glad to think,' he stated, 'we should have met here this evening in a country and a city which have always received Englishmen with hospitality, and that though, not many years ago, there was a time when we were not so friendly as we are now, still that time is past and forgotten . . . and I am convinced that the *Entente Cordiale* which exists between this country and our own is one not likely to change.'

Then he continued in French. '*C'est avec grand plaisir que je viens remercier la nation Française, tant en mon nom qu'au nom de la Commission Royale Britannique, de tout ce qu'elle a fait . . . L'Exposition*

Universelle de 1878 est sans contredit un grand succès. Aussi permettez-moi de vous dire, et dire à la France entière, que la prospérité de ce pays et celle de la Grande Bretagne ont un intérêt essentiellement réciproque. La participation cordiale apportée au triomphe des Arts dans cette lutte pacifique est de la plus haute importance pour nos deux nations et pour le monde entier. L'Exposition Internationale, dans laquelle nous avons tenu à prendre une large part, est le meilleur moyen de sympathie que nous puissions donner au peuple Français auquel nous devons tant.' As Sidney Lee puts it: 'Beyond all misconception had the Prince nailed his French colours to the mast.' In French official and social circles he was at once hailed as the 'accredited representative of courageous Young England which was about to replace decrepit and hesitating Old England.'

On 11 May 1878 Lord Lyons wrote to Lord Salisbury: 'England is very popular here at this moment, and the Prince of Wales' visit has been the principal cause of all this.' Edward had accepted the republicanism of France and he had drawn attention to the importance of the cultural relations between the two countries. It is often in the appreciation of the art, music, literature and architecture of another country that we draw closest to them.

On 18 July 1878 Edward made one of his visits to Paris in the course of which he invited Gambetta to lunch at the Café des Anglais. Lord Lyons was not present but Edward reported to him. 'Gambetta spoke strongly in favour of an alliance between France and England . . . and spoke in the most disparaging terms, not so much of the foreign policy of Russia as of the institutions, the Government and the administration of that country.' Lord Lyons reported to Salisbury: 'I hear from other quarters that Gambetta was extremely pleased with the interview. I am assured that the Prince of Wales acquitted himself with great skill.' On his return to London the Prince was welcomed by Salisbury with a generous acknowledgement of the success of his interview.

'I trust your Royal Highness will not think I am guilty of an intrusion if I venture, on the score of my official position, to thank your

Royal Highness very earnestly for what you have done in Paris. The crisis has been of no little delicacy: and if the leaders of French opinion had definitely turned against us, a disagreeable and even hazardous condition of estrangement between the two countries might have grown up which would have been very much regretted. Your Royal Highness's influence over M. Gambetta, and the skill with which that influence has been exerted, have averted a danger which was not inconsiderable. It has been necessarily my duty to watch anxiously the movement of feeling in France at this moment.'

The Prince replied at once: 'If I have in any way by the personal interview which I had with M. Gambetta tended to allay the irritation which was manifest in France by our taking Cyprus I am beyond measure pleased, as nobody would have deplored more than I would that any estrangement between the two countries should occur.' Cyprus had been wanted by Lord Salisbury as a naval base in the eastern Mediterranean. It figured on the agenda of the Congress of Berlin in 1878 and on 7 July the British took formal possession. The move had been strongly opposed by Gladstone and Lord Derby and the government had been nervous of a hostile intervention by France.

The Berlin Conference lasted from 30 June to 30 July. It concerned the 'Eastern Question'. It was a struggle for the control of the Balkan States. On 28 May Edward wrote to his mother urging that only Disraeli could worthily represent Great Britain: 'The Prime Minister is not only the *right* man to represent us at the conference, he is the *only* man who can go, as he would show Russia and the other Powers that we were really in earnest.'

Victoria immediately disagreed with him; she was afraid that it would put too great a strain on Disraeli's health. 'He is the firm and wise head and hand that rules the Government and who is my great support and comfort, for you cannot think how kind he is to me, how attached. His health and life are of *immense value* to me and the country.' She then moved on to the subject of Russia. 'I don't believe that *without fighting* and giving these detestable Russians a good beating *any* arrangement will be lasting. They will always *hate* us and we can never trust them.'

Disraeli did represent his country at the Berlin Conference and succeeded in getting his way. 'The Russians surrendered unconditionally,' he wrote to Edward, 'and Russia is now more hopelessly than ever excluded from the Mediterranean, to gain which they embarked on the late [Crimean] war.' The only country to vote with the Russians was Germany.

It is interesting to observe that Disraeli found time to write two long and informative letters to the Prince of Wales at one of his busiest moments. This sort of contact with the leading politicians of both France and England had an important formative influence on the Prince and played a significant part in his political education.

Edward, at last, was beginning to find his vocation.

5

Théophile Delcassé

Gambetta died towards the end of 1882; had he lived he would undoubtedly have been one of the chief architects of the *Entente Cordiale*. He might be said to have laid the foundation stone. The mantle of Gambetta fell upon his friend and associate Théophile Delcassé, a man of humble origins whose somewhat love-starved childhood may have paved the way to a passionate devotion to his country and a determination to raise it from the humiliations of the Franco-Prussian War.

It was in July 1870, when he was taking his final exams at school, that he heard of the defeat of France. 'These were moments,' he wrote, 'that I should never be able to forget. It was then that I vowed to devote myself to my country, to make it my ambition to serve her and make my contribution to the reconstruction of her stricken edifice.'

France had failed largely through her hopelessly inadequate military preparation. It cost her fifty billion francs and the loss of Alsace and part of Lorraine. During the negotiation of the Peace of Frankfurt not a single country in Europe had tried to intervene in her favour. She was left to face the humiliating demands of triumphant Germany alone. This was a lesson deeply ingrained in the young Théophile: that it was imperative for France to create a properly trained and equipped army and that she could not survive without allies.

In 1879 he was offered a job by Gambetta as foreign affairs reporter on *La République Française*. It was the oracle of republicanism in France. Here he was a colleague of Eugène Spuller, the chief editor, who had accompanied Gambetta when he escaped by balloon from Paris, and of Gabriel Hanotaux, the future diplomat and historian. These three men were to exercise a formative influence upon him and set him on the path to success.

Spuller was sometimes described as Gambetta's *alter ego*, but Gambetta himself used to come down to the editor's office to discuss with his reporters the earlier debates of the day. He exchanged greetings with everybody and then, having gathered together the leading members of his staff, there would be a brief general discussion on the day's events, after which 'the renowned orator would launch into an eloquent speech on politics and foreign relations. His colleagues wrote down his ideas and his phrases.'

This was Declassé's real schooling in the art of politics. He could not have had a better master and Gambetta could not have had an apter pupil. On one occasion, when Gambetta had concentrated on the internal affairs of France, Delcassé interrupted him with the words: 'it is also necessary to think of remaking Europe and of destroying the work of Bismarck.' Gambetta's overall purpose was to 'reconstruct' France – that is to say to make it a Republic, and to 'complete' it – that is to say to recover Alsace/Lorraine. Years later (1885) Delcassé told his future wife: 'My objective is the resurrection of the country . . . the sacred task undertaken by Gambetta with an ardour, a devotion, a spirit of self-sacrifice and self-effacement that will never be fully comprehended.'

Gambetta's influence was most obvious in Delcassé's devotion to the cause of French colonial expansion as a means of restoring national greatness. Delcassé also inherited from Gambetta both his desire for an *Entente* with England and his reluctance to surrender Egypt to England for the sake of the *Entente*. But he was true to Gambetta's words: 'Be convinced that the English, good politicians as they are, esteem only those allies who take account of their own interests and know how to make themselves respected.'

On 14 November 1881 Gambetta was called to power, but by 26 January the following year he was out again. France was not ready for him. Delcassé left the Chamber with a sinking heart. 'He sat down at his desk,' writes Albéric Neton, 'and started to write. It was five in the morning when he stopped writing. He threw himself on his bed, but sleep would not come. He took up his pen again. He re-read what he had written. He made no corrections . . . He ran to his publisher, who was also his friend, and next morning there appeared a document with the title '*Alerte! Où allons-nous?*'

Neton devotes to it one of his most spirited passages. 'His reasoning, lofty without effort, animated without passion, is irresistible when he denounces those in power, the gaps in the ministerial system, the lack of initiative and even more the lack of continuity in the conduct of our foreign policy, the absence of any definite purpose, the fear which leads to isolation.'

It was essentially an attack on President Freycinet's policy – or lack of policy. Delcassé demanded a complete reorganization of the French military system, including three years compulsory service for all men without distinction. It was not until 1893 that France began to modernize her army.

Delcassé was particularly alarmed at the weakness of the executive branch of the government. The young Republic had not yet got into its stride. He then moved on to foreign policy:

When, on the ruins of the old balance of power, a monstrous and formidable coalition has formed itself (the Triple Alliance of Germany, Austria and Italy) is it possible for France to continue to live in the isolation to which she has been reduced by her disasters without worrying about the future and without any determined purpose?

Do you not see that on all sides of you in Europe there are Powers with interests identical with yours and that the union of these with us would not only be a strong union between these Powers but . . . would form an indestructible *fasces*? For lack of a hand to guide them and draw them together, these interests, instead of seeking each other, disregard each other, flee from each other and you remain isolated, living from day to day at the mercy of events beyond your control because the strings that govern them are not in your hands.

The French seemed to be more interested in establishing the principle of republicanism than in providing the country with a government that was effective.

In particular Delcassé lamented the deterioration of relations with her old ally across the Channel.

England, so firm, so resolute, with a common line of action under the preceding Cabinet (Gambetta's), since your advent to power shows a coldness which you cannot possibly disguise, and which crops up even in the articles of journals most favourable towards you . . . Was not this the moment to display the vigour which you retail with so much facility in your speeches? After a rapid entente with England, energetic action ought to have been taken to put everything back into its proper place and to safeguard our interests. It seemed preferable to you to wait patiently on the course of events . . . Then, disconcerted by your attitude, the London Cabinet detached itself from you and the collective note disappeared.

The last eleven pages of Delcassé's pamphlet (there were thirty-four in all) were devoted to matters of foreign policy. It was this which was to become his dominant interest.

This attack on the government of Freycinet brought Delcassé into the limelight. He soon became one of the most familiar figures among the reporters and leader writers who frequented the lobbies of the Chamber of Deputies – 'a dapper little figure', stated an article in *Le Matin*, 'with a large, smiling mouth; gold-rimmed spectacles over a thickish, slightly upturned nose, big, dark, intelligent eyes, a thatch of dark hair over a flat cranium; a most courteous, amiable little man, grave, precise in speech, ever on the alert for "tips".' He had shown, however, that he could be in deadly earnest.

As a journalist his style, writes his biographer, Charles Porter, was 'devoid of all useless verbiage, was crisp, incisive and convincing, and made foreign affairs intelligible to the man in the street.' Long before he came to occupy any post in the government Delcassé was having an important impact upon public opinion.

In the 1890s the French began an attempt to unify their scattered conquests in West Africa into a single Empire. The motive force behind this logical design was fear of foreign competition. In Italy the Prime Minister, Francesco Crispi, stated that he proposed to make Italy great and strong by giving her an Empire, claiming that 'colonies are a necessity of modern life.'

At its highest, imperialism was bred of a desire to spread civilization to the underdeveloped and often still barbarian races. 'Even the Socialists,' writes Christopher Andrew, 'though deeply hostile to military and financial imperialism, were not altogether unsympathetic to French expansion. The argument of the '*mission civilisatrice*', frequently used to justify French expansion at the turn of the 20th century, was an extension of the earlier tradition, dating from the Revolution, of a French *messianic mission* to lead the oppressed peoples of Europe to liberty.'

To Delcassé the arch-enemy was always Germany. On 11 October 1885 he wrote in *La République Française* that only the machinations and trickery of Bismarck were separating France from Italy.

More than anyone else [Delcassé wrote] we have deplored the misunderstandings which have strained the relations between France and Italy in these last few years; but we have never thought that they could last, because national interests as well as race draw the two countries together and dictate that they should mutually assist each other. All attempts to bring us into conflict in the Mediterranean are in vain. On the contrary, we think Italy has a place marked out for her in the Mediterranean and we shall see with pleasure Italy conquering her just share of influence.

A year later Delcassé accused Italy of being 'the dupe of Bismarck'. As for the other member of the Triple Alliance, Austria, she was no better. 'From the Court of Vienna,' he claimed, 'Italy has received up to this time only signs of humiliating indifference; from Bismarck only sarcasm and menaces . . . Italy has no claim to press against France; why, then, should she ally herself with our enemies?'

Some Italian newspapers, notably *L'Opinione*, continued to support the Triple Alliance. They even preached a 'Mediterranean League' consisting of Italy, Germany, Austria and England. Delcassé was quick to point out the absurdity of including Germany: 'To class Germany among the Mediterranean Powers is a strange thing to do, and denotes a singular state of mind.'

By 1887 Delcassé had more or less left *La République Française* and transferred his allegiance to a new daily paper, *Paris*. On Sunday, 5 June an important article appeared in which he states his own view of the principles of diplomacy.

The only rule which inspires France in her international relations is the defence of her rights, that is, the protection of French interests. Evidently the accomplishment of these obligations can lead her to search for friendship and support on the outside. All the art of diplomacy consists in finding the nation to which the friendship of France appears equally advantageous and her support precious; and when she has found it, to avoid all that might compromise an *entente* founded on reciprocal sympathies and common interests.

Well, this nation exists, and it is our most inveterate enemy, it is Bismarck himself who has taken care to point it out to us. It is he who, on April 26th 1856, in a report to the Prince Regent of Prussia, wrote this sentence which should be continually in the mind of all who give themselves to politics: 'The alliance of France and Russia is a thing so natural that it would be folly not to expect it; because, of all the Powers, they are the only ones which, by reason of their geographic position and political aims, have the least element of hostility, not having any interests which necessarily conflict.'

The idea of a Franco-Russian alliance was somewhat surprising. The Tsar Nicholas II, when still Tsarevitch in 1887, had declared: 'May God preserve us from an alliance with France . . . it would mean the invasion of Russia by Revolution.' But he was to change his mind. In 1891 the Franco-Russian *rapprochement* was made public by the visit of the French fleet to the Russian naval base at Kronstadt. On this occasion Delcassé wrote to his wife: 'For a long time no one, or almost no one, was willing to believe in the Franco-Russian *entente*. And yet it was not difficult to see that it was inevitable. A glance at the map was enough.'

The geographic position was the one which caused most concern to Germany. An alliance between France and Russia could, in the event of war, oblige Germany to fight simultaneously on two opposite frontiers. From a political point of view Imperial Russia and Republican France were strange bed-fellows but they were not incapable of mutual understanding.

Maurice Paléologue, one of France's most distinguished ambassadors to St Petersburg, had made a deep and sympathetic study of the country of his mission.

In order to understand present-day Russia and to foresee the great social tragedy which is being worked out confusedly in the hearts of the masses, behind the pompous facades and Byzantine magnificence of the tsarist regime, there is no shortage of prophets. I name among them the most clairvoyant − or at least those who have made the most vivid impression on myself: Bakunin, Herzen, Prince Kropotkin, Tolstoy, Dostoievsky and their joint predecessor, the one most remarkable for his perceptive intuitions, Joseph de Maistre . . . I have aways suspected that the civilization is several centuries behind that of the west. And I recall the words of Joseph de Maistre during his mission to St Petersburg: 'We deceive ourselves here when we write 1815; we ought to write 1515. We are still in the 16th century.'

On the Russian monarchy Paléologue has much to say.

The omnipotence of the Tsars is not a regime which is the product of chance and which maintains its position by mere force; it springs from the whole history of Russia; it goes hand in hand with the psychology of Russia . . . For several years I have been officially concerned with Russian revolutionaries who are refugees in France; I therefore have some understanding of their mentality; I find in this the most natural explanation of tsarism. I mean by that that the population of Russia is fundamentally and congenitally anarchist. In order to restrain these subversive instincts there is only one which answers to it . . . it is oriental despotism.

It might have been expected that Paléologue would disapprove of such despotism, but he took a practical view of the situation. 'Since Russia is our ally, and since this alliance is absolutely necessary for us to preserve us from German megalomania, we are obliged by our own interests to reinforce, as far as it depends on us, the threatened framework of tsarism.' He might have added that such a regime would require a very firm hand on the tiller. This was the last thing which was to be expected from the new Tsar, Nicholas II.

The early accession of Nicholas on 1 November 1894 was the source of much misgiving in Court circles. Count Wladimir Lamsdorff, the Foreign Minister, stated: 'His Majesty still lacks the external appearance and manner of an Emperor.' According to his sister, the Grand Duchess Olga, Nicholas 'was in despair. He kept saying that he did not know what would become of us all and that he was wholly unfit to reign.' Dominic Lieven, in his biography of the Tsar, sees the same fault in his education which had been the greatest mistake in Edward's. It was to be the same in the education of Nicholas' only son. His tutor made the same observation: 'a child educated in such isolation is deprived of that basic principle which plays the main role in developing judgement. He will always feel the lack of that knowledge which is obtained independently of study through life itself, by means of free relationships with his peers.'

At his coronation Princess Radziwill commented: 'There, where a mighty Monarch had presented himself to the cheers and acclamations of his subjects, one saw a frail, small, insignificant youth, whose imperial crown seemed to crush him to the ground, and whose helplessness gave an appearance of unreality to the whole scene.'

But if the young Tsar did not make much of an impression on the occasion of his coronation, his coronation made an indelible impression on him. In the words of General Alexander Mosolov: 'the Tsar took his role of God's representative with the utmost seriousness.' Nicholas believed, writes Dominic Lieven, 'that through his coronation he had assumed before God a responsibility for the fate of his Empire from which no human being could ever absolve him. Within him rational political calculation was always to co-exist with the conviction that the wisdom which sprang from the instincts and heart of a Tsar, who was the Lord's Lieutenant in the land, was superior to any purely secular reasoning.'

On 26 November 1894 Nicholas married Princess Alix of Hesse, whose mother, Princess Alice, was Victoria's second daughter. Grandmother and grand-daughter had always been very close to each other.

If Nicholas was not cut out for the role of Tsar, no-one could have been less suited to the role of Tsarina than Alix. She was painfully shy and blushed in an unbecoming manner if addressed. Serge Volkonsky, who, as Director of the Imperial Theatre, was frequently in her presence, wrote: 'This characteristic, added to her natural indisposition towards the human race and her wholesale mistrust of people, deprived her of the slightest popularity. She was only a name – a walking picture . . . In her intercourse with others she never emitted a congenial spark.'

To such a couple the immense size of the Winter Palace in St Petersburg did not offer acceptable accommodation. They lived about fifteen miles to the south of St Petersburg at 'the Village of the Tsar' – Tsareskoe Selo. There were two palaces here, the vast Catherine Palace, used only for State occasions, and the smaller Alexander Palace which became the family home. It was here that they experienced their greatest domestic happiness, but it distanced them from the heart of Russian life.

It was this regime with which Delcassé was urging France to form a strong alliance.

Delcassé then proceeded to turn his guns against Germany.

This is the truth today, a truth which Time has fortified, which events have rendered more forceful. To all the causes of friendship between France and Russia described thirty years ago by Bismarck, there has been added one other which makes a close union of these two nations a superior law: that is a common danger. Between them, united Germany raises herself, formidable by her military power, disquieting because of her encroaching tendencies, bruising by her arrogance the most legitimate susceptibilities, ruining the economic interests of her neighbours whose national existence she still menaces. It is against her attacks that France and Russia have to fortify themselves before-hand; it is upon her that they have to press identical claims. To the east and to the west of Europe, they act as counterpoise to the German colossus. Everywhere the same enemies, everywhere the same interests, everywhere the same aspirations. What is puzzling is that an *entente* so natural has been so long in becoming established.

In 1886 the Minister of Foreign Affairs, Flourens, with the support of the Prime Minister, Maurice Rouvier, began to work on an alliance between France and Russia. Delcassé's ultimate vision was a triple alliance between France, Russia and England, but the time was not yet ripe. In the first place relations between Russia and England were particularly tense owing to Russia's threat to India, and in the second place France's relations with England were deteriorating into bitter colonial rivalry. Delcassé had to progress one step at a time and he was wise to have gone no faster. In July 1887 his achievement received recognition from the President, Jules Grévy, who made him a *Chevalier de la Légion d'Honneur*.

In June 1888 Delcassé wrote an answer to those in England who were talking foolishly of the possibility of a war between England and France. 'Why should we make war with England?' he asked. 'To take a strip of land from them? But we acquired our natural frontiers on the north west centuries ago, and it is not on the Channel that we have been mutilated. To take away their colonies? But the exploitation of those which we already possess will keep us employed for a long time to come.'

He insisted that there was no need for enmity between England and Russia and he blamed Lord Salisbury for maintaining this position. 'The Prime Minister of the Queen has not been able to disembarrass himself of the prejudices and hatreds which have it that France and Russia are the born enemies of England. These prevent him from taking well into account the modifications which have taken place in the respective situation of the Powers and from seeing clearly that England's danger now lies elsewhere.'

Delcassé showed himself to be a far-seeing judge of the political trends in England. 'The democracy which is rising, and which is fated to have the government of England, does not share these prejudices. Its arrival in power will lead to a different foreign policy. Lord Randolph Churchill formulated that a year ago on his return from his trip to Russia . . . There is much talk therefore of an *entente* between France, England and Russia.'

Lord Randoph Churchill – the younger son of the Duke of

Marlborough and father of Sir Winston – was a colourful and some-times impetuous character. He had incurred social ostracism by being divorced, but Gladstone valued him and made him Secretary of State for India. He was widely regarded as the apostle of Tory democracy. There was something about Lord Randolph which appealed to Edward, who was one of the first to see him as the man of the future. He was, however, fully aware of his faults. Churchill, he admitted to his mother, 'takes unfortunately strong likes and dislikes.' Victoria disapproved of her son's liaison with Churchill as much as she disapproved of his asso-ciation with Sir Charles Dilke.

Charles Dilke and Joseph Chamberlain represented the radical element in Gladstone's government. Both of them had publicly opposed the principle of the monarchy, but Edward took a very broad-minded view and valued them for what they were. They were both admitted into his social circle. On 4 March 1872 Lord Fife, one of Edward's closer friends, had invited Dilke to meet the Prince at dinner. 'The Prince,' wrote Dilke, 'laid himself out to be pleasant and talked with me nearly all the evening, chiefly about France.' Dilke was very much a francophile.

Edward had a remarkable capacity for crossing lines of social demar-cation and for forming strong ties with political opponents. For Edward was a great listener and a great believer in the value of establishing deep and friendly relationships, both at individual and at international levels. His warm relations with the anti-monarchical Dilke reflected his equally warm relationship with the strongly republican Gambetta. It was these gifts which were to enable Edward to play so important a part in the creation of the *Entente Cordiale*. In their different ways, both Granville and Dilke nourished the Prince's serious interest in the affairs of France.

At the same time Théophile Delcassé, who was steadily rising in his career, was working towards the same end. As a journalist he had gained a reputation and a position which, in France, not infrequently opened the door to ministerial office. At the beginning of 1893, after one of the rather frequent changes of government, Alexandre Ribot was invited to form a new Cabinet. Delcassé had already made a name for himself as a distinguished political correspondent; he had supporters in most of the different Republican groups; he was known to be a hard and conscientious worker. Ribot invited him to take charge of France's colonial Empire. He refused to accept unless the Colonial Administration was given a higher profile.

Only two months previously Delcassé had made the statement: 'A great people, to whom Nature has given a relatively small territory, which mistakes in policy and hazards of war have further diminished, is compelled to make up for this inferiority by her power of expansion.' Now he demanded a more prestigious housing for the Colonial Office. The cramped and unhygienic premises shared with the Ministry of Marine in the Rue Royale were sending out the wrong messages. As luck would have it, the Pavillon de Flore, which formed the south west corner of the Palace of the Tuileries, was available. It had formed part of the Royal Apartments under the Restoration and under Napoleon III. The installation of the Colonial Office in this prominent and prestigious building did not merely provide independence, it conferred status.

Delcassé's first major item on the agenda concerned Egypt. He considered that France had equal rights over this area with England. The English, however, were firmly established in the north of Egypt, but in the south there were still even unexplored areas which might offer opportunities. The Sudan, with its recently established independence, looked like being the soft under-belly of Egypt.

Delcassé was a frank advocate of colonialism. At the beginning of 1885 he had written: 'Europe is stifling within her present boundaries, with production everywhere outstripping demand. Its peoples are therefore driven by necessity to seek new markets far away, and what more secure markets can a nation possess than the countries placed under its influence?'

But there was another, perhaps more important motive for his colonialism. As a pupil of Gambetta he could not fail to respond to the latter's cry of exultation when, after the occupation of Tunisia, Gambetta wrote to the Prime Minister, Jules Ferry: 'I congratulate you from the bottom of my heart. France is becoming a Great Power again.' The Third Republic's bid for Empire was above all a policy of national prestige.

Delcassé was not without enemies, and among the accusations made against him was that of over-spending. He asked what would be France's excuse:

> if one day it could be said that, for some hundreds of thousands of francs, we had allowed our rivals to occupy territories of which we had legitimately dreamed ourselves? Do you think that even the present generation, on whom the expenses of colonial policy weigh, would be pleased by an abstention from which our rivals would profit? No! In this country of France, above all sensible to honour, where the humblest labourer, where the most ignorant peasant has the liveliest feeling for the singular grandeur and superior destiny of his country, no Government would long be tolerated if it could invoke only monetary reasons to explain its lack of enterprise.

As Charles Porter, in his biography of Delcassé, claims: 'Outside of Parliament, critics who were less partisan . . . saw him as a statesman who had bravely answered all of the direct and indirect attacks made against him, who might at times have been wrong, but who had had the singular merit of following a clear and well-conceived colonial policy.' It was not long before Delcassé was back in office.

The position of Minister of the Colonies seems to have been more or less a stepping stone to the more important post of Minister of Foreign Affairs. He ranked second to the Prime Minister. In England the two offices were sometimes held by the same person, so closely were their concerns connected.

On 4 May 1898 Delcassé was re-elected to the Chamber for another four years. On 28 June he was offered the position of Foreign Secretary.

He was to retain it until 6 June 1905. Seven years was a record tenure of office in France at that time. 'Few events in modern history,' wrote Charles Porter, 'are more important than Delcassé's accession to Office on June 29, 1898.' 1898 was a critical year for European diplomacy.

Delcassé had a long and difficult task ahead of him, but he was fortunate in the support of his first Prime Minister, Henri Brisson. Brisson quickly learned to appreciate him. 'You have become a personal friend', he wrote in November 1898; 'your courage, your patriotism, so proud and so enlightened . . . have been an enormous encouragement to me.'

A month after Delcassé's promotion the great Bismarck died. He had already been in retirement for ten years. On coming to the throne Wilhelm II had sent a telegram to George Hinzpeter, his unofficial channel to the press, saying: 'Duty of watch-keeping Officer in the Ship of State has now devolved upon me. The course remains as it was. Full steam ahead.' But, as the famous cartoon by Tenniel so fittingly illustrated, Wilhelm 'dropped the pilot.' The course would not be exactly what it was.

The death of Bismarck, so nearly coinciding with the coming to power of Delcassé, has a symbolic significance. Delcassé's policy was to reverse as much as was possible of Bismarck's work.

By the beginning of February 1899 Delcassé had formulated his policy. Albéric Neton gives an account of the proceedings. 'This programme, a veritable monument of diplomacy, put together by a skilled craftsman, we can see him expounding with admirable lucidity, at a meeting held in his office at which were present M. Paul Cambon [Ambassador to Great Britain], his brother Jules Cambon [future Ambassador to the United States] and M. Camille Barrère, [Ambassador to Rome]. 'The imperial vision,' writes Christopher Andrew, 'which was to dominate the development of his foreign policy was of a Greater France, built round the shores of the Mediterranean, with an African hinterland stretching southward to the Congo.'

Delcassé made his observations in order of urgency. First came the

DROPPING THE PILOT.

'The end of Bismarck's regime.'

alliance with Russia. In October 1898 Count Mouravief, the Russian Minister for Foreign Affairs, came to Paris and spent two days in talks with Delcassé, who found in his approach 'an unexpected stimulant, while at the same time a precious reinforcement of the Franco-Russian alliance.'

The following year Delcassé returned the visit. 'The rumours circulating about this,' writes Neton, 'were considerable. As Delcassé had a holy horror of advertisement, he did not consider it appropriate to inform the Universe of his projects.' He did not often even inform his Cabinet. He had long talks at Peterhof with the Tsar and with each of his Ministers, and at the gala dinner offered in his honour by Mouravief toasts were proposed in which one could feel 'the vibrant allusions to the unalterable intimacy of the two countries.'

Delcassé's first practical step was taken in November 1898, when he negotiated the termination of the long standing tariff war which was embittering relationships without benefiting either side. Speaking in the Chamber in support of the ratification of this measure he put his emphasis not on the articles themselves but on the merit of cordial and confident relationships. As he had written in *Paris*, in November 1888: 'There is between France and Russia a community of interests which renders treaties superfluous and which is a hundred times preferable to the best of treaties.' This was to be the very principle of *Entente Cordiale*.

In August 1899 President Loubet was enjoying a short holiday at Rambouillet which was recorded by Combarieu. On Sunday, 12th he noted: 'Saw Delcassé who is back from St Petersburg and has made his report to the President. The success of his negotiation is more than he had hoped for. He wanted to prepare, in his talks with Mouravief and the Tsar, agreements which could later be signed. And here are the agreements themselves already signed!'

Delcassé had sat up all night to work out the final version, had signed it himself and got it signed by his colleague. 'He brought back the French text on his chest, between his vest and his skin, for fear of it being stolen from him.' A copy was made to be deposited at the Ministry of Foreign Affairs and he handed over the original to the President who put it away in a red portfolio, along with other secret papers, in an iron safe which was fixed into the wall of his office. Meanwhile the British government was moving closer to France.

Germany, however, was doing all that she could to prevent such an alliance. 'What has struck me most,' wrote Delcassé, 'is that since the accession of Nicholas II the Kaiser has tried to impose on him by never ceasing to calumniate, to vituperate France.' As Wilhelm said to Prince Lobanov, the Russian Foreign Minister:

I do not like all these Princely visits coming one after another to Paris; they have the effect of consolidating the Republic by presenting it before the eyes of the people as a regime quite as normal as any other and making them forget that Monarchies are of Divine institution, whereas republics are of human creation. Now, the consolidation of republican France is a danger to all thrones, and, allow me to say, to you, that what is most annoying and most extraordinary is to see the Government which is the most monarchical in Europe maintaining with this republic the most intimate relations . . . On the contrary, we must isolate France, abandon it to the internal strifes of its parties and let it stew in its own juice. And if it shows any inclination to spread beyond its boundaries by means of revolutionary propaganda, the three Emperors ought to unite at once to crush it completely.

One of the most important sources of information on the subject of Divine Right comes from the Kaiser himself – his secret correspondence with the Tsar. These letters were discovered in July 1919 after the murder of Nicholas and his family. They were first published in English by the *Morning Post*, and later in book form by the Editor, Norman Grant. 'It has been left to the Emperor,' he writes, 'to tell us what is most accurate and illuminating about himself.'

There are seventy-five letters, beginning soon after the accession of Nicholas in 1894 and ending in 1914. They were intended for the Tsar's eyes alone. They are written in English and in the Kaiser's handwriting. Wilhelm's most usual form of address is 'to dearest Nicky' and he ended with such expressions as 'Now good-bye, dearest Nicky; best love to Alix, from Ever your most devoted and faithful friend and cousin, Willy.' The correspondence has come to be known as 'the Willy/Nicky letters'.

The object of all this flattery was to prise Russia away from her alliance with Republican France and to focus her attention eastwards, away from Europe.

In letter after letter William attacks the principle of republicanism and exalts that of monarchy by Divine Right. 'We Christian Kings and Emperors have one holy duty imposed on us by Heaven, that is to uphold the Principle *von Gottes Gnaden* [by the Grace of God].' France with her Republic and England with her constitutional monarchy were the glaring exceptions to this principle. In particular he resented the apparent endorsement of republicanism by the frequent visits of European royalty to France.

In Letter no. VII (25 October 1895) he underlines 'the danger which is brought to our Principle of Monarchism through the lifting up of the Republic on a pedestal'. The constant reception of kings and heads of state with great ceremony by the French President:

makes Republicans believe that they are quite honest, excellent people, with whom Princes may consort and feel at home.

The Republicans are Revolutionists *de natura* . . . The République Française is from the source of the Great Revolution and propagates, and is bound to do so, the idea of it. Don't forget that Jaurès sits on the throne of the King and Queen of France *by the grace of God* whose heads French Republicans cut off! The blood of their Majesties is still on that country . . . Nicky, take my word for it, the curse of God has stricken that people for ever.

These letters reveal, among other things, the contrast between Wilhelm and Edward VII. Edward had managed to accommodate his natural taste for monarchy to the republicanism of France. His personal friendship with President Loubet, later to be expressed in their reciprocal visits, was something which the Kaiser could not have achieved had he wanted to. The strong aversion to Edward which recurs throughout these letters reflects Wilhelm's disapproval of his attitude to Republicans. His favourite adjective in writing about the English is 'ridiculous'. In July of the same year he took this a stage further.

I was glad to be able to show [at a Naval Review at Kiel] how our interests were entwined in the Far East . . . that Europe had to be thankful to you that you so quickly had perceived the great future of Russia in the cultivation of Asia and in the defence of the Cross and the old Christian European culture . . . it was natural that, if Russia was engaged in this tremendous work, you wished to have Europe quiet and your back free.

In Letter no. VI, dated September 1895, Wilhelm illustrated his theme in a most original manner.

At last my thoughts developed into a certain form and this I sketched on paper. I worked it out with an artist (Professor Knackfuss) – a first class draughtsman – and after it was finished had it engraved for public use.

It shows the Powers of Europe represented by their respective Genii called together by Arch-Angel-Michael – sent from Heaven – to *unite*, in resisting the inroad of Buddhism and Barbarism, for the defence of the Cross. Stress is specially laid on the *united* resistance of *all* European Powers, which is just as necessary also against our common internal foes: anarchism, republicanism, nihilism. I venture to send you an engraving, begging you to accept it as a token of my warm and sincere friendship to you and to Russia.

This work of art, known as the 'Yellow Peril cartoon', was described in the North German *Gazette*.

On a plateau of rock, bathed in light radiating from the Cross, stand allegorical figures of the civilized Nations. In the foreground is France, shading her eyes with her left hand. She cannot altogether believe in the proximity of danger, but Germany, armed with a shield and sword, follows with attentive eye the approach of calamity. Russia, a beautiful woman with a wealth of hair, leans her arms, as if in close friendship, on the shoulder of her martial companion. Beside the group Austria stands in resolute pose. She extends her right hand in an attitude of invitation as if to win the co-operation of still some-what reluctant England in the common task. At the foot of the rocky plateau stands the vast plain of civilized Europe . . . In the foreground is the Castle of Hohenzollern, but over these peaceful landscapes clouds of calamity are rolling up . . . The path trodden by Asiatic hordes in their onward career is marked by a sea of flame proceeding from a burning city. Dense clouds of smoke are twisting into the form of hellish distorted figures from the conflagration. The threatening danger in the form of Buddha is enthroned in this sombre framework. A Chinese dragon, which at the same time represents the demon of destruction, carries this heathen idol. In an awful onset the Powers of Darkness draw nearer to the banks of the protecting stream.

On 19 January 1904, Paléologue, it seems, got wind of the Willy/Nicky letters. 'We learn from a secret but trustworthy source that the Emperor Wilhelm pursues his course of flattery and incitement with the Tsar Nicholas. He never stops stirring him up against 'dirty little Japan who presumes to defy great and holy Russia.' Not only does he urge him to annexe all the territory of Manchuria, but demonstrates to him that the Korean peninsula . . . is the natural and indispensable pro-longation of Russia's dominions in East Asia.' As Wilhelm wrote: 'Korea and Manchuria ought to belong to you . . . The great combat that you must lead will be the final contest between the religion of Christ and the religion of Buddha.' He looked forward to a joint domination of the two great Oceans: 'Do you know how we will call ourselves henceforth, you and I? I will call you 'Admiral of the Pacific' and you will call me 'Admiral of the Atlantic'.

Nothing could have been more improbable than Nicholas earning any such title. On 10 February 1904 the Mikado declared war on Russia and immediately attacked the Russian ships in Japanese waters. In September Paléologue noted: 'since the squadron of Port Arthur has been sunk and since the Division of Vladivostock is reduced to a few cruisers, it is of the utmost necessity to send out there another fleet.'

It is difficult not to accuse the Kaiser of working on the weakness of the Tsar to manipulate him, in the name of family friendship, into taking action disastrous to Russia and, in the short run, helpful to Germany. Wilhelm was far too intelligent not to realize that in encouraging 'dearest Nicky' to send a second fleet to recover Port Arthur, he was sending it to certain death and destruction. He also used the occasion to try and boost the German dockyards.

The second fleet, which was duly built, was to fare no better than the first. On 20 October 1904 it left for Japanese waters on its first and only voyage. It immediately ran into serious trouble. During the first night, while they were crossing the North Sea, an incident occurred which shook the Chancelleries of Europe and nearly caused a war between Russia and Britain. There were a few British trawlers fishing off the Dogger Bank. The Comander-in-Chief, Admiral Rozhdestvensky, jumped to the unlikely conclusion that they were Japanese torpedo boats and opened fire. One trawler was sunk with all hands and others were badly damaged, causing more casualties. Without stopping to pick up the wounded, the Russian fleet sped on its way.

On Tuesday, 25 October Edward received a telegram from the Tsar. 'Through foreign source have heard of incident in North Sea. Deplore loss of lives of innocent fishermen . . . Having had many warnings that Japanese were lurking in fishing smacks for purpose of destroying our squadron, great precautions were ordered to be taken, especially at night. Trust no complications will arise between our countries owing to this occurrence. Best love. Nicky.'

In replying Edward went straight to the point. 'What has caused me and my country so painful an impression is that your squadron did not stop to offer assistance to the wounded, as your searchlights must have revealed to your Admiral that the ships were British vessels.' Lord Lansdowne, who had been asked to approve the telegram, replied that it was 'most appropriate, and he is particularly glad that your Majesty dwelt upon the callous conduct of the Russian naval officers in making no attempt to succour the victims.'

On the same day Paléologue noted the reaction in Britain. 'There has been an outburst of public opinion in England against Russia . . . they are unanimous in demanding from the tsarist Government a resounding atonement. They demand that the squadron of Rozhdestvensky stops immediately and that, if necessary, the British fleet pursues it.' That evening Delcassé told him that 'in the state of exasperation in which I see public opinion in England, I would not be astonished if war were to break out tomorrow.'

There can be little doubt that Rozhdestvensky, having panicked at the sight of other vessels, had imagined the whole story. As King Edward wrote to Lord Lansdowne: 'One can hardly credit the statement that a Japanese torpedo boat steamed at full speed towards the Russian squadron, which caused the latter to fire at and sink our trawlers.' When the inquest of the International Commission finally reported they found that the Russian Admiral 'was not justified in having opened fire on the trawlers since there was no enemy torpedo boat among them.' Sir Charles Hardinge, who had been the British Ambassador in St Petersburg since May 1904, adds that the Court of Enquiry proved that there were not, and never had been, any Japanese torpedo boats in the North Sea.

The Kaiser, somewhat typically, expressed his belief in the whole story. In a letter written to the Tsar on 30 October he claimed to have 'heard from a private source that the Hull fishermen acknowledged that they had seen foreign steam craft among their boats.' Such a statement from such a man hardly counts as evidence.

The rest of the voyage, which took the Russian fleet right round Africa and up into Japanese waters, presented Delcassé with some very delicate problems. Such a fleet had constantly to put into ports to restock with food and fuel. To permit refuelling could constitute a breach of neutrality. Delcassé managed, with some dexterity, to avoid an actual breach with Japan. On 12 May 1905 Paléologue noted that 'the long time spent by the Russian fleet off the coasts of Annan [which were French waters] had roused the fury of Japanese opinion and the irritation of the English.' *The Times*, he said, asked what France would say if, in the course of a war on which the future of their country hung, their enemy's ships were offered asylum in English ports.

On 27 May the Russian Armada finally reached Japanese waters. It was confronted by Admiral Togo in the straits of Tsushima, between Korea and Japan. Nearly all the Russian ships were sunk or captured; nearly all their crews were killed or taken prisoner. All chance of regaining mastery of the sea had disappeared and with it of avoiding total defeat in the war.

One of the essential requirements, if not the *sine qua non*, of a great diplomat is the ability to deal simultaneously with a large number of different problems and to discern, or if possible foresee, their interconnections. He is like a juggler who is trying to keep half a dozen balls in the air at the same time. This was undoubtedly one of the claims to greatness of Delcassé. He could keep a number of projects moving steadily forward under his hand. He also had the strength which comes from persistence. A considerable number of the principles to which he adhered when he came to the Quai d'Orsay can be traced back to their enunciation in his articles in the press from about 1886 onwards. During his time as a political correspondent his clear command of his subject and his lucid and convincing style of writing had made foreign affairs intelligible to the average reader.

One of his long-term projects was the steady improvement of relationships between France and Italy – still bound by the Triple Alliance to Germany and Austria. The reasons for Italy taking part in this alliance were largely obsolete. Italy did not withdraw from the Triple Alliance but her continuation in it was on the condition that it contained 'nothing directly or indirectly aggressive towards France.' All that Germany and Italy shared was a common hostility to the Vatican.

On 10 July 1902 an exchange of letters between France and Italy declared that 'no divergence now existed between them as to their respective interests in the Mediterranean' and agreeing that in the event of 'direct or indirect aggression' the other would be neutral. Delcassé was able to announce to a vociferously jubilant Parlement that Italy would in no circumstances become the instrument or auxiliary of an act of aggression towards France. This whole negotiation, patiently pursued and triumphantly crowned with success, must be regarded as one of Delcassé's greatest achievements. But it was more than that: it was an important step in the recovery of France's prestige in Europe.

In April 1889 Eugène Spuller, Delcassé's former colleague on the *République Française*, had become Foreign Secretary. He too had been devoted to the cause of a Franco-Italian *Entente*. In the following year Albert Billot, the author of an important work on the subject, *La France et l'Italie*, was appointed Ambassador to Rome. It was a good appointment.

It was made clear to both parties by the discussions that 'the Mediterranean, far from inciting them to conflict, should, on the contrary, serve to draw them together and hold them together'. It was finally agreed on 14 December 1900 that France should have priority in Morocco and that she would not oppose Italy's claim to Tripoli.

The *Entente* between France and Italy did not improve the relationship, already strained, between France and the Vatican. When President Loubet made an official visit to King Victor-Emmanuel III, the Pope protested. In the end Delcassé broke off diplomatic relations with the Vatican.

But Delcassé did not confine his attentions to Europe. 'The success of the United States in the Spanish-American war,' writes Charles Porter, 'opened the eyes of France to this new and growing power beyond the seas.' Frenchmen of all classes who had hitherto sneered at the 'dollar-hunting Yankees', now vied with one another in an effort to embrace Uncle Sam. Delcassé saw another opening for the development of France as a first-rate Power. René Vallier, the author of the *Vingtième Siècle Politique* describes it as '*la conquête des Etats-Unis*'.

Delcassé soon saw that Chinese affairs offered an opportunity for co-operation between France and the USA. On 10 November 1899 the American Ambassador in Paris, General Horace Porter, wrote back to his Secretary of State that Delcassé was 'exceedingly well informed on the subject of the "open door" in China, as he is on all subjects pertaining to foreign relations, which he watches closely and studies personally with great care.'

In February 1902, the German government approached Delcassé, putting out feelers to see if France might join with Germany in a combination of powers to take action to counteract the effect of the growing wealth of the United States upon the trade of Europe. This gave Delcassé the opportunity of assuring the USA that the Germans had met with a prompt and emphatic refusal, saying that France would not be party to such action; that the relations between his country and the United States were of the most friendly character, that the trade between them was increasing, and that there was every desire on the part of France to continue her harmonious intercourse with the American Republic. One feels that Delcassé must have enjoyed the opportunity to use such terms in writing to his enemy.

Another manoeuvre of Delcassé's 'which illustrates his genius', says Charles Porter, 'and exemplifies at the same time the ramifications of the diplomatic art,' was concerned with the channels through which news of European affairs was communicated to America. Paul Cambon expressed himself as 'much perturbed because all the news respecting France came through London and took on a British *nuance*.' Mr M. E.

Stone, of the American Associated Press, was contacted and soon all French Government Departments were communicating directly through Paris. It resulted in a three tier system of telegraphs – one, marked in red, was addressed just to Associated Press; a second bore the message 'Associated Press *très pressé*' and the third 'Associated Press *urgent*'. What the *nuance* was between *très pressé* and *urgent* is not explained. France was soon acting as press agent for Italy and Spain also. It was a small matter, but it was one more step forward in the progress of France's prestige in Europe.

Delcassé also was not unaware of the importance of cultural relations between countries. By the establishment of certain French lectures or debating Prizes at the leading universities of the United States and the Alliance Française to promote the teaching of the French language, and by the founding of Institutes in Paris and other university towns for the reception of American students, Delcassé created something of lasting significance. Jules Cambon, now French Ambassador in Washington, spent much time visiting the colleges and universities of the USA.

Delcassé had acted, and acted successfully, as mediator after a war between America and Spain. This gave him a standing in Spain which he made use of in his negotiations over Morocco. He regarded Spain as one of France's 'natural' allies and thought that, as they had a common interest in Morocco, they should pursue a common policy. Morocco occupied a key position in France's North African Empire – 'a veritable prolongation of France itself'. In an article which he had written in October 1887, Delcassé had already advocated a common policy with Spain. Italy was less involved with Morocco itself but had a concern for the balance of power in the Mediterranean. By agreeing that Italy should have Tripoli, Delcassé 'bought out' any claims she might have on Morocco.

Negotiations with Italy and Spain had been relatively easy. The biggest task which lay before the new Foreign Secretary, however, was neither Spain nor Italy. It was Great Britain. On arrival at his office at the Quai d'Orsay, Delcassé had announced: 'I do not wish to leave here, I do not wish to vacate this *fauteuil*, until I have established a friendly understanding with England.'

His first important move in this direction had been to appoint Paul Cambon to the French Embassy in London. 'In making this selection of the most eminent and capable member of the French Diplomatic Service,' he wrote, 'the French Republic is also choosing an Ambassador well-known to be most friendly and inspired with the best disposition towards England.'

On 8 December 1898 *The Times* duly announced that 'M. Paul Cambon, the new French Ambassador, arrived in London last night, reaching Victoria at 8. 15.' He was met by the outgoing Ambassador, the baron de Courcel, and taken to the French Embassy, situated at the corner of Albert Gate and Kensington Gore. He was to remain in London for twenty two years.

Of all the capitals of Europe [the Baron von Eckardstein wrote] there was never, except for Ancient Rome, a metropolis where the pulse of the world beat so distinctly. The business quarter of the town, the City, has, at least up till now, been to a certain extent the digestive organ of the world's commerce, while the West End has been, both in political and in social respects, the world's centre of gravity. It would, therefore, take much too long even to mention all the foreign politicians and statesmen, Indian Princes, Arab chiefs, Negro Kings and such like that I met in my twenty years in London.

At this time London life was still that of the old fashioned, easy-going, highly-coloured 'Old England'. The four-in-hand still reigned, unmenaced by the motor car. The great Houses and historical clubs were still the centres of social life.

The private palaces of London dominated the green squares and main highways of Mayfair. Devonshire House in Piccadilly, its rather plain facades screened behind a high wall, but offering to those who had the *entrée* some of the richest interior decorations; Lansdowne House, just off Berkeley Square, in the pure classical style of Robert Adam; Stafford House on the Mall, of which Queen Victoria said to the Duchess of Sutherland, 'I have come from my house to your palace;' these and a hundred others gave an architectural distinction to London which has long since been destroyed. But, as Richard Rush, an American Ambassador during the Regency, noticed, these were not the principal residences of the aristocracy. 'They have *houses* in London, but their *homes* are in the country . . . the permanent interests and affection of the most opulent classes centre almost universally in the country.' Among clubs the Beefsteak 'provided not only excellent beef steaks, but intellectual intercourse such as one could get scarcely anywhere else.'

> Manners and customs [continues Eckardstein] were still Victorian; and this was especially evident in dress. What 'gentleman' would have ventured into a West End street otherwise than in a single-breasted morning-coat, striped trousers and top hat? Who would have ventured into a house or club in the evening, whether a guest or no, otherwise than in an evening tail-coat and white tie? This is now all changed by the lounge coat and the evening jacket. We abroad call this latter a 'smoking' – incorrectly, for the smoking jacket was something quite different.
>
> In the Victorian age, it was positively rude to smoke in the company of ladies and unpardonable to smell of tobacco . . . No smoking at all was allowed in the Royal Palaces, not even in the guests' bedrooms. I can remember, on a visit to Windsor, seeing Count Hatzfeldt, who could not live without a cigarette, lying in his pyjamas on his bedroom floor, blowing the smoke up the chimney.

King Edward was notoriously a cigar smoker, and it was he who first broke away from the old interdict.

The day after his arrival in London Paul Cambon was taken to Windsor Castle to present his letters to Victoria. He was shown into his room and sat down immediately to write to his English mother-in-law Mme la Générale Guépratte. 'My dear mother, it is nothing less than that I am writing to you from the palace itself of your Queen, who will be receiving me in a few minutes.' He had already had a visit from Lord Salisbury. 'He has the appearance and the air of a Patriarch . . . He is enormous and seems to be a little asthmatic.' Salisbury conducted him to a very small room where the Queen was standing. 'She looks extremely old and speaks in a low voice. The audience was short. After a few words of welcome, she introduced me to her daughter, the Princess of Battenberg.' He handed her his letters which she passed to Salisbury.

At ten minutes to nine they all assembled in the gallery to await the Queen. At table Cambon was seated on her right. 'The Queen seated,' he observed, 'appears infinitely less old than when standing. She has retained all her faculties and talks with some animation.' But if the conversation was interesting, the food was not. '*La cuisine était détestable* . . . I would not tolerate a dinner like that in my own house.'

What chiefly struck him was the simplicity of it all. After dinner they sat in the Gallery, for the salons had not been used for receptions since the death of Albert. 'She sat down. We were invited to sit, and she remained there for about half an hour saying a few words to each of us. There is no Château in France where everything is done with such simplicity.' The next day they returned to London. 'I have reason to be satisfied by the reception which I received,' he wrote to Delcassé, 'but I fully appreciate that the good behaviour of the Prime Minister does not affect the heart of the matter and that, if the present conflict is allayed for the moment, it could re-appear at the first occasion.'

The political task that lay before Cambon was more than somewhat daunting. Relations between France and Britain could hardly have been worse. Recently, the British Ambassador, Sir Edmund Monson, speaking at the annual dinner of the Chamber of Commerce in Paris, had made a tactless allusion to 'pinpricks' inflicted upon his country by the French government, which was deeply resented. Cambon commented that 'it corresponds so well with the general feeling in

England which has expressed itself through the mouth of the Ambassador.'

One of the 'pins' used by the French press was the political cartoon. Publications such as *Le Rire* and *L'Assiette au Beurre* were merely obscene and for the most part devoid of real wit or artistic skill. Early in the year 1900, soon after the beginning of the Boer War, they mounted a veritable campaign. One showed the exposed legs of Queen Victoria as she hid Joseph Chamberlain under her skirts.

On 20 February 1900 Paul Cambon wrote to his brother Jules to tell him that one of these artists named Léandre had actually been awarded a decoration by the Ministère des Beaux Arts. 'The Prince of Wales,' he wrote, 'had been so exasperated that he was seen to tear up a copy of *Le Rire* – or I don't know what leaflet of that sort.'

Unfortunately the Pretender to the French throne, the duc d'Orléans, a person who had every reason to be grateful to the British government, expressed his approval of the caricatures. Cambon wrote to his mother asking – 'have you heard of the latest outburst by that little noodle the duc d'Orléans? He has written to the cartoonist Wilette a letter of congratulation on his drawings against the Queen.'

By the end of March the matter was becoming politically embarrassing. 'I saw Lord Salisbury,' he wrote to Jules, 'and we talked about the Press . . . The impression created by the caricatures against the Queen – and above all the decoration of Léandre – has not been effaced . . . It goes without saying that the matter has not placed me in a good position.'

Cambon, at the outset of his mission, was confronted by 'a maze of accumulated misunderstandings', but he soon settled into the routine of his work. After a morning of reading letters and despatches he would often walk across Hyde Park to the Foreign Office. 'A small but distinguished figure,' wrote Harold Nicolson, 'with startlingly white hair and beard, with prominent glaucous eyes, would enter the room slowly, place his grey top hat upon its accustomed table, sink into his accustomed leather chair, and exclaim as he drew off first one kid glove and then the other, "Eh bien, mon cher, voici encore votre pain quotidien."' Sir Arthur Nicolson, to whom these words were addressed, was Permanent Under Secretary at the Foreign Office.

Cambon kept closely in touch with the French government and made almost weekly visits to Paris. This enabled him to have frequent and confidential talks with Delcassé. Delcassé had not been at the Quai d'Orsay for more than a fortnight before he was confronted with a crisis which could easily have led to war with England. On 10 July 1898 Captain Marchand, after a journey lasting thirty months, arrived at Fashoda on the White Nile. On 2 September Lord Kitchener won the victory of Omdurman which made him master of the Sudan. Marchand had raised the French flag over Fashoda. Kitchener could not ignore his action.

PLAIN ENGLISH!

JOHN BULL.—" LOOK HERE, MY LITTLE FRIEND, I DON'T WANT TO HURT YOUR LITTLE FEELINGS,—BUT, *COME OFF THAT FLAG !!!* "

'The Spirit of Fashoda.'

6

Fashoda

To understand the Fashoda affair it is necessary to look back over the history of France's relationship with Egypt.

It was Napoleon who first established the position of France in Egypt. In 1798 he commanded the French army in the Mediterranean with the intention of crippling Great Britain by striking at Malta, Alexandria, Egypt and ultimately India. He defeated the Mamelukes and seized Egypt for Europe. He also inspired Mehemet Ali to turn Egypt into a modern state. His immediate objectives were defeated by Nelson at Aboukir Bay, but France remained the dominant force in Egypt for three-quarters of a century. It was the French who created the Suez Canal in 1869, but the opening of a route from the Mediterranean to the Red Sea was of far greater importance to England than to France.

On 24 March 1869 the Prince of Wales, who was on a visit to Egypt, was personally conducted by the Khedive to see the works on the Suez Canal. Here he met Ferdinand de Lesseps, the engineer of this great project. Lesseps was a man after his own heart and the perfect guide. Edward was quick to realize the immense importance of this achievement. He realized how unfortunate it was that the British government had allowed the French a controlling interest. He accused Palmerston of 'a lamentable lack of foresight'.

On 29 October 1875 the Prince passed through the now opened Canal. He wrote to Lord Granville: 'The Suez Canal is certainly an astounding work and it is an everlasting pity that it was not made by an English company and kept in our hands, because it is our highway to India.' A month later, however, Disraeli purchased the Khedive's shares in the canal for four million pounds. The Prince, who was by then at Lucknow, sent him a telegram of warmest congratulations.

This left France and England exercising a dual control over the Canal and acting together to depose Ismael, the extravagant Khedive, and to set about restoring the shattered finances of Egypt. But in 1882 there was a serious threat of a nationalist rebellion under a malcontent, Colonel Arabi. 'From the exercise of that joint responsibility,' writes Maurois, 'France deliberately withdrew, leaving England to quell the revolt of Arabi and to straighten out the financial and administrative tangle left by the deposed Khedive.' The British government made a 'temporary' occupation of Egypt. An indefinite occupation, Gladstone had declared, would have been 'absolutely at variance with the views of Her Majesty's Government.' The 'temporary' occupation, however, lasted for seventy years. It was a curious situation: the Liberal government of Gladstone, hating imperial commitments, anxious to be rid of Egypt at the first convenient opportunity, 'found itself compelled to plunge deeper and deeper into the Nile mud,' says Maurois, 'while the French, who had no compunction about imperialism, and would have given their eyes for Egypt, had, in a sudden paroxysm of timidity, left the palm and the dust to their rivals.'

Paul Cambon, who was later to occupy the French Embassy in London with great distinction, described the English occupation of Egypt as 'almost as disastrous to France as the war of 1870'. It almost led to another war. In March 1895 an article in the *Bulletin du Comité de l'Afrique Française* stated that: 'neither France, Russia, nor Germany can accept that the route to Indo-China, to Madagascar, to Eastern Siberia and to German East Africa should be at the mercy of English troops stationed in Alexandria and Cairo, only a few hours by rail from the great Suez.' It was equally important to Britain that no other country should be able to block her route to India. This made the Sudan an area of international importance. In 1889 Lord Salisbury had stated that 'any European Power, established on the upper Nile, would have Egypt in its grip.' That was exactly what the French desired to do.

Most of the French colonial interests were in north and west Africa, but Théophile Delcassé, French Minister at the time for Colonial Affairs, decided to make a bid for the Sudan. In the spring of 1893 he planned an expedition to Fashoda, on the White Nile, and in May President Sadi Carnot ordered that 'Fashoda must be occupied.' In November the French Cabinet authorized Captain Marchand to lead the expedition. At that time the Sudan was not under Anglo-Egyptian control. It had been conquered by the Mahdi in 1885.

In the middle of all this, on 29 December 1895, an event in Rhodesia, the Jameson Raid, had precipitated another crisis. The Jameson Raid had, in fact, been launched by Cecil Rhodes without the approval and perhaps without the knowledge of the British government. On Sunday, 29 December, writes Andrew Roberts in his biography of Lord Salisbury, Joseph Chamberlain, the Foreign Secretary, sent 'a very tentative warning to Cecil Rhodes not to force the issue,' adding that 'he might have to repudiate the action if it now went ahead.' It had already gone ahead. Dr Leander Jameson, with a force of some five hundred troopers, was galloping towards Johannesburg. At a place called Dorncop, Jameson and his troopers were confronted by a Boer force three times their size. After suffering heavy casualties they surrendered and were taken prisoners.

On Monday, 30 December the Prime Minister, Lord Salisbury – still unaware of the raid – wrote to Chamberlain: 'I am not sorry that at this stage the movement is only partially successful. If we get to actual fighting it will be very difficult to keep the Cape forces – or our own – out of the fray. In such a case we would have an angry controversy with Germany. Of course Germany has no rights in this affair and must be resisted if necessary.' On Tuesday, 31 December at 4 in the morning,

Chamberlain ordered an official at the Foreign Office to denounce the raid. The news had arrived. On the last day of the year 1895, Salisbury wrote to Chamberlain: 'Fortunately no great harm seems to have been done in the Transvaal – except to Rhodes's reputation.'

Considerable harm, however, was to be done to the reputation of Great Britain. Paul Cambon was appalled by the violence of the 'hate Britain' campaign which reached its climax with the outbreak of the Boer War. Prominent among the accusations made against the British was the high mortality of women and children in the so-called 'concentration camps'. The term is unfortunate. In spite of Lloyd George's accusation of a 'settled policy of extermination', no comparison is possible between these concentration camps and those of Nazi Germany.

The high mortality rate – some twenty thousand women and children – was, according to Milner, 'mainly due to the deplorable state of starvation and sickness in which large numbers of people arrived in the camps and which rendered them easy victims to the attack of epidemic diseases.' Winston Churchill states in *My Early Life* that since the outlying camps were 'regularly cut off from supplies by Boer attacks . . . It was difficult to supply those camps with all the necessities of life.' According to Kitchener, the wives and children of soldiers left unprotected from 'the tender mercies of the Kaffirs', flocked into the camps in numbers greatly in excess of what was expected.

That was not all. Jan Christian Smuts, attempting a sortie into the Cape, found 'all along the route evidence of the "scorched earth" policy. Farms were desolate and deserted . . . Dams everywhere filled with rotting animals; water undrinkable; Veld covered with slaughtered herds.' Britain certainly had no cause for pride.

On Wednesday, 1 January 1896 Lord Salisbury had an 'amiable' discussion with the Count von Hatzfeldt, with whom he had a strong relationship. Hatzfeldt, however, although officially the German Ambassador, suffered from ill health which often kept him out of England. The day-to-day business of the Embassy was carried on by the First Secretary, the Baron von Eckardstein. 'The Jameson raid,' he writes, 'in which Cecil Rhodes was prompter and Chamberlain producer, was certainly a badly bungled business; but it does not deserve the severe moral censure that it has generally incurred. The conspiracy of Kruger and his followers was already notorious and, had it [the Jameson Raid] succeeded, a South African war, with all its toll of death and disaster, could probably have been avoided.'

But 1 January happened to mark the twenty-fifth anniversary of the foundation of the Second Reich by Wilhelm I. Wilhelm II celebrated the occasion by announcing that 'the German Empire had become a World Empire [Weltreich].' He ordered Hatzfeldt to request his passports and leave England if there was the slightest indication that the government had had any foreknowledge of the Raid. Andrew Roberts has produced firm evidence that at least Salisbury knew nothing of the raid before it happened.

Not being in possession of proof of any foreknowledge, the Kaiser resorted to other means of making capital out of the occasion. He sent an open telegram to President Kruger.

Paul Kruger was a most remarkable figure. His character is sketched by Jan Christian Smuts. 'As a lad of twelve he had moved off with his parents on the Great Trek, and in the harsh school of this rough-and-tumble life he grew up. The atmosphere of his surroundings, though a godly one, combined deep distrust of the British and hostility to the natives. His education and code of behaviour he took from the Old Testament; his shrewdness from the school of bitter experience.' On another occasion Smuts wrote: 'Kruger was indeed unique in his ancient ruggedness, and might fittingly have stepped back into the days of Abraham and Joshua.' His deep distrust of the British made him draw closer to Germany. The Kaiser's telegram congratulated him 'on the way that you and your own people, by your own energy against the armed bands which have broken into your country as disturbers of the peace, have succeeded in re-establishing peace and defending the independence of the country against attack from without.'

The Boers had certainly not 'succeeded in establishing peace' and the Kaiser had no intention of giving them either help or recognition. When President Kruger, seeking support for his cause, made his unsuccessful tour of Europe in the autumn of 1900, the Kaiser, to the great satisfaction of King Albert of Saxony, refused to receive him. As to any armed help, Joseph Chamberlain leaves no doubt. In a letter to Eckardstein dated 28 December 1899, he wrote: 'I have duly received your letter in which you again assure me that the Kaiser has given the strictest orders against any German officer taking part in the war on the side of the Boers, for which please accept my thanks.'

The Kaiser's implied challenge to British suzerainty, writes Andrew Roberts, 'brought the private response from Salisbury that the Germans' only idea of a diplomatic approach is to stamp heavily on your toes.'

On Tuesday, 7 January 1900 there was a large and distinguished house-party at Hatfield. It is described by Lord Salisbury's daughter-in-law, Lady Milner. In the course of lunch a red dispatch case from London was delivered to him. 'He opened it, read a short note that was in it, scribbled something on a piece of paper, closed the box and handed it back to the servant who had brought it. We were all agog with curiosity as to what was happening, and Princess Christian [of Schleswig-Holstein, Queen Victoria's third daughter] asked him what was the message he had received. He told her that the German Emperor had landed 150 men in Delagoa Bay, and she asked what answer he had given. He said: "I haven't answered; I've sent ships."' The interest of this occasion lay in the fact that Lord Salisbury did not hesitate for a second in his action.

'Little else was spoken of that evening and Princess Christian abounded in abuse of her nephew, the Emperor. "He is more conceited than any peacock that was ever hatched . . . The Queen," she added, "was so upset by his conduct as to be quite ill with it. She had always been very fond of him, and he had – hitherto – behaved very deferentially to her. She had written to him personal letters of reproach which could not be shown to any secretary. Princess Beatrice had written them for her and had sealed them."'

'Without realizing that Germany was drifting into a most serious situation,' wrote Eckardstein, 'Freiherr von Marschall drove us even nearer the breakers by declaring in the Reichstag that the independence of the South African Republic was a vital question for Germany. And, not content with that, an armed expedition to the Transvaal was actually planned and prepared. A force of several hundreds of the colonial troops in German East Africa was to be shipped to Delagoa Bay, in Portuguese territory, and thence, with three German cruisers lying in the port, was to march up to the capital of the Transvaal Republic. The consent of the Portuguese government was requested in a very perfunctory manner, as though it was quite a usual thing for German troops to march through Portuguese territory. The marquis de Soveral (the Foreign Minister at Lisbon and a personal friend of the Prince of Wales) who saw clearly the danger to the peace of the world in the passage of German soldiers in such circumstances, returned a firm and flat refusal.'

Three years later, when Lord Salisbury was discussing this crisis with Eckardstein, he agreed: 'The Jameson raid was certainly a foolish business. It was a failure from the first and never had any prospect of success. But an even sillier business, at least from the point of view of German interests, was the Kruger telegram. And what your Government were thinking about in wanting to send a few hundred men through Portuguese territory to the Transvaal is a complete puzzle to me. What could and would your Government have done there? At any rate it was great luck that this coup did not come off, owing to Soveral's determined attitude. War would have been inevitable from the moment that the first German soldier set foot on Transvaal soil.'

Edward followed the course of events with great interest. 'The Queen,' writes Sidney Lee, 'forwarded to him all communications on the theme which reached her from Germany . . . These letters,' he added, 'are still preserved at Marlborough House in the large envelope which the Queen addressed to the Prince in her own hand. As soon as he read the Kruger message he appealed to Queen Victoria to rebuke her grandson sharply – to administer to him (in his own phrase) "a good snubbing".' But Victoria saw the need for restraint. In a letter to Edward dated 15 January, she warned him that 'those sharp, cutting answers and remarks only irritate and do harm, which one is sorry for. Passion should be most carefully guarded against. William's faults come from impulsiveness as well as conceit. Calmness and firmness are the most powerful weapons in such cases.'

On the subject of the telegram Eckardstein wrote in his Memoirs:

there were the most contradictory stories as to who was the moving spirit in its drafting and despatch. It was generally believed in England that Wilhelm had personally drafted it while on the train and had had it despatched by an *Aide de Camp*; but I had the following account of its origin from the Secretary of the Navy, Admiral von Hollmann.

'The day following the news of the Jameson raid the Kaiser came in from Potsdam to Berlin. I was to have an audience with him in the morning, and after I had finished my report he asked me to go with him to the Foreign Office as the Foreign Secretary, von Marschall and the Director of the Colonial Section were expecting him there. Certain important decisions, he said, had to be taken concerning the Jameson raid. He only referred briefly to the incident and gave me the impression that he did not attach any great importance to it . . . After greeting the Kaiser, von Marschall at once informed him that he had drafted a telegram . . . which he wished to submit to His Majesty for approval. On the Kaiser's seeing the draft telegram he observed: "If this telegram is sent, as drafted, what will happen to our relations with England? Is it really necessary at all that such a telegram be sent to President Kruger?" To which Marschall replied: "I am convinced that it is absolutely indispensable to show the world that the Imperial Government most severely condemns this outrageous raid of English filibusters, both from a moral and also from a juridical standpoint." Thereupon Herr Kayser chimed in with: "in my capacity as Colonial Director I cannot but assent to the view of the Secretary of State . . . We must show that Germany is the most powerful Empire in Europe, and that, in the interests of justice, we will not tolerate such flagrant violence." Whereupon the Kaiser said: "Very well then the telegram can go; only I would prefer that the passage in the middle, which is perhaps rather too strong, should be left out." Freiherr von Marschall then struck a sentence out of the middle of the draft, gave leave for its despatch, and drove back to the palace.'

The foolish telegram to Kruger had raised thunders of applause in Germany, while it had roused a storm of resentment in England. Victoria wrote to her grandson expressing her regret that he had sent such a telegram and commenting that it had made a very painful impression on her country. 'The action of Dr Jameson was, of course, very wrong and totally unwarranted, but considering the very peculiar position in which the Transvaal stands towards Great Britain, I think it would have been far better to have said nothing.'

Sir Thomas Barclay, President of the Chamber of Commerce in Paris, whose *Reminiscences* provide a first-hand account of events there, stated that: 'no event in our time did so much to undermine British prestige abroad as the Jameson Raid. It excited as strong a feeling throughout France against the "perfidious"' British policy, as the Dreyfus affair excited throughout England the feeling that the French 'had lost all sense of national honour and justice.'

By October 1899 a war between Britain and the Boers seemed inevitable, but although it was the Boers who actually declared war, one of the greatest men on the Boer side, Jan Christian Smuts, saw this declaration as the inevitable culmination of the events which preceded it. 'In the worsening conditions that followed [the Jameson Raid] it was not the Boers who were spoiling for a fight but Milner himself, who was determined to bring matters to a head and crush the Republic.'

Sir Alfred Milner had been sent to South Africa by Chamberlain as High Commissioner. He is described by John Buchan, who came out in

August 1901, a year after the war had started, to join his team of promising young men. Of Milner he writes: 'one of the finest scholars of his
age, he had put away his scholarship on a high shelf. On the intellectual side he found that which wholly satisfied him in the problems of
administration . . . He had a mind remarkable both for its scope and for
its mastery of details – the most powerful administrative intelligence, I
think, which Britain has produced in our day. If I may compare him
with others, he was as infallible as Cromer in determining the centre
of gravity in a situation, as brilliant as Alfred Beit in bringing order out
of tangled finances, and he had Curzon's power of keeping a big organization steadily at work.'

Perhaps it was these very qualities which made Milner the wrong
person for the job. For, as Buchan admits, 'he was not very good at
envisaging a world wholly different from his own, and his world and
Kruger's at no point intersected. There was a gnarled magnificence in
the old Transvaal President, but Milner only saw a snuffy, mendacious
savage.' They were, continues Buchan, 'men deeply in earnest who
were striving for things wholly incompatible – an Old Testament patriarchal regime and a modern democracy.' Smuts, whose position as State
Attorney kept him close at Kruger's side, said of Milner: 'From his
German father he had inherited a streak of ruthlessness, from his Irish
mother a certain perversity. There is reason to believe that he came to
South Africa with the fixed idea of forcing the Boer issue.'

In the evening of 9 October 1899 Milner received an ultimatum
from F. W. Reitz, Secretary of State for the Transvaal, threatening war
at 5 p.m. on Wednesday, 11 October unless the demands in it were met.
'In one of the bravest and most foolhardy documents of the 19th
century,' writes Andrew Roberts, 'Pretoria demanded that the troops
on the borders of this Republic shall be instantly withdrawn', and even
included the somewhat unrealistic demand that 'Her Majesty's troops
that are now on the high seas shall not be landed at any port in South
Africa.' They were convinced, continues Roberts, 'that their independence was in mortal danger, so the tiny Republics decided to challenge

the largest empire the world had ever seen.' On this occasion it was Goliath who won, but not without some initial defeats.

'Though it was the Boers and not the British who declared the war,' writes H. A. L. Fisher, 'the sympathy of the Continent was solid for the Republican armies . . . In Germany and in France the waves of anti-English indignation rose mountains high. Even the Tsar of Russia, whose domestic Government was no model of freedom, proposed a general alliance of the Continental Powers against the unpopular, arrogant island.'

In Paris Sir Thomas Barclay records the readings on the political thermometer. The third meeting of his newly established Franco-Scottish Society was due to be held in 1899. It had to be cancelled owing to resentment over the Fashoda situation. Not only were the French excited about Fashoda, but 'the whole country was in a state of nervous tension on account of the Dreyfus conflict and everything was out of focus . . . The violent attitude of British public opinion over the Dreyfus affair further embittered French feeling against England.' The conscience of France was raw.

In December 1894 a young Jewish officer, Captain Alfred Dreyfus, was convicted of betraying military secrets. Lord Salisbury's daughter-in-law Viscountess Milner and a great friend of Clemenceau, the editor of *L'Aurore*, was in Paris at the time and describes the event. 'This extraordinary affair presented an unimaginable spectacle with its traitors and informers, its spies, its intrigues, its crimes. The only thing like it in history is our Popish Plot . . . He was degraded, his uniform was torn off his back, his sword was broken and he was sent in chains to the terrible penal colony of Devil's Island. Everyone in France – except the men who had committed the crime for which he was condemned – believed him to be guilty. Three years later doubt, first as to the legality of his trial, secondly as to the good faith of his judges, and finally as to the guilt of the condemned man, began to trouble men's minds. The Government and the heads of the Army, however, anchored themselves to the *fait accompli* and, by their obvious fear of any form of enquiry, awoke suspicion.' In 1898 some of the evidence which led to his conviction was discovered to have been based on forged documents. The forger, Major Joseph Henry, of the Counter-intelligence Section, had hired the services of a professional forger whose real name was Moise Leeman but who used the alias of Lemercier-Picard.

On 13 January 1898 Clemenceau published Emile Zola's famous diatribe, *J'accuse!* As Voltaire had attacked the authorities of the Catholic Church and the Establishment over the execution of Calas, so Zola attacked the Establishment over the condemnation of Dreyfus.

> *J'accuse* . . . Colonel du Paty de Clam of having been the diabolical agent of the judicial error . . . *J'accuse* . . . General Mercier of having made himself an accomplice of one of the greatest crimes in history . . . *J'accuse* . . . General Billot of having had in his hands the decisive proofs of the innocence of Dreyfus and of having concealed them . . . *J'accuse* . . . General de Boisdeffre and General Gonse of being accomplices in the same crime, the former through religious prejudice and the latter out of *esprit de corps*.

Three more accusations followed and Zola finished up:

> *J'accuse* . . . the first Court Martial of having violated all human rights in condemning a prisoner on testimony kept secret from him . . . *J'accuse* . . . the second Court Martial of having covered up this illegality by order, committing in turn the judicial crime of acquitting a guilty man [Major Esterhazy] with full knowledge of his guilt. . . . Let them dare to carry me to the Court of Appeals and let there be an inquest in the full light of day! I am waiting.

By this time France was polarized. One of the best illustrations of this state of affairs came, appropriately enough, from that prolific cartoonist Caran d'Ache. There are two drawings of a dinner party for ten. In the first they are all happily and politely seated as the first course arrives.

130

The host, at the head of the table, is holding up an authoritative fore-finger. The caption reads '*Surtout ne parlons pas de l'affaire Dreyfus.*' The second scene bears the caption: '*Ils en ont parlé.*' The serene dinner party has become a brawl with everyone at each other's throats.

In March 1898 Moïse Leeman hanged himself. On 22 August Major Henry was accused of forgery. He claimed that he had acted 'solely in the interests of my country'. He could hardly have done it more damage. The vicomte Eugène Melchior de Vogüé admitted: 'Today we have to bow to the evidence; little by little our General Staff has been dragged down by the deplorable moral standards of our times . . . and has itself become entangled in a network of lies.'

On 7 August 1899 a second court martial held at Rennes found Dreyfus guilty 'but with extenuating circumstances'. A few days later the *Daily Telegraph* printed an account of the trial written by J. E. Dillon, who had been an eye-witness. 'Captain Alfred Dreyfus was once more condemned to degradation and imprisonment on Saturday . . . before an auditory trembling with emotion, a city nervous and pas-sionate and a world struck dumb with indignation. Five of his seven Judges have thus put themselves, in the eyes of most, beyond the pale of human reason and outside the reach of appeals to the moral sense. Their verdict is regarded as an outrage on what the bulk of mankind considers as truth and justice . . . Five Officers deliberately closed their ears to unanswerable evidence, shut their eyes to solid facts and opened their hearts to the most odious of human prejudices.' When the verdict of guilty was announced someone near me shouted out to the Judges: 'Ah! You cowards!'

The army closed its ranks; the government rallied in support of the army; the Catholic Church rallied in support of both and mounted an anti-semitic campaign. Half the country rose in support of the Church and the army; half, animated by Emile Zola and Clemenceau, denounced them.

The scandal soon became world-wide. On 19 August 1899 the *General Advertiser* of New South Wales stated that 'when the Dreyfus

Un dîner en famille

– Above all, let's not talk about the Dreyfus Affair!

. . . And then they talked about it . . .

Case is ended, and nobody on this earth knows when that will be, there will be relief to mankind the world over'. To the civilized world, the Dreyfus case represented the classic issue of political expediency versus justice to the individual. The Pope Leo XIII prudently remained silent, but the Jesuit paper *La Civiltà Cattolica* took up arms. 'The Jews have invented the allegation of judicial error . . . the Jews allege an official error. The real error was that of the Constituent Assembly which granted them French nationality. That law must be repealed.'

On 31 August Major Henry committed suicide.

On 2 September 1899 President Emile Loubet and his Secretary General, Abel Combarieu, were trying to get a few days relaxation at Rambouillet, but they could not get away from the cares and worries of the state.

> Beneath the appearance of monotony and calm, wrote Combarieu, the days pass in anxiety. How will the Dreyfus case end? In acquittal or in condemnation? How will the political parties so deeply engaged in the affair react? Will they accept the verdict with equal submission? Will the losers bow to it? Will the winners renounce reprisals? On the one side [that of the General Staff] they declare that they will expel all Jews and take proceeding against the 'syndicate of treason'. The others, [côté Dreyfus] are resolved to prosecute the Generals Mercier and Roget and others. The President and Waldeck-Rousseau [Prime Minister] want the decision of the Court Martial to mark the definite end of this fever. They are loth to perpetuate, on new pretexts, by new trials, between the same adversaries and about the same quarrel, a discord so harmful to the good name of France and to her interests.

A week later they learnt of the result.

Dreyfus is condemned to ten years detention by five votes to two, with unanimous admission of extenuating circumstances. The first reaction was one of stupefaction . . . How could the judges of 1899 have agreed to attenuating circumstances in a crime which they describe as high treason?

The opinion of the President and the Secretary General was unequivocal. 'The innocence of Dreyfus stands out more clearly every day.'

Loubet decided to offer a pardon: 'which would not be a contradiction of the verdict of the War Council. . . . But the partisans of Dreyfus declared that they would proceed with the rehabilitation, which was not implicit in the pardon. It is their right.' Dreyfus himself was reluctant to accept it. 'I had no need whatsoever of clemency,' he said; 'I was thirsty for justice.' But in the end, thinking of the welfare of his family, he accepted. On 19 September 1899 he walked a free man.

But the troubles of France were not yet over.

On the other side of the Atlantic Mark Twain wrote in the *New York Herald*: 'Such cowards, hypocrites and flatterers as the members of military and ecclesiastical courts the world could produce by the million every year. But it takes five centuries to produce a Joan of Arc or a Zola.' In Chicago the *Tribune* delivered the 'most unkindest cut of all'. 'Such a farcical perversion of the methods of justice could not be conceived as occurring in England or America – probably in no other country where courts exist except France and Spain.' Germany, through her Foreign Minister von Bülow, revelled in her rival's discomfiture. 'It is not to be desired,' he stated, 'that France should immediately win liberal and Jewish sympathies by a quick and scintillating reparation of the Dreyfus Affair. It would be best if the Affair would continue to fester, to upset the Army and to scandalize all Europe.'

In England Queen Victoria sent a telegram to the Prime Minister, Lord Salisbury, expressing herself to be 'too horrified for words at this monstrous, horrible sentence . . . If only all Europe would express its horror and indignation! I trust there will be severe retribution.' Lord Salisbury told the Duke of Rutland: 'it is inconceivable that their army, with such traditions, can have reached such a pitch of degradation that forgery is the ordinary recourse of the Intelligence Department.'

In London some fifty thousand demonstrators marched to the French Embassy and hurled abuse at the country responsible for this outrage. The French Ambassador, Paul Cambon, however, was firmly convinced of the innocence of Dreyfus. On 16 June 1899 he wrote to his brother:

The publication of the inquest made by the *Figaro* has thrown a light so penetrating and so clear over the whole affair that unless one were obtuse or dishonest one could not, on reading this inquest, doubt not only the regularity of the procedure but also the innocence of Dreyfus. I have told you that the publication of this enquiry will lead to a terrible reaction . . . What is so heart-breaking is that, thanks to the resistance by successive Ministers, some incompetent and some cowardly, the affair has become a conflict between *the Army* and *Justice*: that should have been avoided at all costs. That is where the ill-fated Boisdeffre [General Raoul de Boisdeffre, Chief of Staff] was guilty of lack of judgement. He was aware of all the irregularities; he knew of all the falsehoods and yet he thought that all could be covered up. The Jewish agitation would have come to nothing if it had not been founded upon the iniquity of the judiciary.

On 12 September 1899 Paul Cambon wrote to his mother: 'I am busy opening abusive letters addressed to me on the occasion of the Rennes Judgement. For France this has caused a moral diminution of which the consequences are incalculable, and of which the many enemies that we have in the world will make capital. No man has ever done more harm to our country than this General Mercier.'

Across the Channel, Clemenceau continued his attack. 'France,' he stated in *l'Aurore*, 'is now a country with no security either for the liberty, the life or the honour of its citizens.' His campaign was gaining ground. 'Belief in Dreyfus' innocence,' writes Barclay, 'gathered strength till the opposing forces became so well defined that the war became one in which, one might almost say, the forces of enlighten-ment and progress were ranged on the side of Dreyfus' innocence and the forces of darkness and reaction against it . . . The subject had the character of intoxicating those who took it up.' In England pro-Dreyfusism raged as an anti-French fever with a violence second only to the anti-Dreyfus fever in France. English newspapers, even politi-cians and statesmen, spoke of France as a country 'fast sinking into a state of moral decay beyond any reasonable prospect of redemption.'

Seven years later Dreyfus triumphed. On 12 July 1906 the Chief Justice Ballot-Beaupré announced the verdict of the Cour de Cassation. The verdict of the Rennes court martial was annulled and Dreyfus unanimously declared to be innocent. The verdict was not to be referred to any military tribunal. On 20 July 1906 *Major* Dreyfus was reinstated into the French army and inducted into the Légion d'Honneur. There were cries of '*Vive Dreyfus!*', but he answered '*Non, Messieurs, non, je vous supplie – Vive la France!*'

Such was the atmosphere in the middle of which the situation con-cerning Fashoda was to be negotiated.

In September 1898 Barclay had recorded a new turn in the course of events.

Suddenly a new and most unfortunate fact had to be dealt with, viz. that a French expedition or mission had reached Fashoda, the chief town of the Sudan province of Bahr-el-Ghazal. Everybody trembled at the idea of what would happen if Captain Marchand defied the victorious general [Kitchener] and a conflict ensued. Any French Officer who had hoisted the French flag at any spot on the globe, I was told rather excitedly, would fight under it until overcome by superior force, and then it would have to be the enemy who hauled it down. If this happened the prevailing anti-English feeling would be roused to frenzy at such an insult to the flag and the two countries would be at war within a fortnight.

136

On 2 September 1898 Kitchener had defeated the Mahdi's successor at Omdurman and the British flag was hoisted once more. He marched south and confronted Marchand.

On 26 September the news reached England of Kitchener's meeting with Marchand. Kitchener had politely requested that the French flag be hauled down and Marchand had politely declined, pending instructions from his government. Kitchener and Marchand, described by Delcassé as the 'two emissaries of civilization', had a merely formal exchange of protests and drank a bottle of champagne together. Kitchener, however, possibly with malice aforethought, provided Marchand with the latest newspapers from Paris. An hour later, records Marchand, 'the ten French officers were trembling and weeping. We learned then and there that the terrible Dreyfus affair had been [re]opened with its dreadful campaign of infamies and for thirty six hours not one of us was able to say anything to the others.'

The British Ambassador in Paris, Sir Edmund Monson, was instructed to deliver an ultimatum demanding Marchand's immediate withdrawal. Delcassé, who had become Minister of Foreign Affairs in June, replied: 'Her Majesty's Government must make no mistake about my desire for an understanding with England . . . nor about my conciliatoriness. I expressed these feelings so freely only because I was sure – and you must be equally sure at this time – that they would not draw me beyond the line marked by national honour. Whilst I may sacrifice material interests, the honour of the nation will remain intact as long as it is in my hands. No capitulation can be expected from the Minister who stands before you.'

To his wife he wrote: 'My course of action is decided on and I have let it be known – 'Recognize an outlet for us on the Nile and we shall withdraw Marchand.' The majority of the British Cabinet opposed any compromise, and public opinion was largely with them. On 24 October Delcassé wrote again: 'If England does not accept my proposition I shall . . . recall the heroic little band.'

On 27 October Lord Salisbury told the French Ambassador, the baron de Courcel, that England would not negotiate while Marchand remained at Fashoda. Delcassé had to accept the inevitable. He admitted the necessity of 'avoiding a war which we are absolutely incapable of carrying on.'

Andrew Roberts, in his biography of Lord Salisbury, states: 'The Fashoda crisis left a strongly Anglophobic feeling in France; it deeply influenced, amongst many others, the eight year old Charles de Gaulle.' It was becoming a very delicate diplomatic issue, but the President, Félix Faure, knew his men. 'We have no Talleyrand,' he said, 'but we have Delcassé and he possesses both subtlety and audacity, besides a good amount of useful cynicism and sound judgement; he is as cool as he is cautious.'

Delcassé was a man of unruffled probity. That made him ready to see his own country's faults and his rivals' virtues. On 9 October 1898 he made his own marginal annotations to a Foreign Office 'Blue Book'. It is as if he were thinking aloud. We find him asking himself: 'if there is not some injustice in harbouring a resentment against England for having been the only one to profit by an operation, in which we did not wish to participate, and in which she took all the risks and all the expenses upon herself?' Or again: 'We resemble the player who, having refused the invitation to join the game on equal terms and with the same stake, is jealous of the gains won by another, more enterprising, who had played his game alone.'

It was this sort of honesty which led Joseph Chamberlain to make no secret of the great admiration which he felt for 'the conduct so worthy and so courageous of Monsieur Delcassé at the time of Fashoda.'

On 21 March 1899 Salisbury agreed with Paul Cambon, the new French Ambassador to the Court of St James's, to a convention which 'keeps the French entirely out of the Nile Valley.' A month later he told Lord Curzon that in Anglo-French relations 'a mutual temper of apathetic tolerance may be cultivated on both sides, without sacrificing the interests of either . . . Anything like hearty goodwill between the two nations will not be possible.'

Perhaps the most significant result of the Fashoda crisis was that it led an important section of *le parti colonial* to abandon the policy of confrontation with England in Egypt for one of compensation for Egypt in Morocco. Eugène Etienne, the leader of *le parti colonial*, had been the first to suggest this solution. The creation of a sub-committee, the *Comité du Maroc*, was an important step in that direction.

Among the members of the *Comité du Maroc*, one of the most interesting was Paul Bourde. On 27 October 1898 he wrote to Etienne: 'M. Delcassé is courageous and patriotic, but I fear that the difference between the interests at stake has not sufficiently impressed itself upon him. On the one hand is Egypt – *lost through our own folly* – and where the only honourable course open to us is to acknowledge our defeat, and the regions of central Africa which can be put to no practical use. On the other hand is one of the finest countries in the world (Morocco) with thirty million hectares of usable land (half the area of France) and the possibility of one day having there fifteen to twenty million of our compatriots. And the country is at our gates, on our national sea – it is not a colony, it is part of France itself. The advantages for us are incontrovertible.' With Egypt out of the way, French diplomacy centred on her interests in Morocco.

Delcassé himself was not optimistic. He was first and foremost a realist. In an address to the Chamber on 1 February he declared: 'On whatever side we look, grave subjects for reflection force themselves upon us. Foreign trade has ceased to expand, industrial production is at a standstill, the population is no longer growing.' This situation, he claimed, 'becomes a veritable decline when we consider the audacious and self-confident ascent of our more redoubtable neighbours.'

As Christopher Andrew writes: 'Delcassé's own personal success could not hide the fact that prospects for the future were far from encouraging. France's international prestige already stood low when he took office, and after the humiliations of the Dreyfus case and the Fashoda crisis, it was to sink lower still . . . many Frenchmen had come to doubt France's future as a great power.'

Andrew illustrates this by describing a caricature by the cartoonist Caran d'Ache. It features Marianne (France) sitting in a third-class railway compartment, along with the smaller states of Europe and complaining, when a carriage containing the Kaiser passes her by: 'only two years ago we were also travelling first-class.'

At the turn of the century the main groupings in Europe were the Dual Alliance between France and Russia and the Triple Alliance, formed by Germany, Austria and Italy. Great Britain was still true to her position of 'glorious isolation'. One of the features of foreign policy in Edward VII's reign was the abandoning of this isolationism and the substitution of a system of *ententes* and alliances.

Two of the most likely causes of trouble in Europe were France's determination to get back Alsace/Lorraine from Germany and the disapproval by most of Europe of Great Britain's war against the Boers, and the resentment of the claim to superiority implicit in the position of isolation. The danger of 'going into Europe' was that of becoming entangled in continental quarrels in which Britain had no interest.

Chamberlain became one of the chief spokesmen against the old isolationism. In November 1899 he made a speech at Leicester. 'No far-seeing statesman could be content with England's permanent isolation on the continent of Europe . . . The natural alliance is between ourselves and the German Empire . . . Both interest and racial sentiment unite the two peoples and a new Triple Alliance between Germany and England and the United States would correspond with the tie that already binds Teutons and Anglo-Saxons.'

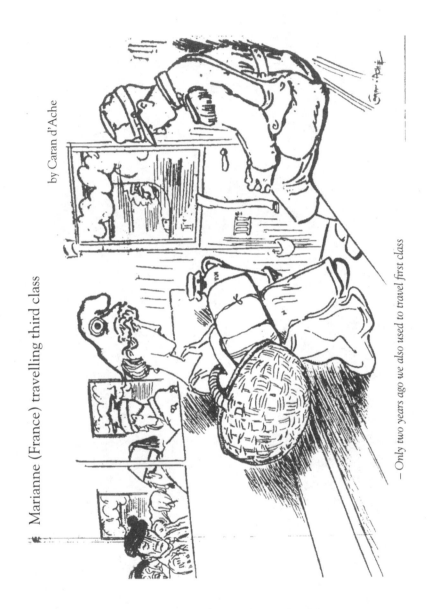

Marianne (France) travelling third class

by Caran d'Ache

– Only two years ago we also used to travel first class

7

Sir Thomas Barclay and the Death of Queen Victoria

At the turn of the century, with European outrage at the British war with the Boers, with France's confusion and guilty conscience over the Dreyfus affair, but above all with the clash between Britain and France at Fashoda, Anglo-French relations were at a low ebb. In 1893 there had nearly been war between the two countries over Siam, and Lord Dufferin, the British Ambassador in Paris, wrote that he could only describe the feelings of all classes in France towards England as 'bitter and unmixed hostility'. The question of Siam concerned a trivial disagreement about the 'rights' of Great Britain over the territories east and west of the Monam basin. That any two civilized countries could even contemplate going to war over anything so unimportant illustrates the atmosphere of hatred and distrust which existed. The matter was decided in the terms of *Entente* in favour of the French. On one occasion, Lord Rosebery, leader of the Liberal Party, on an unofficial visit to Paris accompanied by Lady Warwick, went to a performance of Rostand's *L'Aiglon*. Rosebery was recognized and the house was soon on its feet shouting '*Vive les Boers! A bas les Anglais!*' until the two had to be escorted out by the police.

It is seldom that there are not at least two sides to a case and there can often be different ways of looking at it. Beneath these outward shows of hostility were still lurking the ideas of Gambetta and that the true relationship between France and England would be one of fraternity.

On 24 May 1895, at the annual dinner at the British Embassy in Paris in honour of the Queen's birthday, Lord Dufferin had invited Thomas Barclay, Chairman of the Chamber of Commerce, to discuss with him the forming of a Franco-Scottish Society. He deplored the state of Anglo-French relations.

> The French have a deep-seated, though quite unjustifiable, dislike for the English. I do my best to re-act against it, and so long as I am Ambassador here I shall be able to cope with any difficulties which may arise with the French Government. But there is a danger in this deep-seated popular animosity. Private efforts may be successful where Governments seem to fail. Your Chamber of Commerce is doing good work in the right spirit. But the anti-English feeling is probably least active among the mercantile class, whose material interest might suffer if England retaliated. As regards the lower classes, I doubt if they have any feeling on the subject at all. It is the politicians, and the professional classes from whom they are recruited, who stir up grievances and irritation. Your proposed Society might be the beginning of a change by bringing people belonging to these classes together.

He quoted the adage recorded by Shakespeare: 'If that you will France win, Then with Scotland first begin.'

It was indeed a Scotsman who was to do more than anyone to keep the lamp of Franco-British friendship burning. On Monday, 9 May 1876 the young Thomas Barclay crossed the Channel to take up a job with *The Times* in Paris. It was to remain his home town until 1909.

He was no stranger to France or to French language and literature. 'I had been saturated from my childhood with things French,' he writes in his autobiography.

Louis–Philippe with Queen Victoria and Prince Albert in the royal train. 'I need not tell you again,' Victoria told him, 'how greatly we desire to see confirmed more and more this *entente cordiale* between our two countries, which exists so happily between us personally.'

Victoria arriving at the Château d'Eu in the royal *char-à-bancs*. 'The maintenance of this good understanding,' said Louis-Philippe, 'is the pledge of the peace of the world and the progress of civilization.'

Henri, 8th Marquis de Breteuil, one of Edward's closest friends.

Henry Petty-Fitzmaurice, 5th Marquess of Lansdowne. 'It would be difficult to cite any other man who established himself more rapidly and firmly in the opinion of all alike as an international statesman of the first order.' (Lord Newton)

Sir James Reid, Resident Medical Attendant on Queen Victoria, who died in his arms. 'The Queen kept looking at me and saying "Sir James" frequently.'

Henry Wickham Steed, reporter to *The Times*. 'I can truly say that there is no other work which I would rather have done during the past thirty years.'

The newly married couple – Victoria gazing at the bust of Albert, 10 March 1863.

Kaiser Wilhelm II. General Gallifet said of this portrait:
'That is not a portrait, it is a declaration of war.'

(Left) Spencer Cavendish, 8th Duke of Devonshire. Described by Margot Asquith as 'the last survivor of our Heroic Age.'

(Left) Robert Cecil, 3rd Marquess of Salisbury, 1889. Described by Andrew Roberts as 'one of the most un-Victorian Victorian statesmen.'

(Right) Algernon Freeman-Mitford, 1st Baron Redesdale. 'One of the men who knew Edward best'.

King at last. A constitutional sovereign in the strictest sense of the word, Edward VII was to exercise influence rather than power, and authority rather than autocracy.

The Coronation. Edward helps Archbishop Frederick Temple to his feet.
'It was a kingly act,' wrote Lord Redesdale, 'performed with all the
grace and dignity of which our Lord the King had the secret.'

The reception of President Loubet, 8 July 1903.
'The visit was a spectacular success,' wrote Sidney Lee.

My grandfather was a noted Scottish politician, a Hellenist, a student of French literature and a philosopher who thought Aristotle, Hume and especially Voltaire had got closer to intellectual 'common sense' than did the Edinburgh school who labelled themselves with the term.

He was such a believer in the emancipating character of French culture that he sent all his children to pass some years in Paris . . . In this highly cultured family in Cupar Fife I passed much of my early life. To my young imagination the very name of France seemed to stand for all that was free, brilliant and reasonable. 'What,' said my old Whig grandfather, 'do political systems matter except to put one set of men in office in place of others? They are all the mere tools of the thinkers. What really matters is freedom to think, speculate, talk, write about every conceivable thing.'

Paris was my Mecca. The French intellect, I had been taught, was the motive power which was driving the machinery of the human mind throughout the world.

Brave words, but at least they emphasize the far deeper level at which Barclay and those like him found their *Entente* with France than that of the politicians, diplomats and leaders of the press. It is hardly surprising that he could write of his new appointment to *The Times*, 'I came to France with joy. Here new ideas got a hearing, here all the leaders – the very institutions were young. The country was still a vast political *seminar* – and I was enthusiastic about everything that resembled, in freedom of discussion, the *seminar* in which my mind had learnt how to use its limbs.'

Barclay had come to Paris armed with a number of useful introductions. One of them was to Mr A. J. Wilson, financial editor of *The Times*, whose son Daniel became one of Barclay's best friends. His sister, Mme Pelouze, was one of the *grandes dames* of the French Republic. Politically she was a supporter of President Grévy. Socially she reigned supreme 'No *habitué*,' writes Barclay, 'of the gatherings under the dim red light in her large, cosy smoking room, with the clever men and women she collected round her, can pass the old place at 17, rue de l'Université, without a pang of sadness in his recollection of the sweet woman who was afterwards financially ruined.'

Mme Pelouze is chiefly known today to visitors to the Loire valley. It was she who bought and restored to its original purity of architecture the delightful Château de Chenonceau.

Barclay was convinced that Lord Dufferin and Albert Hanotaux, the French Foreign Secretary, were seeking an *Entente*. The Ambassador, however, was of the opinion that before any diplomatic action could be successful, the French parliamentary atmosphere would have to undergo a change. Somebody was needed who could clear the path.

Barclay was looking for another, deeper, possibility of an *Entente* and this was between the intellectual classes. In 1895 a dinner in Edinburgh led to the foundation of the Franco-Scottish Society. Unlike London, Edinburgh and Paris both contained the oldest and most important universities in their countries. There was a strong intellectual life in both. There was also the background of the Auld Alliance. In the sixteenth century France had provided Scotland with a Queen Consort, Mary of Guise, whose daughter Mary became the reigning Queen of Scots. The French King was still served by the Gardes Ecossaises. Many of the *graffiti* on the chapel walls at Chenonceau are Scottish names.

But the Auld Alliance had been based on a common dislike of England. The *Entente* between France and Scotland was to be built upon an intellectual foundation. 'In the autumn of 1894,' writes Barclay, 'I unfolded this plan to a few French friends in the political world . . . They gave me every possible encouragement . . . On the Scottish side I obtained without difficulty the active co-operation of Lord Reay and Principal Donaldson of St Andrews, who at once appreciated the political value of such an undertaking apart from its educational bearing in which they, however, took a more direct interest.'

The first meeting of the newly founded society was held in the new buildings of the Sorbonne in the spring of 1897. Here was ground on which both parties could meet, proud of their great names. Jules Simon, who presided over this inaugural meeting, used the occasion to pronounce a funeral oration over the old buildings. 'I could not forget that a Boileau, a Balzac, a Voltaire, a Renan had sat on these benches, where I myself had listened to the direct successors of those great masters who make up our intellectual heritage – these real conquerors in the eternal struggle between the freedom of thought and the enslavement of the spirit.' He looked forward to an age when all classes of society would flock to the University: 'se précipiter en foule vers la lumière et la vérité. C'est en vieillard donnant la main à l'avenir que je vous souhaite, Messieurs, la bienvue parmi vos anciens amis.'

At the same time Barclay records the 'excellent work in the same direction by the "Entente Cordiale Society", founded in London by Sir Roper Parkinson, who was a friend of the Prince of Wales." In 1895 there was an *Exposition Internationale* at Bordeaux, and a group of men, including Parkinson, M. Trarieux, Deputy of the Gironde and currently Minister of Justice in M. Ribot's Cabinet, and M. Dutrénit of Bordeaux, had the idea of inviting the Lord Mayor of London, Sir Joseph Renals, to visit the capital of Aquitaine and the magnificent vineyards which surrounded it.

On 6 September the Lord Mayor arrived in Calais with his wife and son and Sir Roper and Lady Parkinson. He was received that afternoon by the President of the Republic, Félix Faure. Two days later Gabriel Hanotaux gave a luncheon at which he declared that 'the two great nations and neighbours always seize with alacrity circumstances which give them an opportunity to reaffirm their friendly relationship, their fruitful rivalry for progress through peace and liberty.' He ended with the words: 'the whole of France, both in the provinces which you are going to visit, and in the capital, offers you a heartfelt welcome.'

On 9 September the party left for Bordeaux, where a *carosse de gala*, such as Louis XV might have used, with coachman and lacqueys in powdered wigs, was waiting at the station for them. Whatever historians of the nineteenth century like Michelet might have written about the iniquities of the *Ancien Régime*, when the French wanted to do something in style it was still in the style of the eighteenth century that they chose to do it.

At the banquet that evening Trarieux made a most impressive speech about the commercial *Entente* between the two countries.

This alliance is not, it is true, confirmed on parchment in the Chancelleries, but its effects will not be the less durable for its roots go deeper. It is the official mission of diplomacy to restrain the egotism of countries, to prepare a peaceful solution to conflicts between neighbours, but its work is three quarters accomplished when the feelings of the people have expressed themselves and the natural sympathies which draw them together have made recourse to justice redundant . . . The immeasurable advantages of this exchange, beneath a clear sky, is to put an end to the artificial animosities which are maintained by parties committed to antagonism.

It was at this level – in the Chambers of Commerce – that the concept of the *Entente Cordiale* found its most natural home.

Another speaker, a M. Hausser, touched on the colonial activities of the two countries. These, he maintained, should not be seen as sources of discord, but a common interest in the progress of humanity. 'The world is open before us,' he claimed; 'may England and France march together side by side . . . What mission could be more noble and more worthy of our nation and yours than that which consists in enabling so many to pass from barbarism to enlightenment and from servitude to liberty!'

But the sky was not as clear as Trarieux had suggested. In 1898 the Franco-Scottish Society had its second meeting, this time in Edinburgh. It again brought eminent Frenchmen and Scotsmen together, and it did undoubtedly pave the way to the breaking down of anti-British feeling in France. But the battle had by no means been won.

Its third meeting [writes Barclay] was to have taken place in France in 1899, and I struggled hard to get the French section to move, but resentment over the Fashoda affair was felt most keenly just among the class of men who were members of the society . . . Besides, the whole country was in a state of nervous tension on account of the Dreyfus conflict, and everything was out of focus. The hostile attitude of British public opinion over the Dreyfus affair further embittered French feeling against England.

In short, the Franco-Scottish scheme had a good beginning, but it had not taken deep enough root to resist the storm which broke out the following year over Marchand's unfortunate though brilliant expedition across Central Africa which had plunged Anglo-French relations into the worst crisis they had undergone under the Republic.

At the beginning of the new millennium, in the January issue of the *Revue de Paris*, the French historian Ernest Lavisse wrote:

A few years ago, if one was looking at the world for causes of possible conflict, one would have found Alsace, the rivalry between England and Russia in Persia and the Far East, that between Russia and Austria in the Balkans . . . to which has been more recently added the foreign policy of the U.S.A. A conflict between France and England would have appeared impossible. Today such an eventuality seems the most to be feared of those which threaten the peace of the world. Between these two countries a hostility, which, however, was not for any serious reasons, is becoming more and more acute: if we are not careful it could become a blind hatred.

No one in France, except for a small band of madmen, is wishing for war with England. All that this country numbers of enlightened people revolts at an idea of so criminal and barbarous a folly. But it is certain that feelings of national antipathy, which lay dormant among the people, have been aroused, and here are sensible people reduced to considering the possibility of so criminal and barbarous a folly.

In September 1899 Thomas Barclay, now Chairman of the Paris branch of the Chamber of Commerce, had put forward the idea of inviting the Association of Chambers of Commerce to have their annual joint meeting in Paris. From the British Ambassador, Sir Edmund Monson, Barclay got no response. 'I believe,' he wrote, 'that at that time the Foreign Office did not believe it possible to determine any more friendly current of French public opinion towards England or any change in the deep-seated British distrust of French policy.'

In March the following year the idea of a joint meeting in Paris was on the agenda. Barclay, moving the motion, made an interesting and in some ways surprising speech.

I should like to make a few remarks about the rumoured ill-feeling in France towards Englishmen. If there is any such ill-feeling it must be of a most superficial character, for it certainly does not in the slightest degree affect the relations of Frenchmen towards Englishmen personally. I have, moreover, the best possible authority, both French and English, for saying that the official relations between the two countries were never more cordial.

Nothing will appeal more to the generous feelings of the French than your disregarding current rumours and stray anglers in troubled waters, for whom peace means empty hands. It was an immense satisfaction to the French to see our future Sovereign at the head of the British section of the Exhibition. No man, not even any Frenchman, is more popular than the Prince of Wales, and if there is any man in the world who has it in his power by a word to make the French nation kind, it is his Royal Highness.

The Exhibition referred to was the third in thirty years to be mounted by France. It was to mark the turn of the century. The second had been in 1889. As the date suggests, it was intended to commemorate the French Revolution. It was not a theme likely to appeal to the monarchies of Europe. Lord Salisbury had made a detailed study of the Revolution. In 1860 he had written about the subject, blaming the 'amiable theories' of men such as Necker, Sieyès and Lafayette, whom he saw as being 'archtypes of the weak-willed liberals whom he so despised . . . they were the proximate causes of a civil convulsion which, for the horror of its calamities, stands alone in human history.' At a more philosophical level he wrote: 'Free institutions, carried beyond the point which the culture of the nation justifies, cease to produce freedom. There is a freedom that makes each man free; and there is a freedom – so called – which makes each man the slave of the majority.' He proclaimed in public that 'the Revolution was an unparalleled time of cruelty, bloodthirstiness, treachery and contempt for every human tie.'

When President Carnot invited the Diplomatic Corps in Paris to the opening ceremony, Lord Salisbury instructed Lord Lytton, the British Ambassador, not to go. But when the Prince of Wales was invited to be President of the Commission of the British section of the exhibition, Salisbury encouraged him to accept. The Queen insisted that he should not. It was unseemly that a member of the royal family should be connected officially with an event so specifically anti-monarchical. Edward followed his mother's advice. On 6 May, when President Carnot opened the exhibition, all the ambassadors of all the major monarchies of Europe left Paris, each leaving a *chargé d'affaires* to represent them.

In spite of this snub, it was hoped once again in 1897, for the millenium Exhibition, that the Prince of Wales would again accept the post of President of the British Commission. Lord Salisbury again urged him to do so: 'for the appointment will conciliate the French and act as a strong spur and encouragement to the British exhibitors.' Edward agreed. His brother-in-law, the Marquess of Lorne, and his old friend the Duke of Devonshire were appointed vice-presidents. For two years, as Barclay relates, the Prince busied himself with the preparations for the Exhibition. But, as the date of the opening approached, Edward began to contemplate withdrawal. On 18 December 1899 Victoria wrote to him: 'It is important that no difficulty should be made about the Paris Exhibition. It is an affair between the two Governments and the French Government is well disposed.'

Unfortunately the press were not. On 28 September 1901 the *Assiette au Beurre* printed a scurrilous cartoon which depicted Albion, seen from behind, with her skirts up to reveal her posterior, with a caricature of Edward painted on her buttocks. The French authorities ordered the posterior to be covered up and in the tenth edition a shawl appeared which conferred respectability upon the cartoon while rendering it pointless. There was also a particularly scurrilous article in *La Patrie*. Against the advice of Lord Salisbury, Edward flatly refused to attend the opening ceremony. 'Many British visitors,' notes Sidney Lee, 'marked their disgust at the Parisian Press by withdrawing their exhibits.'

Barclay was more kind to the press than most. 'No doubt there were some vile caricatures of Her Majesty,' he admitted, 'and they very justly excited the indignation of every loyal Englishman, but we must not hold a nation responsible for the odious acts of individuals in a free country.'

Barclay is open to criticism here. The acts of the press are not the same as the acts of individuals. The cartoons were both vulgar and obscene. It says something about the public at which they were aimed The press prints what it hopes its customers will pay for, and this can lead to the lowest form of playing to the gallery. The cartoon was appealing to something real in the character of its readers.

'At the beginning of 1900,' wrote Thomas Barclay, 'the feeling between France and England was as bad as it could be; the pent-up bitterness engendered by the Fashoda affair was given full reign by the Boer war. The abuse of the gutter Press in Paris and the publication of gross caricatures of our Queen had aroused corresponding anger in England.'

In March 1900, however, the meeting of the combined Chambers of Commerce went ahead as planned. It was, in Barclay's words, 'the largest muster of British Chambers of Commerce on record. The number represented was, if I remember aright, 85, and the number of representatives and their families was somewhere between 500 and 600. The number at the banquet at which I presided was over 800, which included a large number of Frenchmen.' One of the specific aims of the meeting was '*de rendre les français et les anglais amis*'. Unfortunately the British Embassy was closed. They were in mourning for the death of Edward's younger brother Alfred ('Affi') the Duke of Edinburgh.

On 14 April 1900 the Exposition Universelle was opened. '*Voici le grand jour!*' wrote Combarieu. The purpose of the exhibition was made plain in the opening address by M. Alexandre Millerand. 'Labour! Labour! Liberator and sacred! It is you that ennobles, you that consoles. Beneath your feet ignorance is dispersed, evil takes flight. By you Humanity, set free from servitude to darkness, rises – rises without ceasing towards the realms of light, luminous and serene where one day will be realized the ideal and perfect harmony between Power, Justice and Goodness!' It was one of the ironies of fate that Millerand was to become Minister for War.

The President drove to the Salle des Fêtes, where he received a great ovation. So did his speech.

The Republic of France has not only had the thought of getting together a collection of marvels, wonderful to see, and to renew, on the banks of the Seine, our old reputation for elegance, courtesy and hospitality. Our ambitions are more exalted: it goes far beyond the *éclats* of passing fétes . . . This work of harmony, of peace and of progress, ephemeral as the decor is, will not have been in vain. The peaceful encounter of the Governments of the world will not prove sterile . . . I am convinced that, thanks to the persistent affirmation of certain generous thoughts, with which the passing century

153

resounded, the twentieth century will see the dawn of a little increase of fraternity over misery of all sorts, and that, perhaps soon, we will have reached an important stage in the steady evolution of work towards the happiness of man and towards humanity.

Better relations between France and England could have been a step in the right direction.

The report of the British Commisioners stated that:

up to the month of August few British visitors came to the Exhibition. Various reasons contributed to deter Your Majesty's subjects from visiting Paris, and no change was perceptible previous to the visit of the Associated Chambers of Commerce early in September. They were received with marked cordiality and their visit was a striking success, owing largely to the efforts of Lord Avebury and his colleagues, and to the excellent arrangements made by Mr Thomas Barclay, President of the British Chamber of Commerce in Paris. Whether it was due to this or to other causes, British visitors began to come in very large numbers . . . and continued to flock to Paris until the very end of the Exhibition.

On 30 September 1900 the baron Pierre de Coubertin (best known as the founder of the Olympic Games) wrote to Barclay:

to tell you with what interest and pleasure I followed the progress and happy result of your admirable plan. You did the one thing that could, under the present unfavourable circumstances, act most powerfully upon public opinion on both sides. Never mind what incorrigible journalists have to say: the 'reading of the facts' is given to all who are sincere and unprejudiced, and I believe these are far more numerous. When I wrote the article you kindly alluded to, I did it because things were growing worse every day, and I thought it might be good that a Frenchman should denounce the coming danger . . .

Now, as you say, we must help the movement for reconciliation which, chiefly owing to you, has been started.

In September 1900 Barclay recorded that 'a new occasion for anti-English clamour arose which seemed likely to jeopardize the good results of the meeting of the Associated Chambers in Paris.' This was the announcement that President Kruger was about to embark on his mission to Europe for the purpose of enlisting the influence of continental Powers in the preservation of the independence of the republics. On 23 November Kruger arrived at Marseilles to the intense embarrassment of the Mayor, M. Flaissière, and the authorities of the Riviera. These had been losing money since so many of their British regular visitors had withdrawn their custom.

Kruger was received by President Loubet on 25 November. Combarieu was of course present. He puts their predicament clearly. The problem was how to honour, in the person of their President, the unfortunate republics of South Africa – but with moderation. England would be on the look-out and ready to take offence. He wondered if there might not be a risk of her boycotting our commerce and our beaches.

Loubet had stated that he wanted to receive Kruger with all the more consideration because of the misfortunes of his country. He reminded Combarieu that public opinion in France, and especially in Paris, was 'strongly in favour of the Boers and hostile to the English.' The state coach – la voiture de gala – with an escort of cuirassiers was sent to collect Kruger and, to avoid passing in front of the British Embassy, to take the route via the Place de la Concorde, up the Champs Elysées and down the Avenue de Marigny.

There was, however, a very strong feeling among responsible and experienced politicians that the new current of friendship towards England was of infinitely greater value to France than any quixotic manifestations in favour of the republics. Pro-Boer demonstrations could only disaffect Englishmen and would certainly not make them less obdurate in their attitude towards the conquered states. At Kruger's hotel in the Boulevard des Italiens a large crowd was gathered and greeted his appearance with an ovation which did not ruffle his mono-lithic impassibility. 'The behaviour of the crowd,' insists Combarieu, 'was both serious and sincere, in so far as that is possible with the pop-ulation of Paris.'

Among the English present in Paris at that time was the young Alfred Duff Cooper. He records his astonishment at hearing his father discussing with a friend 'the great ill-feeling and even hatred that then existed between the English and the French.' He was ten at the time and an alert observer.

> I was surprised for I had seen no sign of it and everybody had been very kind to me. Shortly afterwards I was taken to an entertainment in which was included what was called the American bioscope, a forerunner of the cinematograph. When Kruger, the Boer President arrived he was greeted with loud applause and enthusiastic cheers. To me he naturally represented the incarnation of evil. I tried to reg-ister my protest by booing and hissing and shaking my small fist. I felt how right the English were to hate the French and I shared their hatred. Then my attention was caught by the tall figure of a bearded man standing beside me. There could be no doubt as to his nation-ality, but he was looking down at me with an expression of so much amusement and such sweet benevolence that all my hatred melted and I returned his smile.

In spite of the outbreaks of enthusiasm for Kruger, Barclay records that 'the Government did the official minimum in accordance with the etiquette governing incognito State visits. Both President Loubet and M. Delcassé were heartily thankful when, on December 1st, he took his departure for Cologne.' He ends on a typical note: 'It is due to French public opinion to say here that the attitude of its responsible organs was one of dignified self-restraint.' The first phase of the Boer War had seen a succession of defeats for Britain, but 'Frenchmen have told me that at the time they had never realized the true greatness of England till they saw how she bore defeat.'

At the same time M. Cornély, writing in the *Figaro*, echoed this theme. After extolling the calm and Christian spirit in which the Boers had defended their country, he wrote: 'On their side the English teach us how a great people bears reverses . . . Sensible men must have sympathy both for the Boers and the English . . . The English are an example for us.'

It was typical of Barclay also to try to see both sides of the case and to emphasize the existence of a calm reasonableness not always credited to the French by the English. He records 'what all sensible private people thought'. This was not often what the press was interested in publicizing. The turn of the century began to mark a turn in the tide of public opinion.

All the pessimistic anticipations with which it opened and apprehensions which disturbed its course [claims Barclay] were dissipated by the end of the first year of the new century.

Never in my time had circumstances seemed more favourable for the starting of a vast popular agitation for the burying of the Anglo-French hatchet. Unfortunately no occasion for any specific demonstration was in sight. At the Quai d'Orsay, moreover, there was still a conviction that Lord Salisbury, who still controlled British foreign policy, did not believe an enduring *entente* possible. Sir Edmund Monson's attitude in 1900 seemed at best to reflect an incredulous indifference.

In 1898 Lord Salisbury was already beginning to recognize that 'the work of the Foreign Office was very heavy and getting heavier.' In October 1900 Arthur Balfour, who was soon to succeed Salisbury as Prime Minister, combined with the Queen and the Chief Whip, Aretas Akers-Douglas, to 'ease Salisbury out of the Foreign Office'. They were successful. Salisbury said that he 'was ready to do whatever was most agreeable to the Queen.' He added that the only possible successor would be Lord Lansdowne.

Henry Charles Keith Petty-Fitzmaurice, 5th Marquess of Lansdowne, was born in January 1845. He started life with the title Viscount Clanmaurice and was always known to his friends as 'Clan' and to his grandchildren as 'Daddy Clan'. At Eton his housemaster was the Dr Birch who had tutored the young Prince of Wales. From Eton he went to Balliol where he was under the aegis of Benjamin Jowett, who soon formed a high opinion of him. In January 1864 Jowett wrote to his father: 'He has a great deal of ability and promise. There are very few undergraduates to whose career I look forward with as much confidence as his.' Later he expanded on this: 'I am surprised at his abilities, which are very good and he has excellent taste. I have rarely known anyone quicker at apprehending a new or difficult subject. He sees the point of a thing in a moment.'

Two years later his father died and he became the 5th Marquess of Lansdowne, and as such the owner of Bowood in Wiltshire and a stately home in Berkeley Square originally known as Shelburn House and later as Lansdowne House. Jowett wrote to him: 'When I pass by your splendid house in London I feel a sort of wonder that the owner should be reading quietly at Oxford. But you could not do a wiser or a better thing. Wealth and rank are means and not ends, and may be the greater evils or the greater goods as they are used.'

To his mother Emily, Lansdowne wrote a letter every week without fail until she died. Her father, the comte de Flahaut, was one of Napoleon's most trusted aides de camp and later Ambassador in London. It was widely believed, however, that Lansdowne's grandfather was not Flahaut but Talleyrand. In either case both France and diplomacy would have been part of his inheritance.

Lansdowne could be said to have represented the best and highest traditions of the British aristocracy. In the autumn of 1869 he married Lady Maud Hamilton, daughter of the Duke of Abercorn, a family renowned for its 'good looks, high spirits and general brilliance'. His brother-in-law, Lord Ernest Hamilton, paints a warmly appreciative picture of him. He was grateful, among other things, for the fact that he never mentioned politics in a household where everyone else did. Lansdowne's tastes were simple and abstemious: 'but though the port decanter may have passed him by unnoticed – and in fact it generally did – it was no gloomy ascetic that it left behind, but a uniformly bright and cheery neighbour, ready and able to talk on any subject – always excepting the ponderous machinery of State.' He was always 'the most courteous of listeners and the most intelligent of critics'.

In the country, 'away from the burdens of office and the ceremonies and problems of State, Clan was genuinely and boyishly happy. Fishing was his favourite relaxation.' In fact, the highest tribute paid to Lansdowne was, in Lord Ernest's eyes, 'the bond between him and his subordinates. Diplomats and Courtiers may wear convenient masks, but not keepers and boatmen. Their faces are an open book.' Lord Ernest regarded his brother-in-law as 'possibly the greatest gentleman of his day, I don't use that word in a *Grand Seigneur* sense, though he was that too – very markedly – but in all the qualities that really mark a great gentleman he may be said to have stood out a little from his peers. Most people in society would, I think, have nominated him as our representative in any international competition for gentlemen.'

He was to represent his country as Governor-General of Canada and Viceroy of India. In June 1885 Lord Salisbury offered him the position of Secretary for War. As his biographer, Lord Newton, puts it: 'there has never been a more thankless post in any British Administration than that of Secretary of State for War; and in the selection of Lord Lansdowne, Lord Salisbury was probably influenced by the fact that for ten years he had taken no part in party politics and that, consequently, his record was blameless.'

In October 1900, at Salisbury's request, the Queen offered Lansdowne the post of Foreign Secretary. He wrote to her: 'Lord

Lansdowne has been made aware by the Prime Minister that you have been pleased to think of me for the Foreign Office. He is most grateful for this mark of Her Majesty's confidence in him. He values it the more because he does not disguise from himself that as Secretary of State for War, he must often have seemed to Your Majesty to fall short of expectations.' Later in life he was to speak of his tenure of the Foreign Office as 'incomparably the most interesting period of my life.'

The life of Lord Lansdowne, written shortly after his death by Lord Newton, provides the best summary of his particular gifts and abilities.

The main qualifications required by a Foreign Minister are extreme patience and tact, a judicial disposition, a willingness to listen to experienced opinion, some knowledge of other countries and of foreign tongues, the faculty of knowing when to make a stand when the national interest requires it, and the power of defining the national policy, both in the written and in the spoken word, in dignified and courteous language.

These qualifications he possessed to perfection. No one ever excelled him in his conscientious attention to details, or in the application needed to master the innumerable dry and complicated questions with which the Secretary of State is confronted daily. No one was ever more accessible to those who served under him, and certainly no other Foreign Secretary inspired a stronger feeling of confidence among foreign representatives here; while his position and the ability to entertain on a magnificent scale, naturally tended to facilitate social relations.

All this, combined with the administrative experience which he had already acquired in the public service, gave him perhaps greater advantages than any other occupant of the post, and it may be truthfully asserted that it would be difficult to cite any other man who established himself more rapidly and firmly in the opinion of all alike as an international statesman of the first order.

The replacement of Salisbury by Lansdowne opened the door to the negotiations for the *Entente*. On 14 February 1901 the French Ambassador in London, Paul Cambon, had written to his brother Jules complaining of Salisbury's lethargy. 'Every time that I was led incidentally to speak of Nova Scotia, Lord Salisbury replied: "It is a dispute that has been going on for sixty years and can go on longer without inconvenience."'

On 1 January 1901 Queen Victoria wrote in her Journal: 'Another year begun, and I am feeling so weak and unwell that I enter upon it sadly.' It was, in fact, the beginning of the end. The decline and death of Victoria is chronicled by the one man most qualified to do so, the Resident Medical Attendant to the Queen, Sir James Reid. He had held the post since July 1881.

Sir James Reid was in constant attendance and his wife Susan contributes to the chronicle. Victoria had refused to see Sir Francis Laking, Physician in Ordinary to the Prince of Wales, who had summoned him to Osborne House. 'The Queen will not see him,' wrote Susan on 12 January, 'at least not about her health, and she can hardly bear Jamie out of her sight . . . She does depend on him entirely now and happily *he is very well*.' 'Reid at that time was the only one who realized that the monarch whom he had served for twenty years was rapidly declining,' writes his biographer Michaela Reid (wife of his grandson), 'but it is doubtful whether even he imagined that within ten days of Susan's letter the Queen would be dead.'

On 19 January Reid rang Marlborough House and asked Sir Francis Knollys, Edward's Private Secretary, 'to tell the Prince that in my opinion he ought not to go to Sandringham but to remain in London ready to come here at a moment's notice; that I consider the Queen's condition is a most serious one, and that I think it is quite possible she might be dead in a few days.' The Prince arrived at Osborne at 5 p.m. The official bulletin for that day stated: 'The Queen is suffering from great physical prostration accompanied by symptoms which cause anxiety.'

161

It had not been an easy day for Reid. Victoria's daughter, Princess Christian of Schleswig-Holstein, had sent a telegram to her brother stating the opposite to the doctor's report. She did not want the Prince of Wales to come and she had an angry scene with Reid. Both she and her sister, Princess Beatrice of Battenburg, had learned that the Kaiser was coming to Osborne and agreed that 'he must be stopped at all hazards.' Reid had sent a private telegram to the Kaiser reporting his grandmother's state of health. Fortunately the two princesses did not know of his telegram.

Towards evening that day the Queen showed signs of improvement and Reid began to feel that she might almost pull through. 'At 6 o' clock she was clear and talked with me coherently, though with difficulty.' Later she announced that she wanted 'everybody to go out except Sir James, so they all went out, leaving me alone with her. When I told her they had all gone out, she looked in my face and said: 'I should like to live a little longer, as I have a few things to settle. I have arranged most things, but there are still some left and I want to live a little longer.' She appealed to me in this pathetic way with great trust, as if she thought *I* could make her live.' On 20 January Edward returned to London to receive the Kaiser.

The bulletin that evening was slightly more optimistic. 'The Queen's strength has been fairly maintained throughout the day, and there are indications of slight improvement in the symptoms this evening.' That night Victoria was not so well again and very weak.

The next day, 21 January, the Prince of Wales was advised to come back as quickly as possible and to bring the Kaiser with him. 'We even thought that, in the uncertainty as to how soon anything might happen, they might have to travel by night.' Sir James recorded: 'I was up all night. Powell [Sir Richard, Physician in Ordinary] was with me and we gave her oxygen frequently. We thought perhaps she was going to die quickly, but we did not fetch any of the Princesses, who never came to enquire at night.'

It was a difficult time for Sir James. Not only were his professional duties unremitting, but he had to exercise authority over the members of the royal family.

It was a difficult time also for the Queen's Equerry, Sir Frederick Ponsonby. He also kept a diary. 'On January 21st,' he records, 'a long telegram about the war in South Africa arrived and I went off to ask Reid what should be done with it. He said, with a grave face, that there had been a change for the worse and that he feared the end might come at any time during the night. I therefore despatched a mounted groom to summon Edwards [Keeper of the Privy Purse and extra Equerry] and Bigge [Sir Arthur, Assistant Private Secretary] and I also sent a carriage for the Bishop of Winchester.' This was Randall Davidson, who had been Dean of Windsor and was one of the clergy closest to Victoria. He was staying at Whippingham Rectory with the parish priest. 'They all came and we had a long consultation and it was decided that the Prince of Wales should be told at once. The telephone in those days for long-distance calls was very uncertain, but after some delay I managed to get onto the Prince of Wales himself, and he decided to come at once by special train.' With him came the Duke of Connaught, the Duke of York and the Kaiser. 'Although the rest of the Royal Family seemed to resent his coming,' continues Ponsonby, 'and no one had asked him to come, he behaved in the most dignified and admirable manner. He said to the Princesses, 'My first wish is not to be in the light. I should like to see Grandmama before she dies, but if that is impossible I shall quite understand.' Nothing could have been better.

'When the Prince of Wales went to see the Queen she became conscious for a moment and recognized him. She put out her arms and said 'Bertie', whereupon he embraced her and broke down completely.' After the Prince had left Reid went to her bedside. 'Her Majesty took my hand' he wrote 'and repeatedly kissed it. She evidently, in her semi-conscious state, did not realize that the Prince had gone and thought it was *his* hand she was kissing.'

'Another time, during a moment of consciousness, she sent for her dog and called it by its name.' His name was 'Turi' . . . He was taken and put on the Queen's bed, who patted him and seemed pleased to have him beside her.'

'In the afternoon I saw the Kaiser who was most anxious to know about his grandmother and thanked me for my telegram which he said had at once decided him to come. I told him that I was anxious that he should see the Queen alone and talk to her, for which he thanked me, for it was the one thing he desired . . . I meant to take him to see the Queen when none of the family was there. He was very grateful and said, "Did you notice this morning that everybody's name in the room was mentioned to her except mine?" I replied *Yes*, and that is one reason why *I* specially wish to take you there . . . I went to the Prince of Wales to report about the Queen and said I would like to take the Kaiser to see her. He replied, "Certainly, and tell him the Prince of Wales wishes it." I took the Kaiser to see her and sent all the maids out and took him up to the bedside and said, "Your Majesty, your grandson the Emperor is here; he has come to see you" . . . and she smiled and understood. I went out and left him for five minutes with her alone. She said to me afterwards, "The Emperor is very kind."'

At 4 p.m. on 22 January the bulletin was sent: 'The Queen is sinking.' 'I returned to the room after five minutes' absence, and did not leave until she died at 6.30 p.m . . . A few minutes before she died her eyes turned fixedly to the right and gazed on the picture of Christ in 'The Entombment of Christ' over the fireplace.' It is a portrait by Gustav Jager which still hangs in Victoria's bedroom at Osborne House.

'Her pulse,' continues Sir James, 'kept beating well till the end when she died with my arm around her. I gently let her down on the pillow and kissed her hand before I got up. When she died at 6.30, I had for the last half hour been kneeling at her right side with my right hand on her right pulse all this time, my left arm supporting her in a semi upright position, helped by the Kaiser who knelt on the opposite side of the bed . . . The Bishop of Winchester was saying prayers. The Queen kept looking at me and saying 'Sir James' frequently.'

'The behaviour of the German Emperor,' writes Ponsonby, 'was

164

beyond all praise. He kept in the background until they were all summoned. The Prince and Princess of Wales, Princess Christian, Princess Louise and Princess Beatrice stood around the bed, while the German Emperor knelt down and supported the Queen with his arm, while Reid held her up on the other side. The Emperor never moved for two and a half hours and remained quite still. His devotion to the Queen quite disarmed all the Royal Family.'

Sir James continues: 'When all was over most of the family shook hands with me and thanked me by the bedside, and the Kaiser also squeezed my hand in silence. I told the Prince of Wales to close her eyes. Later the Prince and Princess of Wales sent for me and thanked me together in their room, and the Prince said: 'You are an honest straightforward Scotchman and I shall never forget all you did for the Queen.'

The bulletin that evening needed only four words: 'The Queen is dead.'

8

King at Last

The Queen was dead and with her died the symbol of an age. She had inherited a crown which had sunk low in the estimation of the people: she left it respected and beloved. The feelings of most of Victoria's subjects are summed up in the story, quoted by Elizabeth Longford, of a London policeman on the occasion of one of her fairly rare visits to Buckingham Palace. He pointed to the Royal Standard and said to a bystander: 'Mother's come 'ome.'

To many at that time it was impossible to imagine Great Britain without her. Princess May of Teck spoke for the majority when she exclaimed: 'The thought of England without the Queen is dreadful even to think of. God help us all!' This could be taken, at least in part, as an expression of no confidence in Victoria's successor.

All eyes now turned to the Prince of Wales who, setting aside his first name of Albert, ostensibly in deference to his august father, took the title of Edward VII.

'There is no position,' stated an article in *The Times* the following morning, 'more difficult to fill than that of Heir Apparent to the throne.' It dwelt on the manifold temptations to which such an individual was necessarily exposed. But it ends: 'The King has passed through that tremendous ordeal, prolonged through youth and

167

manhood to middle age . . . The Prince of Wales, in all his public relations has been as unique among those who have occupied the same position as was his mother among sovereigns. He has never failed in his duty to the throne and to the nation.'

Not many people knew much about the real Edward. What they saw in him was the leader of the fast set – the Marlborough House set. It was a society in which etiquette had been relaxed and smoking permitted. An atmosphere of easy hedonism prevailed. Edward himself was a pronounced *bon viveur* who had learnt in France to appreciate the refinements of the *haute cuisine* and the perfection of the great vintages of Château d'Yquem and Haut Brion.

More serious, in the eyes of many, were his departures from chastity during his earlier years and his more recent infidelities to his wife – a pattern of behaviour, however, not unknown when royal marriages were arrangements based on purely dynastic considerations. 'The hospitalities of Marlborough House and Sandringham,' writes Lord Redesdale, one of the men closest to Edward, 'were lavishly magnificent, while the small and very intimate society at Abergeldie was delightful. The Prince of Wales and the Princess shone as host and hostess . . . We must remember,' he added, 'that when the Prince of Wales married he was very young – only just twenty-one. He was full of high spirits and endowed with a vitality such as I have seldom seen equalled.'

But there was a serious side to his entertaining. 'The invitations to Marlborough House and Sandringham were by no means confined to the butterflies of society. As often as not the Prince might be seen standing apart in earnest talk with Lord Granville, Lord Clarendon, Mr Gladstone, Mr Disraeli, Bishop Wilberforce . . . Generals and Admirals, men of science.' This was his true education.

At a more profound level, those who knew more about the new King might also have had misgivings. One of the greatest reproaches that could be made against Victoria was her stubborn refusal to allow the heir to the throne any apprenticeship in the business of government.

'In 1882,' writes Sidney Lee, 'Edward pointed out to his mother that he was less trusted with official information than the secretaries of Ministers.' Three years later Mr Gladstone 'deliberately sought a remedy from the witholding from the Prince of all information about Cabinet deliberations.' He promised to invite the Queen's sanction for his sending to the Prince 'anything of importance that takes place in the Cabinet.' The Queen merely reiterated her old, disparaging plea that 'secrets' ought not to be divulged to one who talked too much. To Mr Gladstone's questioning of the validity of her argument she replied that 'it would be quite irregular and improper for the Prince to receive copies of the Cabinet reports with which she alone was furnished.' Attempts to persuade her to allow the Prime Minister to choose the confidential intelligence fell on deaf ears. The Queen answered that the Prime Minister 'can only report to the Sovereign and it would not be desirable that W.G. and H.R.H. should have discussions which she knew nothing about.' Anything Edward learned he must learn from her.

To Laurence Oliphant, an author who had met the Prince, the causes of Edward's character defects were largely due to 'a position which never allowed him responsibility or forced him to action.' As the editor of the *Review of Reviews*, W. D. Stead, argued: 'if the Prince of Wales had been saddled with his father's duties he might have developed somewhat more of his father's virtues.' It was no use talking to Victoria like that. Any suggestion from the Prime Minister of useful employment for the Prince of Wales was immediately turned down. She came very near to saying that he could not be given a job that would have been a useful experience because he was too inexperienced.

It does not seem that Victoria was looking towards the future. 'No-one who knows the character of the Queen and of the Heir Apparent,' wrote Sir James Clark, Victoria's Physician, 'can look forward to the future without seeing troubles in that quarter.' It was clearly in the interests of the country that the heir to the throne should receive a political education which would enable him to become a worthy successor. Victoria's attitude may even have been connected with her life-long obsession with Albert. Elizabeth Longford, one of the Queen's many biographers, writes: 'For close on thirty years she obstinately kept Prince Albert's golden key to the Foreign Office despatches out of hands which seemed to her both grasping and incompetent.' The idea of Edward's stepping into Albert's shoes in any capacity was abhorrent to her.

The leaders of the government, taking the long-term view, continued to press the point. Some took it into their own hands. Lord Rosebery, during his short period as Foreign Secretary in 1886, caused foreign despatches to be forwarded to Edward without the Queen's specific authority. It was not until Lord Salisbury became Prime Minister that proper access to documents was obtained. It had taken thirty-six years.

Sidney Lee draws attention to the political education which the Prince had received by the end of Victoria's reign. 'It was not generally known that for some fifteen years every important foreign despatch had been placed at his disposal and that for some nine years the reports and proceedings of the Cabinet had been regularly submitted to him. Although he had not figured publicly on the political stage, he had moved almost continuously behind the scenes and the prominent actors had often taken their cue from him.'

But Edward had been learning about statesmanship and diplomacy from other sources. Among these were Lord Granville and Sir Charles Dilke and, indeed, Gambetta. Granville was a personal friend of his, and his appointment to the Foreign Office in 1880 brought Edward into a more serious relationship with France. The same was true of his relations with Dilke. Dilke was a francophile and a friend of Gambetta. In their different ways Granville and Dilke nourished in the Prince a serious interest in the affairs of France.

Not many people knew of the wideness of interests, the breadth of experience and the depth of the understanding of men and of affairs which Edward had acquired during his long years as Heir Apparent. Not many knew of the outgoing personality and of that rare gift of being able to speak, and to speak brilliantly and to the point, without notes, in English, French and German. Many who did know wondered whether these were sufficient to sustain the weight of the Imperial Crown. The contrast between the characters of mother and son, writes Sidney Lee, 'was so great as to give rise to grave fears concerning the future trend of the British Monarchy. That King Edward would be popular there was no doubt, but whether he would be a wise King and a great King was a question that few dared to answer when he ascended the throne.'

On Friday, 25 January 1901 Lord Salisbury moved, in the House of Lords, an address of condolence to the new King on the death of his mother. He spoke of the country's 'deep and heart-felt feeling – deeper than I ever remember – of sorrow at a singular loss.' As Andrew Roberts comments: 'nobody was better placed to pay such a tribute. He sums up her supreme virtue as no-one else could.' No-one knew her as well as he did. He had, as *The Times* reminded its readers, been Prime Minister for a longer period than any other statesman during the past seventy years. 'It was always a dangerous matter,' continued Salisbury, 'to press on her any course of the expediency of which she was not thoroughly convinced. She had an extraordinary knowledge of what her people would think – extraordinary because it could not have come from any personal intercourse. I have said for years that when I knew what the Queen thought I knew pretty certainly what view her subjects would take, especially the middle classes of her subjects, such was the extraordinary penetration of her mind.' It was this strange capacity which enabled her to symbolize the age to which she gave her name and which died with her.

On 9 January 1901 the Baron von Eckardstein had received an invitation from the Duchess of Devonshire to stay for a few days at Chatsworth. In 1895 he had begun his 'Ten Years at the Court of Saint James' (the title of his memoirs). In 1899 he had become First Secretary and, during the long absences of the ailing Count von Hatzfeltd, was acting Ambassador.

171

'Pray come without fail,' the Duchess urged, 'as the Duke has several urgent political questions to discuss with you. You will also find here Joseph Chamberlain. As we shall have a house party of fifty or so for the theatricals you will easily get an opportunity for a quiet talk with the Duke and Jos . . . There are in the *schloss* plenty of rooms where you will be able to talk without any one noticing you. The Duke makes a great point of your coming.'

Spencer Compton Cavendish – 'Cav' to his friends – Marquess of Hartington and 8th Duke of Devonshire, had played a leading role in Queen Victoria's government. Patrick Jackson, author of a recent and valuable biography, has given his book the title *The Last of the Whigs*. Born in 1833, the future Duke was educated at home before going to Cambridge where he took no interest in politics and never spoke in the Union. Thanks, however, to the influence of Lord Granville, whose mother was a sister of the 6th Duke, politics were to become his foremost interest in life. He spent thirty-four years in the Commons as Marquess of Hartington and sixteen in the Lords as the 8th Duke of Devonshire, during which time he was three times asked to form a government but on each occasion declined. Like King Edward, he was a man more suited to exercise influence than to wield power. Many of the portraits and cartoons of him depict him with a slightly puzzled look and a slightly open mouth, which is the expression of a man who ponders deeply but has not yet reached a decision.

It was perhaps this which made him the outstanding speaker of his time. His obituary in the *Daily News* claimed that his speeches had 'an extraordinary effect on the audience . . . they were unrhetorical, totally unadorned, lacking all traces of grace or energy in delivery. They gave the impression of a man thinking aloud.'

On 4 June 1857 he made his maiden speech in the House of Commons. It only lasted five minutes but that was long enough to give him time to yawn halfway through. Disraeli commented that 'to any man who can betray such complete langour under such circumstances the highest post in the gift of the Commons should be open.' Two years later he made a fifty-minute speech which was very well received. Lord John Russell wrote to the Duke: 'Hartington has only to go on to become not only a very good speaker but a man to influence the House of Commons in time to come.'

In 1869 he had his first government office – that of Postmaster General. It was the occasion of a cartoon by Carlo Peregrini in *Vanity Fair* which depicts him walking past a pillar box. It bears the caption: 'His ability and industry would deserve respect even in a man: in a Marquis they command admiration.' Such was the man who, together with Joseph Chamberlain, was to initiate a new foreign policy and open the door which was ultimately to lead to the *Entente Cordiale*.

At Chatsworth, after dinner on the 16th, 'the two Ministers definitely formulated their position,' writes Eckardstein; 'their statement was embodied by me in an official dispatch after consultation with Count Hatzfeldt.' On 18 January Hatzfeldt wrote to the Chancellor, now *Prinz* Bernard von Bülow, 'The Colonial Minister [Chamberlain] and his friends in the Cabinet had made up their minds that the day of a policy of isolation was over for England. England must look about for allies for the future.'

It is perhaps significant that this meeting took place when Salisbury, the opponent of commitment to alliances, was absent in France. The death of Victoria was a great blow to him. The night before the Queen died Violet Cecil wrote in her diary: 'Lord Salisbury is very unhappy. The break for him is fearful.' But it was not only the end of a great partnership: it was the end of an era. Salisbury was soon to follow the Queen.

On 26 September 1900 a double cartoon had appeared in the Westminster Gazette showing Lord Salisbury and the Duke of Devonshire asleep on their benches. It bore the title 'No Change', but it marked the beginning of a very great change. In October, just when Salisbury was leaving the Foreign Office, Lord Esher described him as 'sitting in a crumpled heap . . . evidently wearied out.' On Saturday, 22 August 1903 he died. Devonshire was notoriously somnolent, but he still had several years to go.

XIII.—NO CHANGES.—(I.)

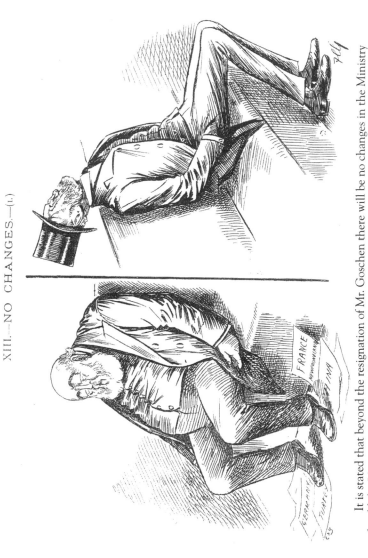

It is stated that beyond the resignation of Mr. Goschen there will be no changes in the Ministry should the Unionists return to Office after the General Election. – DAILY PAPER.

Lord Salisbury will continue to watch over the interests of the Empire in all parts of the world.

The Duke of Devonshire will continue to look after the important interests of Education and will keep the reformers "in their proper places."

[WESTMINSTER GAZETTE, September 26, 1900.]

On Friday, 11 July 1902 Lord Salisbury had delivered his seals of office
to the King. George Buckle, the Editor of *The Times*, wrote to him: 'You
are indeed happy in the political end to which you have come. You leave
your country ... prosperous and wealthy, on good terms with all her powerful neighbours, on better terms with those we specially desire to be our
friends, than ever before; and you leave your Party at the height of prosperity with a majority ... such as you never could have dreamed of in your
early political career. The destructive movements you dreaded have lost
ground, the principles you contended for are in the ascendant. Finally
you are able to hand over your proud position to your pupil and nephew.'

The Duke of Devonshire died on 4 March 1908. Arthur Balfour, now
Prime Minister, pronounced his obituary.

Of all the statesmen I have known, the Duke of Devonshire was the
most persuasive speaker; and he was persuasive because he never
attempted to conceal the strength of the case against him.

He brought before the public in absolutely clear and unmistakable
terms the very arguments he had been going through, patiently and
honestly, before he arrived at his conclusions ... He had that quality
in a far greater measure than any man I have ever known, and it gave
him a dominant position in any assembly. His listeners felt 'here is one
addressing us who had done his best to master every aspect of this question, who had been driven by logic to arrive at certain conclusions and
who is disguising from us no argument on either side which weighed
with him, or moved him to come to the conclusion at which he had
arrived.'

As a man he had a singular gift. He had that transparent simplicity
of character which gave him the power of arousing and retaining the
affections of all those with whom he came into personal touch.

Almeric Fitzroy, who was his Private Secretary in the Privy Council
Office for eight years, gives the same picture. 'The integrity of his method
made it impossible for him to overlook anything that could be said in

favour of a course from which he shrank; for his first step was to seek out all that could be urged on its behalf, just as he was wont to challenge investigation of every objection to the line he intended to pursue. His was the most transparently sincere and unsophisticated mind with which I have ever been brought into contact. Its massive honesty must have proved inconvenient.'

Margot Asquith, in her autobiography, introduces him as 'a man whose like we shall never see again . . . He had the figure and appearance of an artisan, with the brevity of a peasant, the courtesy of a King and the noisy sense of humour of a Falstaff. He was possessed of endless wisdom. He was perfectly disengaged from himself and without pettiness of any kind.' Balfour said that 'in the Duke of Devonshire we had lost almost the last survivor of our heroic age.' By a certain irony of fate it was at Chatsworth that the decision had been made to move on to a new age.

The funeral of Queen Victoria presented a problem. It was sixty-four years since the funeral of the last sovereign. Frederick Ponsonby had a considerable share in the arrangements, but, he admitted, 'no one seemed to know what the procedure was. We spent the evening looking up what had been done when George IV and William IV had died.' The 60th Rifles were summoned from Parkhurst to provide the guard, but 'the men had never been taught to reverse arms and the drill book was dumb on the subject.'

It then turned out that this duty was the prerogative of the Queen's Company of the Grenadier Guards, who took over. Fortunately Captain Arthur Lloyd, their Commanding Officer, was both competent and resourceful. 'The changing of the sentries,' observed Ponsonby, 'became a most impressive sight, all done in slow time.' The Dining Room was turned into a mortuary Chapel and decked out with great magnificence – 'all was gorgeous with colour and most impressive.'

Ponsonby was put in charge of the funeral procession in Windsor, but this turned out to be the responsibility of the Earl Marshal. 'I rushed off to London and went at once to the Earl Marshal's office, where I found absolute chaos.'

An amused spectator of all this chaos was the French Ambassador, Paul Cambon. Thirty-six hours before the actual funeral he wrote: 'They do and undo; everything is mixed up and it is impossible to obtain precise information. The funniest thing is that the disorder is not causing any trouble. Lord Lansdowne's secretary has only just told me, very quietly, "We are very stupid." But the superiority of the British is that it is a matter of complete indifference to them if they appear to be stupid.'

On the day of the funeral Cambon sat in the seat of one of the Knights of the Garter in Saint George's Chapel at Windsor, shivering with cold. 'I had opposite me Lord Salisbury all wrapped up in his mantle and with a velvet bonnet on his head [presumably his Garter robes].' As he was leaving the Kaiser came up to him. 'My dear Cambon,' he said, 'you know already my sentiments for your country. I consider France indispensable for the equilibrium of Europe; a strong France is necessary for me; if you have any difficulty, count on me; I will lend you my help.' Cambon replied a little coldly: 'I am deeply touched by the sentiments of your Majesty and will transmit them to Paris. But France asks only to live in peace and I hope and believe that she will never have need of the help of your Majesty.'

Across the Channel Thomas Barclay records the reaction to the Queen's death. 'The mourning of the whole British Empire for its Queen struck a sympathetic chord in the generous nature of the French. That all the political, commercial and industrial life of an Empire should stand still, even for a few hours, to express, as it did, the feelings of hundreds of millions of her subjects for the loss of their Sovereign produced a profound impression on the French. At the meeting of the deceased Queen's subjects, held in the large hall of the Hôtel Continental, the contagiousness of the prevailing emotion was such that I could hardly command my voice when, as Chairman, I opened the proceedings.'

Between eight hundred and a thousand persons were present and the meeting was duly reported in the Daily Messenger. In his speech Thomas Barclay gave one of the best definitions of the place of a hereditary sovereign as opposed to an elected President.

The Queen has been to us more than a sovereign. She has been the embodiment of all that in the public and private life of men and women of our race we hold to be sacred. From the earliest recollection of the oldest of us she has been the model and pride of her nation. We have remembered her in our prayers, and we have never forgotten her in our joys. Her image as a wife, a mother and a Queen, has been our most familiar figure throughout our lives. We have always held her, without a single note of reservation, in the honoured first place of the national heart. And wherever the national heart beats, there is a sense of loss which we can only feel for those whose love and care for us never failed. To cease all our daily wranglings and differences and stand together as one man in this hour of mourning is what all England, all the Empire, is doing and we, who love England none the less because we are in a foreign land, feel the same need to express the grief that we have in common.

I should like also, in conclusion, to mention the deep and wide-spread sympathy with us in our mourning shown throughout France, and the expressions of warm admiration and deep respect for the Queen which her death has called forth. Englishmen will always remember this with gratitude, and if at any time of late we may have doubted the real feeling of France and Frenchmen, we know that it is one of delicate and earnest sympathy for us when we need it.

Sir Edward Sassoon MP then stood up to second the motion. In conclusion 'he recalled to our minds the good work done by Mr Thomas Barclay and the British Chamber of Commerce in Paris over which he presides, in promoting good feeling between France and England, and he referred with unfeigned satisfaction to the deep sympathy which the French nation had shown in these circumstances. He was convinced that no two nations were better fitted to be on terms of solid friendship with each other.'

Barclay reminds us that Victoria's death took place just thirteen months after the publication of the caricatures which had caused such indignation in England. 'The change in the public attitude of Frenchmen towards this country showed that the seeds of *rapprochement* had already taken root.'

The Kaiser had remained in England after Victoria's funeral until 15 February. The King gave a luncheon for him before his departure at which he proposed his health in the most cordial terms. Wilhelm replied, saying: 'I believe there is a Providence which has decreed that two nations which have produced such men as Shakespeare, Schiller, Luther and Goethe must have a great future before them; I believe that the two Teutonic nations will, bit by bit, learn to know each other better, and that they will stand together in keeping the peace of the World. We ought to form an Anglo-German alliance, you to keep the seas while we would be responsible for the land; with such an alliance not a mouse could stir in Europe without our permission, and the nations would, in time, come to see the necessity of reducing their armaments.'

He also had a conversation with Lord Lansdowne who jotted down some notes. Wilhelm had described the Tsar as 'only fit to live in a country house and grow turnips – the only way to deal with him is to be the last to leave the room – French bitterly disappointed with Russia and Russian Emperor – no real love between the two countries.'

Lansdowne's jottings are significant. Wilhelm's contemptuous remarks about the Tsar are in complete disaccord with the attitude revealed in his secret letters to Nicholas. His remarks about the French disappointment with Russia look like wishful thinking. In the same correspondence Wilhelm made the most strenuous efforts to turn Russia against France and without much success.

In spite of the apparently friendly attitude of the Kaiser, negotiations between the two countries rather hung fire. Sir Valentine Chirol, a distinguished journalist on the staff of *The Times*, was invited to Berlin for unofficial talks with Count Bülow. At the end of the interview Bülow clasped Chirol with both hands and assured him of his good faith. 'Believe me, and I give you my word of honour as the Chancellor of the German Empire, not only shall I never countenance the hostile attacks upon your country of which I know a large – too large – section of the German press is often guilty, but I shall never allow . . . the anti-British sentiments of an ignorant public to deflect me so much as a hair's breadth from the policy of true friendliness towards England which lies nearest to my heart.' Fine words – but a few days later Bülow, speaking in the Reichstag, delivered, according to Lord Newton, 'an almost unparalleled outburst of Anglophobia.'

'The private letters from Sir Frank Lascelles, our Ambassador in Berlin,' continues Lord Newton, 'leave very little doubt, in spite of their optimism, as to the hostile feelings entertained towards us by important personages in Germany. The Kaiser's entourage was notoriously anti-British and, whenever he received reports from his own representatives in London that the British Government was in reality more friendly than was believed, elaborate efforts were made to convince him to the contrary.'

On 22 April 1902 Lord Lansdowne wrote to Lascelles: 'I am sanguine enough to hope that the bitter feeling against us in Germany may not last for ever. Have we not a right to ascribe a good deal of it to the South African war, and would the Emperor, Bülow and Holstein have contemplated, as they did, an Anglo-German alliance if hatred of Great Britain was for all time inherent in the sentiments of the German people?'

Three days later Lascelles replied: 'I have always been an optimist as to the relations between England and Germany for the simple reason that the interests of the two countries demand a good understanding between them. It is true that bitter feeling against England existed before the war began, and was partly due to jealousy of our success in colonizing, and partly a feeling that the position of Germany as a first class Power had not been adequately recognized by us. The Germans are quite extraordinarily sensitive. They are always on the look-out for fear they should be insulted.'

The Germans, Lascelles continued: 'cannot understand that if England were to cease to exist as a Great Power, Germany would be at the mercy of Russia and France if those two Powers united against them.'

She would have to fight on both her frontiers and alone. 'It is therefore unlikely,' he concluded, 'that Germany would lend her hand to anything that would seriously weaken the power of England.'

The Baron von Eckardstein's Memoirs were written after the end of the Great War, after the defeat and humiliation of Germany and the fall of the Hohenzollern dynasty. Looking back to the days of his ministry, Eckardstein writes with a bitterness and sometimes an exaggeration which put a question mark against the accuracy of some of his information. Tyler Whittle describes the Memoirs as 'studded with inconsistencies and contradictions'. This does not, of course, mean that none of his reportings and anecdotes were true. What he says is often corroborated by Paléologue.

Professor George Young, in his preface to Eckardstein's Memoirs, describes him as 'very much in the good graces of our Court and Cabinet and the ally of those English statesmen who were trying to establish the peace of Europe upon the firm foundation of an Anglo-German Alliance. How and why they failed – when the first rifts appeared that ended finally in rupture and ruin – can be seen, I think, more clearly in these memoirs than in any elaborate analysis of pre-war politics. As the reader follows the story, he realizes that he is watching from the wings the first scene of the first act of the tragedy of modern civilization. He sees the impending storm cloud, dark with the doom of Empires and the death of millions, draw visibly nearer.'

The blame for this, Eckardstein felt, 'must be ascribed primarily to the idiosyncrasies of Wilhelm II, and, with a few exceptions, to the responsible and irresponsible advisers chosen by him . . . With these lay the real power. The real inspirer and the one head of German diplomacy is no other than one of the leading *fonctionnaires* of the Wilhelmstrasse . . . the Baron von Holstein.' Bismarck had taken him into his personal service. 'From this moment,' writes Paléologue, 'Holstein is omnipotent . . . He keeps up a correspondence of his own with all the Ambassadors, outside the official correspondence and over the head of the Secretary of State. He sends them instructions, gives them orders, ticks them off, snubs them, threatens them.' His position became so secure that even the fall of Bismarck did not weaken it.

He desired nothing more. 'He never accepted the post of Secretary of State; he was never seen on social occasions; he allowed himself no private liaisons; he had no friends, no confidants; he revealed to none the secret of his thoughts . . . In this impenetrable solitude, for sixteen hours a day, he consecrates himself stubbornly to his hard labour with a fanatical zeal. From this obscure *fonctionnaire* the theatrical megalomania of Wilhelm II need fear no competition.' He became the *Eminence Grise* behind the throne.

Paléologue gives a dramatic description of his first sight of this extraordinary man. On a misty morning in Berlin in January 1899, he was walking along the Wilhelmstrasse with the French Ambassador, the marquis de Noailles. They saw a man approaching. 'Do you see this man coming towards us?', said the marquis; 'take a good look at him.'

He saw a man, tall but bent, who walked with a firm but rapid step. His clothes were modest, a shabby old hat and his fur coat threadbare; his white hair was over-long and his beard unkempt. 'Suddenly he recognized Noailles; he greeted him with an affected politeness, but quickening his step and distancing himself as if to escape conversation. Nevertheless I had time to look him in the face. He had a high forehead, the face bony, the nose aquiline, the lips pursed but with a fascinating expression of wiliness and energy, of mistrust and tenacity. Noailles said to me: "you have just seen our most redoubtable enemy – Holstein," and I began to understand the mysterious power of this *Eminence Grise*.' After the fall of Bismarck, Holstein took over the same place in the confidence of the Kaiser.

Bismarck had been succeeded as Chancellor by General von Caprivi. His foreign policy was, according to Eckardstein, 'on the whole sensible and sound in principle. Towards England it was indeed identical with that of Bismarck, namely a persistent pursuit of an alliance with Great Britain. His Secretary of State, Herbert Bismarck, though he was a pygmy compared to his father, yet he was still head and shoulders above his successor, von Marschall. Marschall was acclaimed in Germany as one of the greatest statesmen in the world. The Foreign Mission had, however, taken his measure more accurately when they referred to this *Ministre des Affaires Etrangers* as *Ministre Etranger aux Affaires.'*

The Count Paul von Hatzfeldt-Wildenburg, decribed by Bismarck as 'the best horse in his diplomatic stable', had been Foreign Secretary of State from 1880 to 1885, when he was transferred to London. 'It was fortunate for the German Empire,' wrote Paléologue, 'that during the first half of the Wilhelmic era Diplomacy contained men like Hatzfeldt, who could correct to some extent the compassless course laid by Wilhelm II and the vagaries of Holstein. Hatzfeldt, unfortunately, suffered from a chronic illness which obliged him to live as seldom as possible in foggy London. At the end of September 1891, Eckardstein received instructions that he was to be trasferred from Paris to London and should take up his duties there in November as First Secretary under Hatzfeldt. Eckardstein was the permanent resident and he thoroughly enjoyed it.

'London life was very pleasant and easy under the old Queen. It was the good old days, not only for England but for all Europe. And, apart from excitements caused by the Kaiser, Anglo-German relations were very tolerably good. There was not the least ill-feeling against Germany, either public or in the Government. On the other hand there was in the German Empire, from 1890 onwards, an absurd and quite artificial agitation against England and everything English. It was sad that the last days of the ageing Queen should have been thus overshadowed.' The advent of Edward, however, held out new hopes and new fears.

'Nothing could be further from the truth,' wrote Eckardstein, 'than the conviction current in Germany that King Edward was a sworn enemy of Germany. All those who knew him at this time would have been outspoken in their opinion that up to a certain point he always had the friendliest feelings towards Germany. Today King Edward is often represented as having brought about the encirclement of the German Empire by his fanatical hatred of Germany. Nothing could be more mistaken than this view.'

To the Kaiser, however, the Triple Entente between Great Britain, France and Russia was seen as an act of aggression. '*Deutschland ganzlich einzukreisen*' [to encircle Germany completely] was the self-evident aim of the Triple Alliance. The German press saw Edward VII as the villain of the piece. 'King Edward is the Napoleon of the 20th century, except that he operates in time of peace, using dextrous diplomatic methods instead of brute force.' They seemed to believe that Edward was an autocrat and not the strictly constitutional King that he was.

Wilhelm II had always maintained an affectionate relationship with his grandmother, Queen Victoria. She was herself instinctively pro-German and her relations with Wilhelm were good. This encouraged him to make more or less annual visits to England. Owing to the proximity of Osborne House to Cowes, Wilhelm had every opportunity to become a competent and enthusiastic yachtsman. But behind this enthusiasm for yachting there were deeper motives. His visits to Cowes enabled him to take a good look at the British navy. He was beginning to entertain ambitions of forming a German navy that would rival that of England. The Kaiser, ably assisted by Admiral von Tirpitz, set about the steady building up of a fleet. 'Our future,' he said, 'is on the sea. We must seize the Trident.' It was easily construed as a plan of aggression against Britain.

Early in January 1904, the Kaiser made a remarkable speech at Bremen.

My study of history led me to take counsel with myself, and inwardly to vow that never would I strive for a vain empire of the world. For what was the end of all the great so-called World-Empires? Alexander, Napoleon, all the mighty conquerors – had they not waded through blood and left behind them subjugated peoples who cast off the yoke as quickly as might be, and brought those vaunted Empires to decay?

The World Dominion of my dream consists above all in this – that the new-made German Empire should everywhere be regarded with the most absolute confidence, should enjoy the reputation of a tranquil, fair-dealing pacific neighbour; and that if ever, in the future, history should tell of German world-dominion or a Hohenzollern hegemony, neither of these things should have been founded on conquests by the sword, but on the mutual confidence of nations animated by a similar ambition.

A minute later he was on to the subject of armaments. 'The fleet is launched and being built . . . Its spirit is the same as that which inspired Prussian officers at Hohenfriedberg, Königgratz and Sedan; and with every German warship that leaves the docks another guarantee of peace on earth is launched upon the waters.'

The question that needs to be asked is whether re-armament is defensive or offensive. There is much sense in the words of Vegetius '*Qui desiderat pacem, praeparet bellum* . . . Let him that desires peace prepare for war.' The Kaiser sometimes speaks as if he had been a pupil of Vegetius.

In April 1901, in order to announce his succession in accordance with tradition, Edward had appointed special envoys to the major countries of Europe. Lord Carrington, an old friend and later to become Marquess of Lincolnshire, was to visit France, Spain and Portugal and the Duke of Abercorn was to visit Norway, Sweden, Denmark, Russia and Germany. The Kaiser wrote enthusiastically to Edward: 'We have just had the great pleasure of entertaining the gentlemen of the Special Mission which you kindly sent to announce your accession. They made an excellent impression here and were most respectfully treated by the public.'

It seemed as if Germany and Great Britain were moving towards an alliance. One of the first things that Lansdowne did as Foreign Secretary had been to write to the British Ambassador in Berlin, Sir Francis Lascelles. He claimed that he had approached his new job with very few preconceptions, but he did admit to one. He was convinced that 'we should use every effort to maintain, and if possible to strengthen, the good relations which at present exist between the Queen's Government and that of the Emperor.' Lascelles replied that he was optimistic about this. The German Foreign Minister, Count Bülow, and his Under Secretary, the Baron von Richthofen, were both in favour of such an alliance, but he warned that public opinion, and above all the press, was hostile to Britain.

Wilhelm, who described the British ministers as 'a set of unmitigated Noodles', insisted that only by a definite and binding treaty could a satisfactory relationship be established. In May 1901 Hatzfeldt renewed conversations with a view to furthering an Anglo-German alliance.

Meanwhile Carrington had been paying a similar visit to France. Lansdowne had warned him that he might get a hostile reception in Paris, where sympathy for the Boers was still strong. But President Loubet – 'a simple, sincere sort of man' – asked him to luncheon to meet Théophile Delcassé, still Foreign Secretary – 'a sharp, clever, dark man of about forty five, sociable and civil' – who pressed Carrington 'to assure the King that no effort would be spared on his part to foster and maintain happy relations between France and England.'

Carrington wrote in his Diary: 'I told the King that my impressions of Paris were very favourable and that President Loubet and all his Ministers were very civil, willing and anxious to talk openly on any subject, and that I felt certain that there would not be much difficulty in coming to a very friendly understanding with France if Ministers so desired. I also said that his [the King's] immense personal popularity in Paris would go a long way to smooth the path for this if it was thought worth while. I said that I could tell him all this plainly . . . His Majesty said that I had better put my impressions before Lansdowne and let him judge for himself.'

At a later meeting between the Kaiser and Lord Lansdowne, recorded by Eckardstein, Lansdowne raised the question of the balance of power among the European nations, which lay in England's hands. The Kaiser retorted that 'the balance of power now lay with the German 22nd army corps and that England was no longer in a position to isolate herself, as in former years, from the rest of Europe, but must move together with the Continent.'

There was also a number of merely domestic issues confronting the new King. Sir Charles Hardinge, who had served as Secretary at the Embassy in St Petersburg since 1898, and one of the leading diplomats of the times, makes an interesting comment.

There is little doubt that during the last few years of Queen Victoria's reign, when her energy and industry began to fail . . . the power of the Cabinet gradually grew and many important decisions of the Cabinet were carried out without the usual reference to the Queen. As far as I know there was no abuse of power by the Cabinet, but gradually the sovereign was – chiefly on account of her health – consulted less. When the King ascended the throne, he demanded, and very rightly too, that he should not be ignored and that he should be consulted, especially in connection with Foreign affairs. To this demand he experienced at first a certain opposition, especially on the part of the Foreign Office, and had, in my opinion, good grounds for complaint.

However, he was not the sort of man to be thwarted by any Cabinet or Minister and he very soon levelled all the barriers opposed to him by the soundness of his views on all matters referred to him, and soon convinced the Government that from his knowledge of men and his shrewd appreciation of events his advice was well worth taking on all questions of the hour.

On 23 January 1901 Edward attended a meeting of the Privy Council at St James's Palace. The Archbishop of Canterbury, the ageing Frederick Temple, administered the customary oaths. The King then addressed the gathering. He had sought no advice as to what to say and he had written no notes. The words came directly from his heart. 'My first and melancholy duty is to announce to you the death of my beloved mother, the Queen, and I know how deeply you, the whole nation, and I think I may say the whole world, sympathize with me in the irreparable loss which I have sustained. In undertaking the heavy load which now devolves upon me, I am fully determined to be a constitutional sovereign in the strictest sense of the word.' The speech was reconstructed by some of the listeners, who all averred that what they had produced was 'nothing like so good as the speech which the King actually delivered . . . the original words were full of dignity and pathos.'

Edward, in fact, possessed the fundamental charisma needed by all who would move the hearts and address the minds of their fellow men – that sense of friendly ease between the speaker and the listener. Contact must be made. He recognized that the art of conversation is not just the ability to talk but the ability to listen. This was remarked on by Edward's Private Secretary and Equerry, Sir Frederick Ponsonby. 'The King's great attraction,' he wrote, 'was that he was a very good listener. During the interviews and audiences, no matter on what subject, he was always able to fix attention on his visitor. Men who came from central Africa, or from some other remote place, were delighted at being asked questions and came away with great admiration for the King, who really had only listened intently. I have seen the King apparently deeply interested in something I knew bored him.'

In public speaking he had the confidence bred of the knowledge that what he said was worth saying. His understanding of European diplomacy was thorough and he had the details at his finger tips. It was this confidence which enabled him to speak without notes. It was the despair of the press correspondents who expected a copy in advance of what he was going to say.

Two days after his first speech as King at the Privy Council meeting, the Prime Minister, Lord Salisbury said of Edward: 'He has been familiar with our political and social life for more than one generation and he enjoys an enormous popularity. Moreover he is loved in foreign countries and Courts almost as much as our beloved Queen was.' Salisbury is being over tactful about the Queen. Edward commanded a far deeper affection in foreign hearts. Sir Henry Campbell-Bannerman, Leader of the Opposition, seconded Lord Salisbury's address. He laid stress, writes Sidney Lee, 'on the new Sovereign's manifold public services which he had rendered to practical schemes for the benefit of the country, and confidently anticipated increased efforts for the promotion of the people's welfare. He was the only speaker to mention Queen Alexandra – a reference that was loudly cheered by both sides of the House.'

Edward had undertaken to be 'a constitutional sovereign in the strictest sense of the word' – the question was how that phrase should be interpreted. It was soon apparent that he did not intend to be a mere figurehead, a rubber stamper of democratic decisions, a gramophone for other people's words. But he was to exercise influence rather than power, and authority rather than autocracy. The word suggests the scene in *King Lear* when Kent, in disguise, offers his services.

'Thou hast that in thine eye which I would fain call master.'

'What's that?'

'Authority.'

It was not long before Edward gave his ministers a taste of it. On 14 February he opened his first Parliament. Before he made his speech he was called upon by the Lord Chancellor, Lord Halsbury, to repeat a Declaration of his allegiance to the Church of England. The wording of this Declaration dated from the Bill of Rights in 1689. It repudiated the doctrine of Transubstantiation and affirmed that the invocation or adoration of the Virgin Mary and the sacrifice of the Mass 'as they are now used in the Church of Rome, are superstitious and idolatrous'. He was called upon to state that his declaration was made 'without any evasion, equivocation or mental reservation whatever'. It was noticed that he pronounced these words in a low voice.

Next day Cardinal Vaughan sent a protest to this insult to the Catholic Church which Edward passed on to Lord Salisbury. The Cabinet acknowledged the need for some change in the wording and Edward expressed the hope that 'it will be the last time that I or any of my successors may have to make a declaration in such crude language.' But as the Bill of Rights was an act of Parliament it could only be altered by another act of Parliament. On 13 June a committee of peers, which included the Prime Minister and the Lord Chancellor, met to revise the formula. Unfortunately the document which they produced was published before it had been submitted to the King.

On 10 July Edward wrote to Lord Halsbury complaining that he was 'naturally surprised that he had received no intimation, previous to his having read it in the newspapers, of this Report, as it was an important matter concerning the Sovereign regarding which he ought to have been consulted.' He drew attention to the strange omission of the Archbishop of Canterbury, or of any other Bishop, from the Committee and insisted that the matter 'ought surely to be dealt with this session or there may be agitation in the country' and he ended with the words 'thanks to the Lord Chancellor's bungling from the beginning.'

The whole affair was mismanaged and it was only after his death that the new formula was actually agreed. The Sovereign was to undertake to 'secure the Protestant Succession to the throne.' The issue at stake is now long dead, but in the new King's reaction to the somewhat unimaginative way in which it was handled he showed what he meant by authority. Edward's only aim was to rid the Declaration of any matter offensive to those Catholics who were his subjects.

One of the rather rare beams of light on Edward's personal religion is shed by Lord Redesdale. 'He was a convinced Christian,' he claims, 'devoutly observing all the ordinances of the Church. In Scotland he regularly attended the Parish Church at Crathie. I can call to mind one Sunday at Abergeldie in 1870 when so fierce a storm was blustering outside that it was impossible to leave the castle. The Prince, then a very young man [he was twenty-nine], read the Church of England service at home. Never did I hear that beautiful liturgy more impressively rendered. The music of his voice, the perfect diction – so conspicuous in his public utterances – gave value to every word of those inspired prayers. They struck home. He made us feel. The devotional sense, obviously genuine and true, would have been contagious in a crowded Cathedral. It was no less so in that little room in the old grey castle.' Edward seems to have been endowed with a charisma which is all too rare among the clergy.

The year 1902 was the Coronation year of King Edward,' [wrote Sydney Holland, later Viscount Knutsford] and the date had been fixed for June 26th. By that date all the representatives of the foreign nations were gathered in London, where the big hotels and houses had been specially taken for them. My wife and I were looking forward greatly to the ceremony as the Queen had kindly sent us both seats in her own private box in the Abbey.

On the 23rd I was at the London Hospital when a telegram came from Sir Frederick Treves telling us to send up a nurse to Buckingham Palace at once as the King was very ill. He had peritonitis. The fact was to be kept quite secret. Then a messenger came from him to tell us that he had settled to operate on the King the next day . . . There was a dinner party that night at the Palace, but the Queen was not told of the impending operation until after the dinner was over.

Next day, to the dismay of the whole world, it was announced that the Coronation was postponed. The news struck everyone dumb.

The operation took place at midday, and the Queen told me afterwards that the King had walked into the operating room unaided and had got onto the table without any help. He was wearing his oldest dressing gown and she was 'quite ashamed of it'. She had stayed in the room until the King was insensible and then left him.

The operation was a very severe one, and I have been told that at one moment all those present except Sir Frederick Treves wondered whether it would be safe to go further with it. All went well, however, and next day the King was better. But the sudden cancellation of the Coronation had caused problems.

Dinners had been laid on everywhere to celebrate the Coronation and the King had specially desired that they should not be put off. I attended the very large dinner that had been arranged in the Out-Patients' Department of the hospital and spoke to the 1,100 people who were present. The tragedy of his illness, of course, made the dinner rather a sad affair, but the King's consideration in not wishing it postponed was wonderfully appreciated.

The most immediate problems were, in fact, chiefly of a gastronomic nature. In the royal kitchens M. Menager had been preparing a banquet for two hundred and fifty guests. The sudden cancellation of this resulted in a distribution of the full menu among the poor of Whitechapel, who unexpectedly found their frugal fare enriched by the arrival of gallons of *consommé de faisan aux quenelles*, two thousand five hundred quails, sole poached in Chablis and garnished with oysters and prawns, snipe stuffed with *foie gras*, three hundred legs of lamb, and other delicacies with which they were doubtless not familiar.

The Coronation finally took place on 9 August. Lord Redesdale was among the many who described the event.

Great as Westminster Abbey is, full of immemorial traditions, it can never have looked more splendid than it did on that day when princes, peers and commoners, subjects from lands lying far away across the seas, were all gathered together to acclaim their King.

Never before in the history of man had such a world's gathering been brought under one roof. And when we listened to the salvos of artillery, and remembered that eight thousand miles beneath our feet the booming of the cannon would in the Antipodes thunder out the joy of men who were fellow subjects with us, we felt the power of which that royal figure on the throne was the symbol.

One touching episode will never be forgotten. When the venerable Archbishop of Canterbury [Frederick Temple] did homage he was weak and tired, and failed by himself to rise. The King leant forward, and grasping the old man's hand, which had anointed him, bore it to his lips and helped him to stand upright. It was a kingly act, performed with all the grace and dignity of which our Lord the King had the secret.

9

A Tour in Europe, May 1903

On 6 August 1902 Lord Lansdowne and Paul Cambon had an important conversation. Lansdowne noted that 'the first symptoms of an inclination to come to terms on the subject of Siam and Morocco became apparent.' Cambon stated that France's colonial dominion sufficed for their needs and that they had no desire to extend it. It ought to be possible to *marcher d'accord avec vous*. So far as Siam was concerned there should be no difficulty in disposing of the 'trivial questions'.

On 23 August Sir Edmund Monson, the British Ambassador in Paris, wrote to Lansdowne that Cambon's words 'entirely represent the opinion which Delcassé had frequently stated.' He added that 'it is certainly a novelty that His Excellency should have termed the questions which have so long been in dispute as "trivial".'

The question of Siam concerned a disagreement as to the relative 'rights' of Britain and France over the territories east and west of the Menam basin. That any two civilized countries could even contemplate going to war over anything so unimportant illustrates the atmosphere of distrust and hatred between them at that time. Once the distrust and hatred had been removed the matter was decided in favour of the French claim by a stroke of the pen.

On 28 December Lansdowne wrote to Monson: 'Fortunately we have no very thorny questions at issue with the French just now.' He was, however, deeply concerned about the position of Morocco. 'They [the French] are, I believe, convinced that we have designs of our own, although we do not reveal them. I wish I could persuade M. Delcassé of our absolute sincerity and disinterestedness. Do what you can to impress this on M. Delcassé.'

During the evening of Thursday, 31 December 1902 King Edward wrote a long letter to Lord Lansdowne. He had received a report from Sir Charles Scott, the newly appointed Ambassador at St Petersburg, which Lansdowne had forwarded to him. 'I have just read Sir C. Scott's letter to you with the greatest possible interest. You will, I am sure agree that it was most desirable for him to have a conversation with Count Benckendorff before the latter comes over here as Ambassador . . . Being old friends they could talk over matters with far greater freedom. I fear that there is hardly a country that exists concerning which England and Russia hold similar views, and both distrust the other. I feel, however, convinced that Count Benckendorff will endeavour to be most friendly and amiable and make a good impression.'

He ends on an optimistic note. 'In a few hours the year 1902 will be a thing of the past, and in wishing you a happy New Year I express the ardent hope that in 1903 we may have peace and prosperity, but I confess that there are heavy clouds over us which I fear will not be easily dispelled.' By the end of 1903 it was well recognized by statesmen on both sides of the Channel that the projected Anglo-French convention required for its full effect a good understanding between France's ally, Russia, and England.

In March 1903 Lansdowne intimated to Monson that Edward was intending to make a cruise in the Mediterranean and that on his return journey it would give him much pleasure to meet President Loubet on French soil. Monson passed this on and on 13 March reported that 'the intimation of His Majesty's desire was welcomed by the President with unmistakeable delight. He said that a visit from the King would, in the present temper of France, do an amount of good which is probably not recognized in England.'

It was at least recognized by Chamberlain. Just after Edward had started out he said to Eckardstein: 'Here in England the King's visit is very popular; and if Paris gives him a good reception then everything will go well between us in future.'

Monson hoped that 'His Majesty's Government were already aware of the extent to which cordiality to England had increased in France, but probably the public at large were not to the same extent informed as to the growth of that sentiment in Paris and throughout the country. In this capital His Majesty, while Prince of Wales, had acquired an exceptional personal popularity, and his many old friends would be overjoyed to see him again; but this statement was not confined to his old friends and was general among all classes. The hope that it [the visit] might be realized,' concludes Monson, 'has been constantly present in my mind, and has been strengthened by the steadily increasing manifestation of the French that it should come to pass and the current of popular feeling has set in favour of friendliness with England.'

The importance of Edward's role is underlined by Maurice Bompard, the French Ambassador in Russia at the time. 'Never has England had a King,' he writes, 'who had a better understanding of the French nor had so deep a sympathy with them. Being sure of his ground he did not hesitate to announce his official visit to Paris. It was on his part a bold, not to say reckless decision, for twenty years of disagreement between the two countries could not have failed to impress upon the French at that time a turn of mind that was not exactly favourable to England.'

Edward had already visited most of the countries of Europe. The Kaiser had also made a number of official visits, travelling in all the panoply of state, with a view to enhancing the prestige of Germany. Edward travelled armed only with his astonishing capacity to get across to people and win their hearts. He was attended by only a few members of his household, two equerries and a physician. He also took Sir

Charles Hardinge, 'a rising man in diplomacy.' As Sidney Lee writes:
'It was an almost irresistible combination. The King would pave the
way by creating a favourable impression and Hardinge would follow up
with conversations on detailed points.'

Lord Newton makes the same point in his life of Lansdowne. 'The
King's visit to France had caused a good deal of apprehension at home,
but Lord Lansdowne had always been confident of success . . . Various
writers have acclaimed it as the genesis of the *Entente*, which is manifestly absurd, but undoubtedly it assisted greatly towards the creation of
a more favourable atmosphere. The real moral, however, conveyed by
it seems to be the advantage of a monarchical system. Royal rank makes
just as strong an appeal to democratic states as to private individuals,
and the visit of a monarch makes an impression in every country which
cannot be rivalled by any republican president, however blameless.'

Edward's plan was to make a Mediterranean cruise in his yacht the
Victoria and Albert. Portugal was to be his first stop in order to make a
return visit to the King, Don Carlos. The Marquis de Soveral, the
Portuguese Minister in London and one of Edward's closest friends, saw
to it that a brilliant reception awaited him.

On Tuesday, 31 March, after a delay caused by heavy weather, the
royal yacht, the *Victoria and Albert*, set sail from Portsmouth. A
detailed commentary on the visit by Sir Frederick Ponsonby brings the
scene into clear focus. It happened to be Holy Week, but that did not
appear to cramp their style. Their arrival in the estuary of the Tagus
was like a return to the eighteenth century. King Carlos came out to
welcome them in a green and gold state barge, rowed by eighty
oarsmen in red jackets. They proceeded, writes Gordon Brook
Shepherd, 'in a Canaletto-like procession of smaller boats rowing
respecfully in the wake of the State barge.' Once on shore a procession
of coaches took over from the barges. The first four were each drawn
by six white Arab ponies. The King's coach was the one presented to
the King of Portugal by Louis XIV. The others, described by Ponsonby
as 'not unlike the one that Cinderella had to take her to the ball,' were

adorned with exquisitely painted panels in the style of Boucher, but the one he was in was so aged that he feared that the floor boards might fall out and that they would have to run inside the coach. The caval-cade took an hour and a half to drive round Lisbon.

On the following day, Ponsonby describes the reception of the entire Diplomatic Corps. The ambassadors, ministers and their staffs were drawn up round the room and the King was required to speak to each one. 'The King was a past master at this and never seemed to find any difficulty in doing it quite naturally. His method was to talk to A and then draw B into the conversation, move on imperceptibly and while apparently listening to B, draw C into the conversation; but it required a very alert mind not to make a mistake and to recognize each country by the uniforms and decorations, so that the Peruvian Ambassador was not mistaken for the Bulgarian Ambassador.' At the State Banquet on the last evening, records Ponsonby, 'the King of Portugal read a speech of welcome in French, and the King replied in French without a note.'

But King Edward did not merely visit the royal palace. He made an important speech to the Chamber of Commerce. It sounded the key note for his whole embassy. 'It is my most fervent and cherished hope that . . . our two countries may, side by side, tread the peaceful path of progress and civilization, and that by unity of purpose in our commer-cial policy, we may jointly contribute to the further expansion of trade and industry in our respective countries and colonies, the integrity and preservation of which is one of my dearest aims and objects . . . I think I may confidently predict that in the peaceful development of civiliza-tion and progress, wherever the Portuguese and British flags have been raised, the future history of our countries will present an even more glo-rious vista than the history of the past.' His words were greeted with tremendous applause.

On 7 April the royal party went on board the *Victoria and Albert* and left Lisbon. Their next stop was at Gibraltar, where they stayed for five days. It was here, Hardinge records, that Edward learnt that President Loubet was making a visit to Algiers.

As Anglo-French relations had been very unsatisfactory during the Boer War, owing to the sympathy shown by the French to the Boers, and also on account of the disgusting caricatures of Queen Victoria that had been current in the French press, King Edward decided to make an effort to place Anglo-French relations on a better footing. He had the happy idea of sending four battleships of the Channel Squadron . . . to Algiers to salute the French President on his arrival.

M. Loubet was delighted with this unexpected act of courtesy and sent a very friendly telegram to the King, thanking him and expressing the hope that His Majesty would visit Paris on his way home . . . The Cabinet were averse to his doing so, fearing that public opinion in Paris would be hostile and that an unpleasant incident might occur, but King Edward knew the public of Paris better than his Cabinet and persisted in his intention to go to Paris. Later events proved just how right the King was and his wisdom in going. The history of Europe might have been very different but for his decision.

From Gibraltar the royal yacht proceeded to Malta. 'As the *Victoria and Albert* entered the harbour of Valetta in the most brilliant sunshine,' continues Hardinge, 'the scene was one which could not easily be forgotten.' King Edward was the first British sovereign to set foot on the island. 'All the vessels in the harbour were gaily decked with bunting, and, as the King's yacht proceeded up the Grand Harbour, the guns from the forts and ships thundered their salutes, the crews cheered and the bands played "God save the King". The enthusiasm was very remarkable and the sight thrilling for those who witnessed it.' Before leaving Malta, Edward was entertained by a 'Water Carnival'. Ponsonby describes how each man-of-war had a steam launch made up to represent in miniature some period in shipbuilding, beginning with the Ark. This did not contain the passengers usually attributed to it, but as it passed the royal yacht a dove was released from it.

On Thursday, 28 April Edward arrived in Rome and was driven to the Quirinal in an open carriage. 'The crowd,' noted Ponsonby, 'was

198

most enthusiastic, as the Italians have always had a great love of England and they were delighted at the visit of an English King.' Arrived at the Quirinal, Ponsonby was lodged in a suite of 'most comfortable rooms'.

The visit to Rome raised the delicate problem of a possible visit to the Pope, Leo XIII. 'When it was known in England that the King was to visit Rome,' wrote Ponsonby, 'the Roman Catholics, headed by the Duke of Norfolk, took the view that it would be an act of discourtesy if the King did not visit the Pope, while Protestant Societies stirred up anti-Catholic feelings vigorously. All this was reflected in the mass of letters and telegrams and resolutions passed by these societies that were sent to the King at Rome. I took all the telegrams to the King, who read them carefully and said he did not intend to be guided by such narrow-minded people.'

The King's attitude was quite simply that 'among his subjects there were millions of Roman Catholics and that they would be inclined to take offence if he took no notice of the Pope while he was in Rome. There was no doubt that he firmly intended to pay this visit and the Cabinet in London had been told that such was His Majesty's intention.'

While in Rome King Edward made the same gestures as he had made in Lisbon. He was received everywhere with the same enthusiasm. Wherever the King went, claims Sidney Lee, 'he listened attentively, even respectfully and did not presume in any way on his high position ... His smile, the intonation of his voice, his acts, his words, all these were accommodated with infinite delicacy to the person whom he was addressing ... He was more than the right man in the right place: he was the right man in every place. A fine gentleman in the strictest sense of the word, he knew how to remain a King while stooping to intimacy and even to familiarity.'

There were, however, problems of protocol. 'The Vatican,' Combarieu explains, 'insisted that the ruler of a Catholic State must visit the Pope first and the King second. The ruler of a non-Catholic

State could visit the King first but he was obliged to spend some time at his own Embassy before proceeding to the Vatican.' The reason for this curious requirement is that an embassy was regarded as an extension of the country to which it belonged. Thus the British Embassy in Rome was actually regarded as being British soil and the King could be considered to have left his own country to visit the Pope. On Saturday, 30 April Edward drove from the British Embassy to the Vatican, where he was received with great courtesy.

The evening of the State Banquet turned out to be a difficult time for Edward. The King 'seemed overcome with heat and was distinctly peppery in his temper.' Ponsonby noticed, however, that 'while he seemed to resent trivial matters, he became quite calm when anything important required his decision.' At the dinner he made a speech in which he spoke with confidence of the mutual friendship which had always existed between the two countries. 'We both love liberty and free institutions . . . and have marched together in the paths of civilization and progress . . . I am certain that we shall always be united for the cause of liberty and civilization as well as for the universal well-being and the prosperity of all the nations.' He struck exactly the right note.

Sir Rennell Rodd, the Councillor at the Embassy, had been besieged by the press with applications for an advance copy of what the King was going to say, as it was customary on such ceremonial occasions to read a speech that had been carefully prepared. But Edward could never be induced to follow that practice, and what he said would be the expression of his feelings at the moment he rose.

Unfortunately the Italian Prime Minister had sent his Private Secretary to ask for a copy of the King's speech at the forthcoming banquet. 'The King was dangerously calm about it and explained that he always spoke extempore, that he never attempted to commit a speech to memory, nor did he ever read it.' This meant that it would have to be taken down in shorthand. But none of those who could manage shorthand in Italian could manage it in English. There was nothing to be done but for Ponsonby to take it down himself. He was placed at table directly opposite the two Kings and when Edward rose to speak Ponsonby had to stand, note book in hand, and take it down. 'There was I in full uniform, the scarlet coat of an Equerry with aiguillettes and decorations, standing up in front of two Kings with a lovely Italian lady on each side wondering what on earth I was doing.'

On 5 May Sir Francis Bertie, the British Ambassador in Rome, wrote to Lord Lansdowne: 'The stay of the King in Rome has been very successful. The public generally are better pleased with the King than with the Kaiser. The latter's ostentatious display, all the state, and particularly the escort of his own soldiers on his visit to the Pope, have given offence . . . The King's speech, which was in English, was spoken in a very clear voice and in a tone which conveyed a conviction that what he said was said in all sincerity. There was absolutely nothing in it that could offend any foreign country in the slightest degree.'

The forthcoming visit to Paris posed problems. Lord Lansdowne had drawn Edward's attention to the frequent displays of hostility to England in France. Sir Edmund Monson was also hesitant and asked how the King wished to be received. The answer came: 'as officially as possible and that the more honours that were paid to him the better it would be.'

On 8 April President Loubet told Monson that the idea 'had been welcomed with extreme pleasure in every direction.' Loubet knew all about Edward's popularity with the Parisians and added significantly: 'we shall always think of him as Prince of Wales.' At last Monson became enthusiastic. 'There can be no question of the genuineness of the pleasure which the prospect affords to M. Loubet and the French Government.' By the end of April all preparations had been made and Europe awaited the arrival of the King in Paris – some with bated breath. The recent hostilities over Siam and Fashoda, the disapproval by the French of the British action in the Transvaal and their own uneasy national conscience aroused by the Dreyfus case did not give promise of an enthusiastic welcome.

The German Ambassador to France, Count von Radolin, reported on 20 April to Bülow: 'The nearer we approach the day of the King of England's arrival, the more energetically do the nationalist papers oppose an Anglo-French alliance . . . The general impression is this: King Edward will be given a courtly and brilliant reception, but it will not come up to the inspired enthusiasm as was witnessed during the visit of the Tsar.'

At first the German attempt to play down the event seemed to be justified. The King arrived at the Bois de Boulogne station (now the Porte Dauphine) where he was met by President Loubet with an impressive cortège. They processed up to the Arc de Triomphe, down the Champs Elysées and along the Faubourg Saint-Honoré to the British Embassy. The coaches were greeted with a silence broken by occasional cries of *'Vive les Boers! Vive Fashoda! Vive Marchand!'*, even *'Vive Jeanne d'Arc!'* One of his suite said to the King, 'The French don't seem to like us.' He replied, 'Why should they?'

That evening at the Embassy Edward made his first public pronouncement to a deputation of the Chamber of Commerce. He began by stressing his personal affection for Paris and his 'happy associations that time can never efface.' Then he moved on to more important ground. 'The days of conflict between the two countries are, I trust, happily over, and I hope that future historians, in alluding to Anglo-French relations in the present century may be able only to record a friendly rivalry in the field of commercial and industrial developments, and that, in the future as in the past, England and France may be regarded as champions and pioneers of peaceful progress and civilization and as the home of all that is best and noblest in literature, art and science.'

He touched lightly on recent events. 'There may have been misunderstandings and causes of dissension in the past, but all such differences are, I believe, happily removed and forgotten, and I trust that the friendship and admiration which we all feel for the French nation and their glorious traditions may in the near future develop into a sentiment of the warmest affection and attachment between the peoples of the two countries. The achievement of this aim is my constant desire and, Gentlemen, I count upon your Institution, and each of its members severally, who reside in this beautiful city and enjoy the hospitality of the French Republic, to assist me in the attainment of this object.' The reports in the press of this speech profoundly affected French sentiment.

Later that evening the King went to a performance of Donnay's play *L'Autre Danger*. During the interval he wandered into the lobby where he immediately recognized a French actress. 'Ah! Mademoiselle,' he exclaimed, 'I remember how I applauded you in London. You personified there all the grace, all the *esprit* of France.' Of course this was overheard and became widely known. It was very much the right note to have struck.

Next day at the Hôtel de Ville he assured his audience that 'it is with the greatest of pleasure that I return each time to Paris, where I am treated exactly as if I were at home.' These words lived on in the memory of the French. They were repeated to George V when he visited Paris for the tenth anniversary of the *Entente Cordiale*.

The State Banquet at the Elysée is described by Ponsonby. 'I was amused to see that, although France was a republic, everything was done in exactly the same way as in monarchical countries. There were hundreds of footmen with powdered hair and the whole banquet was precisely the same as we had in Rome and Lisbon, the only difference being Monsieur et Madame Loubet instead of a King and Queen.'

The President, of course, proposed the King's health. His speech had been written for him by the Protocole. 'He was obviously nervous,' noted Ponsonby, 'and had pinned his speech to one of the candlesticks in front of him which necessitated his leaning forward to read it. The result was that only a certain number of people near him could hear what he said.' After his health had been proposed, Edward had to reply. He replied in French. 'He never seemed to be at a loss for a word,' Ponsonby assures us, 'and without any notes or papers in his hand he

made an admirable speech, speaking like a Frenchman, which captivated all the guests. The King spoke clearly and distinctly so that all
the people at the further ends of the long tables were able to hear, and
this no doubt accounted for the enthusiastic ovation which he received
when he sat down. There are,' concluded Ponsonby, 'very few people
who can make a telling speech in a foreign language.'

Edward expressed his appreciation of this occasion, 'which will
strengthen the bonds of friendship and contribute to the friendship of
our two countries in their common interest. Our great desire is that we
may march together in the path of civilization and of peace.'

Ponsonby's final comment is of a political nature. 'The visit to Paris
seemed to strain the limitations of a constitutional monarch to breaking point. The King went to Paris with no Cabinet Minister [Hardinge
had no official standing] to advise him or to act as liaison between him
and the Government, and yet he reversed the whole policy of this
country.' Ponsonby is going a little too far with this assertion. It is not
quite true to say that Edward 'reversed the *whole policy* of this country'.
He was not negotiating with a government: he was changing the
outlook of a whole nation. No Cabinet Minister could have done
that.

On Monday, 4 May the King, accompanied by the President, was
driven to the Gare des Invalides. The crowds this time were really
enthusiastic and cries of '*Vive notre Roi!*' were heard. Sir Edmund
Monson reported to the Foreign Office that the visit had exceeded all
expectations, largely owing to the King's personal charm of speech and
manner.

More disinterested, a Belgian representative reported to his Foreign
Office:

The welcome accorded to the King of England by the people of Paris,
a trifle reserved at the beginning of King Edward's stay, became sub-
sequently much more sympathetic. On two occasions the King had
the opportunity of expressing his attitude, during his reception at the

Hôtel [de Ville] and at the Elysée banquet. Each time the King spoke in terms which appear to express his thoughts clearly and to define the aim of his visits: His Majesty spoke of *rapprochement*, and indeed it is a rapprochement that has been effected between France and Great Britain. Every class of the population is glad to see the friendship of France sought by a great neighbouring nation, without this improvement in international relations leading to a weakening of the alliance with Russia. Prince Ouroussow, the Russian Ambassador, seems to be very well satisfied with the Anglo-French rapprochement; he is much impressed and he does not hide his satisfaction.

The impression produced in France by King Edward VII's visit could not be better. Everybody remarked on the Sovereign's efforts to obliterate any misunderstandings which might exist between the two countries. His Majesty has been completely successful. Not a word, not an action which was not appropriate to the circumstances and to the persons. It is said here that Edward VII has won the hearts of all the French. Seldom can such a complete change of attitude have been seen as that which has taken place in this country during the last fortnight towards England and her Sovereign.

It is not quite the same with regard to Germany. A certain reserve is noticeable from that quarter in their comments on the royal visit ... Germany regarded the whole affair with amused suspicion. Count Paul Metternich, the Kaiser's Ambassador in London, wrote at some length to the Chancellor, Count von Bülow. In the course of the letter he stated that 'the idea of an Anglo-French alliance is the result of a general aversion to Germany.' He goes on to say that Edward's visit to Paris was 'a most odd affair and, as I know for certain, was the result of his own initiative.' He did, however, add 'I am far from assuming that King Edward meant to aim a blow at Germany by this visit ... The English Government, in the approaching reconciliation with France, desires to create no opposition with Germany.'

205

The Baron von Eckardstein, after ten years as effectively German Ambassador in London, continued to be an interested observer. 'When King Edward paid his visit to Paris in 1903,' he writes, 'I went over in order to get an idea of the political atmosphere as between France and England. I had already satisfied myself in London that negotiations were proceeding with France for an agreement along the whole line, and this was confirmed by what I saw and heard in Paris. But when I got to Berlin, I soon found that they had been completely left in the dark by Count Metternich and by Prince Radolin.'

He immediately wrote to Bülow.

Conversations I have had recently with British Ministers and leading personages in Paris convince me that negotiations are proceeding between the two governments for a general settlement of all impending questions . . . The excitement of public opinion on both sides over Fashoda and the Boer War can probably account for these negotiations having more than once broken down . . . Today things are very different. The fact that it was at all possible for King Edward to go officially to Paris, and the friendly, if not altogether enthusiastic reception given him by the Paris public, proves that the previous passionate bitterness has given way to a friendly feeling . . . There is now on both sides a firm wish for a general political *rapprochement*.

Even before Edward's visit to Paris preparations were begun for a return State Visit by President Loubet to London. Paul Cambon, was, of course, deeply involved in the planning. He had certain reserves about the principles involved. A President, after all, is not the same as a Sovereign. 'He is only an elected, temporary Magistrate.' If making State Visits were to become routine a President might be out of the country more often than he was in it. Nevertheless the project was pursued.

Ponsonby had remarked on the strongly regal aspect of Edward's reception at the Elysée. In the planning of the return visit an apparently trivial detail of republicanism nearly wrecked the whole project.

It was all about *les culottes*. The word refers to the knee-breeches worn by the French aristocracy before the Revolution. The soldiers of the Revolution refused to wear anything so undemocratic. They proudly accepted the title of *Sans-Culottes*.

At the time of Edward VII's reign trousers were the every day garment of the male sex. But for the aristocracy – those who belonged to some order of knighthood or were otherwise entitled or obliged to wear Court dress on state occasions – knee-breeches and silk stockings were the order of the day. Edward made it clear that, at the receptions during the President's visit, all the French officials would be expected to appear in *culottes*. It was, however, out of the question. In vain did the King argue that representatives of the much older Republic of the United States had no objection to this sartorial distinction. Cambon asserted that if the President appeared in knee breeches 'all Paris would laugh at him' and he would be a butt for the ribaldry of the press. But Edward was intending to confer the Order of the Garter upon Loubet, a ritual which would have been impossible if the recipient was wearing trousers. Loubet, however, declined the Order. The Foreign Secretary, Monsieur Delcassé, was asked to submit to being *culotté*. He replied that London must either accept a Minister *sans-culottes* or the *culottes* without the Minister.

On Monday, 6 July there was a State dinner at Buckingham Palace. The King proposed the toast with a warmth unusual on such occasions. In doing so Edward said: 'France and England, formerly enemies, are now friends and allies . . . The cup which I raise in your honour, Monsieur le Président, was offered to me by the City of Paris and I have had it brought here in order to drink to your health . . . I hope that the welcome you have received today has convinced you of the true friendship, indeed, I will say affection, which my country receives from France.'

The populace of London had been eagerly demonstrative in their welcome. Their feelings were expressed, writes Combarieu, 'by prolonged acclamations, in the forecourt of the station and along the

THE *ENTENTE CORDIALE*.

– Arm in arm on the Champs Elysées
by J.-C. Gould (*The Westminster Budget*, 8 May 1903).

FRIENDS

His Majesty the King – Look M. Loubet, he's giving you his paw.
by Linley Sambourne (*Punch*, 8 July 1903).

official route, and by the inscriptions – sometimes naïve – which we could read on strips of calico across the streets.' By the word 'naïve' Combarieu was referring to the somewhat irregular translation into French of certain texts. 'Long live the President,' on one of them was rendered 'Vive le long Président.' The English have traditional difficulties with the gallic tongue.

The whole visit, writes Sidney Lee, 'was a spectacular success. Emile Loubet, who came of yeoman stock, and was Prime Minister before he became President of the Republic, was the delight of all who met him in London. His beaming, ruddy face, his pleased smile and cheery manner made him a great favourite.'

It is remarkable how the French officials, none of whom came from an aristocratic background, felt – or were made to feel – completely at their ease on such occasions. The French seem to like Kings provided they do not sit on the throne of France.

One of the important results of the visit was that the two Foreign Secretaries, Lansdowne and Delcassé, had the opportunity of having a long conversation.

Delcassé [writes Albéric Neton] had a thorough knowledge of his file; he kept it, as it were, wide open in front of him. He had recourse once again to his preferred method . . . He divided each difficulty into as many problems as were susceptible of a clear solution . . . He had the firm purpose, in only bringing into the discussion those values which were equally acceptable to the one and to the other, to settle the back-log of errors in an inclusive and lasting agreement.

His logic is firm, compact, precise. Delcassé puts into his words his usual stamp of sincerity, which adds to the force of his reasoning. Let us resume it. France does not entertain any fanciful thoughts. She does not indulge in any rash delusions and, once her higher interests are safeguarded, where the security of frontiers demand it, as in Morocco and Siam, she is ready to discuss the other questions in a spirit of wider and more friendly understanding, following a system of concessions, no longer unilateral, against which Delcassé has always stood out, but reciprocal and equivalent.

Neton recalls the formula prescribed by Gambetta which had been Delcassé's guiding principle: 'Be convinced that the English, good politicians as they are, esteem only those allies who take account of their own interests and know how to make themselves respected.'

Both Delcassé and Lansdowne were men of stature and of undoubted probity. Both were desirous of finding the means of achieving the ultimate rapprochement. Neither of them could ignore their responsibility to their respective governments. Both had to carry their Cabinets and ultimately their parties with them. It is possible that Lansdowne and Delcassé were the only two men in England and France who could have carried the negotiations through to a successful conclusion. It is probable that they would not have been able even to start if Edward had not so skilfully prepared the ground.

The next item on the programme was a dinner at Lansdowne House. To mark the importance of the occasion, and perhaps to remind his guests of his own French connection, Lord Lansdowne used the great dinner service and *surtout de table* of Sèvres porcelain which had belonged to the Cardinal Prince de Rohan, the one who had played such an unfortunate role in the affair of Marie-Antoinette and the Diamond Necklace.

Combarieu records some of his conversations at Lansdowne House. He was asked by the lady next to him what had struck him most in the course of the visit. He replied: 'It is the unitedness of all the British people when patriotic interests are involved; it is the unaffected simplicity of the Court and the King's *entourage*. In this *milieu* one has the impression of a family; etiquette is observed and so is rank, but as it might be within the family.'

Combarieu was particularly impressed by the fact that Lord Lansdowne had invited to the dinner, in order to present them to the

President, 'the leaders of the Opposition – Sir Henry Campbell-Bannerman and Lord Rosebery. It was a very English courtesy, the courtesy of a gentleman, and at the same time another mark of amity to the President, who could take note of the fact that all parties were united to receive him. Add to that there was a similar sentiment on our side, though less developed: the full expenses of the visit had been voted unanimously by the Chamber and the Senate, which had impressed and flattered the English.'

Later in the evening Combarieu asked Colonel d'Amade, the military attaché at the Embassy, 'whether the warmth with which the President had been received was not artificial, for it seemed to me that a nation so respectful of its dynasty and its aristocracy would have some difficulty in understanding our democratic regime with its elected President.' 'Don't you believe it,' replied the Colonel, 'the enthusiasm of the whole of the British people is without reserve and without reticence. For them the President *is* France just as Edward represents England, that is the reason for this outburst. Add to that, and without flattery, the open countenance of the President, his simple and perfect manners add a touch of personal sympathy to respect for his position. Do not forget that the English aristocracy is not a caste. Its ranks are always open to merit. Every year the King gives it new blood by creating Lords, Earls and Marquesses; it does not stand aloof from economic activity.'

'This new sympathy,' asked Combarieu, 'which pushes the English towards us, is it not partly due to their animosity towards . . .' 'Towards Germany?' – interrupted the Colonel – 'No doubt about it. It is, however, not so much animosity as an instinctive distrust. Germany is developing its Navy so fast that England feels threatened. William II has said: 'Our future is on the seas.' His telegram to Kruger, exhorting him not to yield, exasperated the English. And the words of the Chancellor von Bülow to the Reichstag – 'It is to offer an insult to a German soldier to compare him with a French soldier' – is another reason for the sympathy of the English people towards the representative of the country which is the front line enemy of Germany.'

211

One of the most interesting of sources for the history of Europe during the last years of the nineteenth and first years of the twentieth century is not the work of a historian but the work of a journalist. His name was Henry Wickham Steed. Looking back over his career in 1924 he claimed that he could 'truly say that there is no other work which I would rather have done during the past thirty years, or any other branch of public service in which I would have preferred to have been engaged.' He had, in fact, a lofty view of the responsibility of the press, 'the only medium of education that affects the majority of literate human beings when once school or university has been left behind.'

All these visits were carefully observed by Wickham Steed. As he wrote of Edward's visit to Paris: 'few, even among the King's friends, then knew that he had conceived the visit as part of a far wider policy which was maturing in his mind. Not until the conclusion of the *Entente Cordiale* in April, 1904 – two months after the outbreak of the Russo-Japanese war – which might otherwise have compelled France and England to fight each other in support of their respective allies – did the world at large begin to understand the method that had lain behind King Edward's apparently aimless round of visits to European capitals.'

10

The Signing of the *Entente*

On 1 July 1903 Cambon wrote to Delcassé saying that he had told Lord Lansdowne that the visits of Edward to Paris and Loubet to London 'would have no significance if they did not give rise to an exchange of views between the two Governments on all the subjects of possible interest to them and that you could be able to have a serious conversation with him.' Lansdowne appeared to share this feeling, but, with his customary reserve, retained the right of consulting the Prime Minister and no doubt the King. 'Today he was somewhat warmer about it.' It was agreed that the meeting should take place at Lansdowne House on Tuesday, 7 July at 9.30 in the morning where they could talk at leisure.

On Tuesday, 7 July at nine thirty Delcassé duly visited Lansdowne House and the two Foreign Secretaries had a long and momentous conversation which could be regarded as marking the beginning of the actual negotiation of the *Entente*. All the questions were brought up, including Egypt and Morocco. As Delcassé reported: 'It was recognized that it was not impossible to find for each of the problems with which we were confronted a solution equally advantageous to both parties.' 'That evening at the Embassy,' Cambon adds, 'I could have wished that you had been there seated between Lord Lansdowne and Mr Chamberlain, because at this moment Mr Chamberlain *is* the

Government of England, and I know that, disgusted with the Germans, he is wanting to turn in our direction.' Chamberlain, he added, 'is pride personified; he proclaimed the necessity of an Anglo-German alliance after a quarter of an hour's conversation with the Emperor William, who gave him a sprinkling of compliments. I think you could talk with him more usefully than the Emperor.'

Unfortunately it was not a straightforward issue. Spain had certain claims which could not be overlooked. In a letter dated 14 July to Sir Mortimer Durand, British Ambassador in Madrid, Lansdowne expressed his hopes. 'My own impression is that it would not be diffi-cult for us come to terms with France if Spain were out of the way.' But, perfect gentleman that he was, he added: 'Nothing will, however, induce me to be disloyal to her or to make a backstairs arrangement with the French Goverment to her detriment . . . The question seems to me,' he added, 'whether this country and Spain could not afford to acquiesce in such a preponderance [in Morocco] if it were carefully limited in the manner which I indicated.' In the eyes of the English by far the most important issue was Egypt.

Delcassé's views were submitted to Lord Cromer, who was Consul-General in Egypt. On Cromer's retirement four years later, Lord Lansdowne, speaking in the House of Lords, stated that 'the Anglo-French *Entente* would hardly have been obtainable, in its existing shape, but for Cromer's high authority among foreign representatives in Egypt.' On 17 July 1903 Cromer wrote to Lansdowne saying that Delcassé's language appeared 'eminently satisfactory' and admitting that he himself 'did not anticipate that he would open out anything like so hopeful a prospect of settling our various outstanding differences with France.'

Lord Cromer had a first-class mind and he had thoroughly mastered all the details. He gives one of the clearest pictures of the situation.

What it really amounts to is this: that everything depends on our attitude as regards Morocco. M. Delcassé, you say, 'did not attempt

214

to disguise from me the immense importance which the French Government attached to attaining from us a recognition of the predominance which they desired to obtain in Morocco.' I rather anticipated something of the sort, but certainly I did not expect M. Delcassé to go so far as to say that he was 'entirely in favour of a comprehensive settlement and that the Egyptian formed part of the larger African quesion, which could, he felt sure, be disposed of satisfactorily if only we could come to an agreement as to the position of France and Morocco.'

I cannot help thinking 'that, in making these remarks, Delcassé went rather further than he intended, and that it may consequently be found that, under pressure exerted by the permanent officials at the Quai d'Orsay, and others, he will be reluctant to face the French Chamber with any Egyptian proposals which would be thoroughly satisfactory to us.

'There are six outstanding questions, viz: (1) Newfoundland; (2) Morocco; (3) Siam; (4) the New Hebrides; (5) Sokoto; (6) Egypt. In Morocco, Siam and Sokoto the French want various things which we have it in our power to give. In Newfoundland and Egypt the situation is reversed. In these latter cases we depend to a greater extent on the goodwill of France.

'The New Hebrides question does not fall distinctly into one or other of these two groups. There would not appear to be any great difficulty as regards meeting the French views on Siam. Possibly some concession in Sokoto might be made for counter-concessions on their part in Newfoundland, But the main question is manifestly Morocco. My own opinion is distinctly in favour of making concessions in Morocco in return for counter-concessions in Egypt and elsewhere.

'The question therefore in my mind is this: have we any objection to Morocco becoming a French province? Personally I see none, provided always (1) that we get an adequate *quid pro quo* in Egypt or elsewhere; and (2) that the French comply with your three conditions as regards Morocco. These, if I understand rightly, are (1) the sea-board is to be neutralized; (2) a proper regard is to be shown to Spanish interests and susceptibilities; and (3) a guarantee is to be obtained that British trade will not be placed at any legal disadvantage.'

But there was also in Cromer's mind, a sense of urgency. 'In all diplomatic negotiations there is always a danger of moving either too fast or too slow. In the present case, possibly, the danger lies rather on the side of moving too slow. Personally I would be inclined not to delay too long but to take advantage of the present phase of Anglo-French tendencies and relations. It is conceivable that it may not last.'

The French, however, seemed to be playing for time. On 29 July Cambon came to the Foreign Office for further discussions. Lansdowne tried to bring up the question of Egypt. Cambon merely answered that he had no instructions from Delcassé to mention the matter. The fact was, as Lord Newton observes, 'that the French, as was only natural, were endeavouring to obtain their objects in Morocco at the price of minimum concessions to us with regard to Egypt, and M. Delcassé was no doubt in great fear as to how any surrender to us there would be received by his countrymen. It must be remembered that the French had never forgiven themselves for having missed their opportunity in 1882 and that, for many years, their chief aims in foreign policy had been our expulsion from Egypt.'

One French diplomat, relates Newton, had even refused to accept the post of Ambassador to Britain on the ground that he would be expected to get the British out of Egypt. As he wisely observed, 'It can't be done.'

Nevertheless, on 1 November 1903 Lord Cromer could write to Lansdowne: 'I am not at all discouraged by the French answer.' He then listed the points already gained. 'Certainly this is not enough, but when we consider the difficulties of the subject, the general course of diplomatic negotiations of this sort and the frame of mind of the French only so recently as the Fashoda period, I cannot think we have any reason to be dissatisfied. Who would have imagined, only a short period ago, that we should have got so far?' Six months later the negotiations were concluded.

On Sunday, 3 April 1904 Paléologue wrote: 'The Franco-British agreement, which will be the *Magnum Opus* of Delcassé, is nearing its conclusion. Lord Lansdowne and Paul Cambon are putting the finishing touches. 'Consequently all the Chancellries of Europe are most impatient to learn at least the exact range of this great and mysterious agreement which had been in gestation for the last nine months.' Germany was no exception.

'Three weeks before the signing of the Entente,' writes Count von Bülow in his Memoirs, 'M. Delcassé had informed our Ambassador in Paris, Prince Radolin, of the chief clauses of the Agreement and assured him that rights of third party states, including Germany, would not be affected by them. I had immediately acknowledged this information in a polite manner by saying in the Reichstag on April 12, that we had no occasion to presume that the Anglo-French Colonial agreement was pointedly directed at any other Power . . . German interests were not affected.'

In Germany, on 25 March, shortly before the signing of the *Entente*, the semi-official *Norddeutscher Allgemeine Zeitung* had predicted that 'in view of the repeated assurance given officially that France has in view neither conquest nor occupation, but seeks merely to open up the Sultanate of North-West Africa to European civilization, the belief is warranted that German commercial interests in Morocco are not exposed to any risk.' Two days after the signing it reassured its readers that the Sultanate was 'in no peril of being interfered with. On the contrary, successful endeavours on the part of France to give greater stability to public affairs in Morocco would presumably benefit German as well as other commerce . . . There is, therefore, no reason, from the German point of view, to regard the Anglo-French *Entente* in preparation with hostile eyes.'

217

The *Populo Romano*, always well informed, announces the coming event as being 'without precedent and without parallel in the annals of diplomacy' and states prophetically: 'All the politics of the twentieth century could be affected by it; for the arrangements which are about to be concluded will ensure, for an unlimited period, the common action of France and England in the world.' The article ended with the words: 'the Franco-British *entente* does not seem to imply any threat to the Franco-Russian agreement.' The more important question was how the *entente* would be received in Germany.

Two days later, on 5 April, the baron de Courcel, who had been Ambassador in Berlin and had preceded Cambon in the French Embassy in London, paid a visit to Paléologue and expressed his admiration for Delcassé's achievement 'of having so skilfully reconciled France and England'. But, he said: 'All the courage and all the tenacity of Delcassé would not have been sufficient to transform into friendship an age-old antagonism between the two peoples if the English were not beginning to be apprehensive of the rivalry of Germany, even of the *German Peril* – "*la crainte du péril allemand, voilà ce qui a surtout rapproché l'Angleterre et la France.*"'

On 8 April 1904 Lord Lansdowne and Paul Cambon signed the Agreement. Delcassé had asked to be informed by telephone the moment the deed was done. But Cambon, writes his biographer Keith Eubank, 'was none too familiar with this new method of communication. Returning to the Embassy he entered the telephone booth which was the pride of the establishment. Connections were made with France and finally with Delcassé. Not trusting the electronic transmission of sound, the Ambassador filled his lungs and yelled: "*C'EST SIGNÉ!*"'

The first to be informed was, of course, King Edward, who was in Copenhagen. He sent at once a telegram to Lord Lansdowne: 'I sincerely congratulate you on having brought the difficult negotiations to a successful termination. I hope the House of Lords may meet at the same time as the House of Commons so that you may be able to make a statement of arrangement at once.'

On the same day Paléologue wrote the triumphant words:

Today our Ambassador in London, Paul Cambon, and the Secretary of State at the Foreign Office, Lord Lansdowne, have signed the Franco-British agreement, that is to say: (1) A Declaration concerning Egypt and Morocco. (2) A Convention concerning Newfoundland and Africa. (3) A Declaration concerning Siam, Madagascar and the New Hebrides. This great act of diplomacy touches on an infinity of questions which it solves in the most equable spirit; no difference, no litigation continues between the two countries. Of all the stipulations the most important is the one which concerns Egypt and Morocco: we are abandoning Egypt to England and England, on her part, is abandoning Morocco to us.

This agreement, which has just been concluded, is not just a liquidation. It opens up, in the relations between France and England, a new era; it is the preface to common action in the general politics of Europe. Is it directed against Germany? Explicitly, No. But implicitly, Yes; for to the ambitious outlook of germanism, with its avowed intentions of preponderance and invasion, it opposes the balance of Europe.

As might be expected, the leading article in *The Times* of Saturday, 9 April contained a concise account of the terms of the Agreement and a sound assessment of their significance.

The signature yesterday in London of the documents which embody a comprehensive Agreement between this country and France, touching our mutual interests all over the globe, is an event of high historic importance. No consummation, it may safely be said, has been more earnestly desired by the best public opinion of the two nations; none is more likely to cement in the future that sense of common aims and common interests which is the surest pledge of universal peace.

It is not very long, as time is computed in the political world, since the realization of such a design might well have seemed outside the compass of the most patient and most optimistic statesman. The more honour, therefore, to those who, interpreting surely and sagaciously the growing wish of the two peoples to draw closer together, have guided their diplomatic intercourse in such a way as to attain this supremely important aim.

We, in this country, have always recognized how great a part has been played in the furtherance of Anglo-French cordiality by the KING, nor have our neighbours across the Channel been slow to acknowledge the fact. KING EDWARD'S visit to Paris last year, followed as it was later in the summer by the arrival of PRESIDENT LOUBET as a warmly welcomed guest in England, furnished the most favourable of opportunities for an expression of mutual good will, and fittingly initiated the negotiations which have now ended in a concrete understanding. The statesmen who on both sides had the by no means easy task of embodying that understanding in all its complex details deserve no less the gratitude of their fellow countrymen.

M. Delcassé has always been recognized here as a Foreign Minister of great insight and dexterity, and his sincere desire for friendly relations with Great Britain, ably seconded by M. Cambon, the distinguished representative of the French Republic in London, has been still more warmly appreciated. For LORD LANSDOWNE the present Agreement marks the culminating point of a highly successful administration of our Foreign Policy since he took charge of it some three years ago.

It may be said of Lord Lansdowne that he has handled skilfully and successfully the threads of diplomacy which he took over from his eminent predecessor and that the signing of the present Agreement is a result which any of the British Statesmen who have occupied the post of Foreign Secretary might legitimately have envied.

Summing up the career of Lansdowne at the Foreign Office, Lord Newton, himself a distinguished diplomat, wrote:

The first outstanding feature of his period of office is the abandonment of the old British policy of isolation and the substitution for it of understandings and alliances. The second is the gradual but clearly defined tendency to move closer to France and to Russia and further from Germany.

Lord Lansdowne will be best remembered in connection with the Anglo-Japanese Treaty of January 30th, 1902 and the Anglo-French *entente*. In the former case it was decision and the courage to face responsibility which were required; in the latter, infinite patience combined with firmness, and there can be little doubt that his perfect knowledge of the French language and his own partial French origin contributed largely towards gaining the confidence of a race somewhat prone to suspicion. Perhaps the best tribute to his success during five critical years is that his policy was never seriously impugned, and that his successor followed implicitly in his footsteps. The fact is that he was exactly suited to the Foreign Office, both by training and by hereditary natural aptitude. His instinct was essentially diplomatic and he possessed all the requisite qualities.

Lord Newton then proceeds to give his own definition of the qualities required in a Foreign Secretary:

extreme patience and tact, a judicial disposition, a willingness to listen to experienced opinion, some knowledge of other countries and of foreign tongues, the faculty of knowing when to make a stand when the national interest requires it, and the power of defining the national policy, both in the written and the spoken word, in dignified and courteous language.

These qualifications he possessed to perfection. No-one ever excelled him in his conscientious attention to details, or in the application needed to master the innumerable dry and complicated questions with which the Secretary of State is confronted daily. No-one was ever more accessible to those who served under him, and certainly no other Foreign Secretary inspired a stronger feeling of confidence amongst foreign representatives here; while his position and the ability to entertain on a magnificent scale, naturally tended to facilitate social relations. All this, combined with the administrative experience which he had already acquired in the public service, gave him perhaps greater advantages than any other occupant of the post, and it may truthfully be asserted that it would be difficult to cite any man who established himself more rapidly and firmly in the opinion of all alike as an international statesman of the first order.

The Times provides the details of the understanding.

Our Paris Correspondent sends us particulars of the Agreement which is embodied in three diplomatic documents. Each differs somewhat in form, according to the subject matter with which it deals. A convention regulates the various points for settlement in Newfoundland and West Africa. The very important questions of Egypt and Morocco are dealt with in a Declaration, and another instrument, called a *déclaration annexe*, defines outstanding matters in Siam, Madagascar and the New Hebrides. The whole Agreement covers, it will be seen, a great field of detail, and, until the complete text of the document is available, it would be premature to discuss each separate question with the minute attention which it deserves.

But the general significance of the various arrangements is sufficiently plain. In Newfoundland, France, while securing some facilities withheld from her fishermen at present, renounces the exclusive rights of fishery which she derived from article 13 of the Treaty of Utrecht (1713). With this renunciation the oldest existing subject of diplomatic dispute between us passes from the field of controversy.

The French Shore question bristled with irritating technicalities [such as whether lobsters counted as fish!] and restrictions; and it involved Newfoundland in an Imperial problem of a particularly baffling kind. The disappearance of a difficulty so petty in itself, and yet so full of inflammable materials, is something on which we may all congratulate ourselves.

The arrangements with regard to Egypt and Morocco hang naturally together and form, probably, the most important section of the Agreement. While we once more declare – as our practice has long openly shown – that we do not intend to modify the political *status* of Egypt, France does not ask us to limit the time fixed for the British occupation. She therefore affords plain recognition of the extent to which her large material interests in Egypt have benefited since the country has been under our control . . .

Broadly speaking, what France undertakes to do is not to prevent the Egyptian Government from exerting fuller freedom in the disposal of its fiscal surpluses. She abandons the old policy of obstruction which has benefited her so little in the past. It is elsewhere stipulated that France and England shall afford each other diplomatic assistance in executing the Egyptian and Moroccan engagements; and in Egypt, France, with financial interests only second to our own, should find no difficulty in making her own influence so felt as to give full effect to the altered policy to which she pledges herself.

We recognize in return the prominent position of France in Morocco, but a stipulation provides against the fortification of the Moroccan coast at the Straits of Gibraltar, and we secure, for thirty years at least, the open door for trade.

It is important to notice that the Agreement stipulates that the commerce of the two countries will be treated on the same footing in transit through the French and English possessions in Africa – a stipulation which ought to be sufficient to guarantee automatically the equality of opportunity which we both desire.

In discussing the various particulars embraced within this

extensive Agreement, it is difficult to avoid representing them as compensations from one of the Powers to the other, as the case may be. And this aspect of the case is so far correct that in order to secure various objects of importance and above all the extremely important object of a definite understanding as a whole, we have in the Agreement made territorial concessions of a kind which we are not very accustomed to make every day or to any comer. The rectification in West Africa of a frontier determined upon only six years ago – a rectification carrying with it no small adjustment of territory in France's favour – and the more explicit and extended recognition of the French sphere of influence in Siam – again in revision of an Agreement only eight years old – show that we are prepared to waive no slight points of form to secure a solid and permanent understanding with our neighbours.

But we venture to say that the whole significance of the Agreement will be missed if it is jealously scrutinized as a mere barter of concessions from one country to the other. Its importance and its worth are really of a deeper kind. It is a landmark in the policy of the two nations, because it represents for the first time a serious attempt to see their worldwide relations steadily and to see them whole. It cannot, we think, be called anything but a satisfactory settlement of the material points at issue. But transcending its significance in this respect is the value it must possess and the weight it must carry as a substantial pledge of the essential unity of our interests and desires. That value, as a great factor in the peace of nations, we believe it will retain, because it gives expression to the general and heartfelt wishes of the two great democracies whom it concerns.

On 12 April 1904 Count von Bülow, in a speech to the Reichstag on the subject of Morocco, stated that 'we know of nothing that leads us to think that this agreement is directed at any Power whatsoever. What it seems to indicate is an attempt to settle a series of disputes between France and England by means of amicable understanding. From the point of view of German interest, we have no objection to make against it.' All seemed to be well.

On 23 June 1904 Edward paid a visit to the Kaiser at Kiel and they dined together on board the *Hohenzollern*. On the next day, at a luncheon on board the *Meteor*, von Bülow writes: 'the King conversed with me for nearly an hour . . . Towards the end of our talk King Edward, on his own initiative, touched on "the Agreement" (of April 8th) concluded by Balfour's cabinet with France.' He listed the main items and commented: 'On this very important agreement [to whose conclusion he himself had greatly contributed] no such particular agreements would be necessary between England and Germany, since there are no concrete, conflicting political interests.

'With France, things are different. Understanding, in her case, with regard to old and difficult points of contention, had become an absolute necessity. But this understanding was not directed against Germany. There is no thought of isolating Germany. On the contrary, my one desire is to reduce all points of friction between the Great Powers, and to secure for as long as possible for Europe that universal peace which is as much to England's interest as to Germany's. I shall do my uttermost to reduce the points of conflict between England and Russia. Peace is a universal necessity since all countries groan alike under the burden of their armaments taxation.'

Von Bülow added: 'I have reproduced this talk almost textually. On account of its historic importance I noted it down almost at once. I reproduce it here from my notes.'

The Times leader had rightly drawn attention to the important roles of the King, Lord Lansdowne, Delcassé and Cambon as the four architects of the *Entente*. There was, however, one other name which was not mentioned: Thomas Barclay. But Edward knew of the unremitting efforts, often in the face of serious set-backs, to foster more friendly relations between Britain and France. In June he conferred a knighthood upon him and at the same time the French President made Sir Thomas an officer of the Légion d'Honneur.

Ernest Beckett, later Lord Grimthorpe, wrote enthusiastically to congratulate him. 'I am delighted that your most brilliant and useful services to humanity at large, and your own country in particular, have met with recognition, and I can honestly say that, in my opinion . . . no honour that has been conferred upon any individual for many years has been so entirely merited. The Government, in honouring your successful efforts on behalf of peace and good will between nations that should always be friends, in the teeth of difficulties and discouragements that would long ago have deterred most men, have honoured themselves more than you.'

Sir Thomas Barclay, however, was not one to rest upon his laurels. There was still one possible danger to the success of the *Entente* – the reaction of Germany. To this he now turned his attention. During the winter of 1904 Barclay made a visit to Germany. On his return the *Standard* asked him for an interview. The interviewer posed the question: 'Is Anglo-German *rapprochement* possible in view of the very strong animus displayed in both countries?' Sir Thomas replied that: 'The feeling against us in Germany is not half as strong as the Press in both countries would have us believe.' He reminded the reporter that 'at the beginning of 1900 the feeling between France and England was as bad as it could be . . . In the *Revue de Paris* so weighty a writer as M. Ernest Lavisse took an almost despairing view of the situation.'

Sir Thomas then briefly sketched the beginnings of the present Anglo-French *Entente*, 'modestly omitting the strenuous part which he himself took in its accomplishment.' He was then asked if he really thought a similar good feeling could be established between England and Germany.

'Most emphatically,' he replied; 'remember that only four years ago the bitterness between France and England was such that war had seemed inevitable. At present there is no such extreme tension between England and Germany. We judge here far too much by the attitude of Berlin. Neither London nor the London Press can speak for England; to a still greater degree is it true that the voice of Berlin does not represent the feeling of Germany. Leave Berlin aside, then, and the feeling in Germany is fairly evenly divided. Germany cannot afford the ever increasing burden of naval expense, but she is driven to build battleships by the hostile tone of the British Press. Do not forget this; that every anti-German article in an English newspaper means more votes in Germany for the increase of the naval estimates.'

The last question was: 'How would an Anglo-German *rapprochement* affect the Anglo-French *Entente?*' Barclay answered confidently: 'Surely not for the worse. No, the French would welcome such a *rapprochement* because it would largely secure the peace of Europe.' Certainly one of the most important results of the signing of the *Entente* was the effect which it produced upon Germany.

Barclay's evident concern for Germany was reflected in an invitation from the *Handelstag* – the Association of Chambers of Commerce – in Berlin to a banquet on 15 February. In preparation for this he made certain soundings in France and satisfied himself that 'beyond *the latent feeling about the lost provinces*, there was at that time no hostility on the part of Frenchmen to Germany.' The wound caused by the annexation of Alsace and Lorraine, however, had not healed.

On Wednesday, 13 April Paléologue reports: 'the Chancellor Bülow was challenged by the National Liberals on the Franco-British agreement of April 8th. According to the authors of the challenge this agreement will place Germany in a painful, humiliating situation by reason of the enormous privileges which France has obtained in Morocco.'

The Count von Bülow replied very wisely: 'It seems to be an attempt to eliminate the points of difference between France and Great Britain by means of an amicable understanding. From the point of view of German interests we have nothing to object to, for we do not wish to see strained relations between Great Britain and France, if only for the reason that such a state of affairs would endanger the peace of the world, the maintenance of which we sincerely desire.'

More importantly Professor Schliemann, described by Barclay as one whose 'long and close attention to all the passing events of current

227

international politics and keen practical intelligence have given him a unique place among the leading men of Germany', says the same. On 29 June 1904 he wrote: 'The Anglo-French agreements contain, we may say with certainty, nothing that can disturb our equanimity. They have in fact considerably contracted the area of possible differences between the two western Powers, and that can only be satisfactory.' That was the voice of Reason. The voice of wounded pride is sometimes politically more important.

Paléologue preferred to listen to the voice of the people. 'In spite of the wise declarations which the Chancellor Bülow had pronounced a few days previously before the Reichstag, German opinion does not take the side of the Franco-British agreement; it continues to see it as an intolerable diminution of Germany. "We cannot admit that France and England should regulate, apart from us, such important questions. . . . We cannot tolerate that France should obtain in Morocco a preponderant position."'

There were practical reasons also for Germany to be interested in Morocco, other than those connected with her commerce. Germany had a rising population: might not Morocco offer a suitable ground for colonization? Germany was increasing her navy: might not Morocco offer a port in the Mediterranean?

'In Nationalist circles,' continued Paléologue, 'they affect to believe that the language of the Chancellor to the Reichstag in no way corresponded with imperial policy and they hoped for a prompt rectification by the Kaiser.' But the Kaiser was biding his time.

On 31 May the Bill for the ratification of the *Entente* was read in the House of Commons for the second time and was passed without a division. The leaders of the Opposition, Sir Edward Grey and Sir Henry Campbell-Bannerman, expressed their personal approval. Only in the House of Lords was there a significant exception. The Earl of Rosebery uttered a prophetic warning, predicting that sooner or later it must lead to war.

11

Morocco and the Fall of Delcassé

On 24 December 1904 Paul Cambon was in a state of depression which contrasts strongly with the exultation of the earlier months of the year.

> Alas! we are finishing the year very badly. The affairs of Morocco are charged with threatening contingencies. We have lost too much time. From the moment of the signature of the Anglo-French agreement we should have given the Sultan the assurance of our pacific intentions . . . But time has passed; the Moroccans, at first dumbfounded, pulled themselves together; advice was received from religious leaders in Cairo and Constantinople – and suddenly they dismissed all Europeans in their employ, including our military mission. We have been forced back into a threatening position which, if it does not produce an immediate effect, would lead us fairly quickly to an armed intervention.
>
> The situation at home is deplorable, mutual recrimination in the army, disorganization in the navy, the religious war pushed to extremes, the absence of recognized leaders of the Parties. The Emperor William multiplies his approaches to Russia. Opinion in Russia is unsettled by it; she forgets all her old grievances against

Germany and accuses us of betraying the Alliance for the benefit of England . . . In fact they no longer regard us as constituting a force in Europe.'

Back in March 1904 Paléologue had noted: 'While a great war is flaring up in the far East [between Russia and Japan] and the Governments of every country were anxiously wondering whether some spark from over there did not threaten to spread the sparks to other parts of the world, our President of the Council, Emile Combes thinks only of closing down Convents and Schools and preventing the recruitment of novitiates, of removing Crucifixes from Law Courts, in short of unleashing the passions of anti-clericalism and destroying the basis of the Country's conscience.'

In January 1905 Cambon was invited to stay at Windsor Castle. The conversation was mostly about the war between Russia and Japan, but it was just at the time that Combes had resigned and a new Cabinet was being formed. On the second day Cambon wrote to Delcassé: 'The King has told me, and charged me to tell you, how pleased he is that you have maintained your position at the Ministry of Foreign Affairs.' Lord Lansdowne had expressed the same sentiments. 'Where would we be without Delcassé?' he had asked.

All, however, was not well with Delcassé. He was a man whose whole life had been focussed on a single objective. The words of William Wilberforce might have been engraved on his heart: 'This one thing will I do.' He had no outside interests, no private life, no capacity for relaxation. All his relentless efforts were concentrated on the fulfilment of his youthful ambition to serve his country and 'to make my contribution to the reconstruction of her stricken edifice' – to see France once more among the foremost powers of Europe. In practical terms this meant the diminishment of Germany and the recovery for France of Alsace-Lorraine. In spite of the undoubted success of the *Entente Cordiale*, this still seemed a long way off. The government of France had been chiefly concerned with lesser matters.

A week later Paléologue tells of a visit to Delcassé.

This evening I take Delcassé some of my current affairs. He has what I call his migraine face; the complexion yellow, the eyes troubled and swollen. I shorten my report, for he is not listening. His mind is obviously far away. When I have finished, I rise to go. 'No!' he says. 'Sit down again. I want to talk to you . . . in secret . . . here it is. For some time I have been experiencing extreme fatigue; I do not sleep; I have no appetite; I am always hearing the knocking of a hammer in my head; or, if I am in the dark I see sparks and flashes of light before my eyes. It is absolutely essential that I have a rest.'

'Yes. Of course you must have some repose. Why don't you go and relax on the Côte d'Azur? You have all the leisure to before you accompany the President of the Republic to Rome.'

'No. I am thinking of a much longer rest; of one that is infinite . . . Very seriously I am thinking of abandoning my power.'

Paléologue objected that the Franco-English *rapprochement*:

which is his capital work, is still in its early stages; that he alone is capable of deriving all the useful results from it; that in any case no one would understand his abandoning his power just because of a simple feeling of fatigue which would certainly yield after a few days of rest. After a long silence Delcassé said: 'My task has become too heavy. It becomes more complex every day. *They* will make it impossible. Not only do they not facilitate it, they thwart it, they paralyse it; they demolish it. M. Combes thinks of nothing but *manger du Prêtre et fomenter la guerre religieuse*. M. le Général André is preparing for us to reduce military service to two years and in the meanwhile he abandons the army to all the blackguards of Freemasonry; M. Pelletan [an ardent socialist] disorganizes our Navy and teaches the workmen in our arsenals to go on strike; all that is the very negation of my policies. Well! I have had enough.'

231

It was the first time Paléologue had heard him talk like this, but he knew that Delcassé was right. 'It is an illogicality – a paradox – to try to give to diplomacy a vigorous and creative activity when the country itself, wounded in its vitals, has lost its moral cohesion, when anarchy reigns among the crews of its fleet and the workers in its arsenals.' At the end of the year 1904 the government of France was indeed at a low ebb.

At the beginning of 1905 Europe was, as Sidney Lee writes: 'like a vast powder magazine which a spark might ignite with the direst results. The rapid growth of suspicion between Germany and Britain, the rising hope of France of recovering the provinces wrested from her in 1870 and the developing ambition in the Balkan States to free themselves from Turkish suzerainty and Austrian influence, were all aggressive sentiments which threatened a well nigh universal conflagration.'

In all this King Edward had appeared as the peacemaker. On 12 January he had a long interview with the German naval attaché, Captain Coerper, who duly reported back to Berlin. 'He told me I could inform the Kaiser of the following matters: in the first place he was determined to keep peace with all the nations; and secondly that England would never prepare a war with any other nation, least of all with Germany, for the simple reason that there was no cause for such a thing and that such a war between the two nations would do infinite injury to both.'

It was the question of Morocco which next began to sow the seeds of violent contention throughout Europe, not only between France and Germany but between Germany and Britain.

On 12 March 1905 the German Chancellor, Count von Bülow, who had in the previous year stated that the affairs of Morocco were outside the interests of Germany, now declared to the Reichstag the urgent need of asserting Germany's 'rights' in Morocco. This led to a personal visit by the Kaiser to Tangier, in the course of which he persuaded the Sultan to ask for a European conference on Morocco.

The Kaiser's move was not made until nearly a year after the signing of the *Entente*. By this time the defeat of Russia by Japan had effectively deprived France of her main ally. Von Bülow was ready to strike a blow which would shatter the Anglo-French-Russian alignment. He persuaded the Kaiser, in the course of a cruise in the Mediterranean, to make a political visit to the Sultan of Morocco. In his own words: 'I did not hesitate to confront France with the possibility of a war, because I had confidence in my own skill and caution. I felt that I could prevent matters coming to a head, cause Delcassé's downfall, stem the flow of aggressive French policy, knock the continental dagger out of the hands of Edward VII and, at the same time, ensure peace, preserve German honour and enhance German prestige.'

On Monday, 17 March Paléologue wrote: 'The coming visit of the Emperor William arouses the enthusiasm of the population of Tangier. At the express order of the Fez the local authorities are preparing a brilliant reception for the Kaiser; they display an eagerness and an activity of which their customary apathy would permit one to believe them incapable. Evidently Morocco sees, in the visit of William II, the arrival of the Saviour.'

The Kaiser professed that the aim of his visit was 'with their help to maintain and develop, in a free Morocco, the interest of the German Fatherland.' The German Empire, he declared, 'had great and growing interests in Morocco,' and he concluded by saying that 'commerce can only progress if all the Powers have equal rights and respect the independence of the country.'

At nine in the morning on 31 March 1905 the German liner *Hamburger* dropped anchor in Tangier harbour. The landing was delayed by an extremely rough sea, but at 11.45 the Kaiser came ashore. 'The Emperor William has thrown down his gauntlet and sounded his fanfare.'

'Delcassé reckons,' continues Paléologue, 'that the real cause of this agitation and these threats is the new *entente* between France and England. He is concerned but not disquieted. The Emperor will not make war on us, Delcassé thinks, and he will not succeed in getting our treaties with England and with Spain torn up. Germany has, in the

English people, an adversary whose hostility is less inspired by their sympathy with the French than by their fear of an economic competition which becomes daily more menacing... England has felt no less vividly the thrust of William's manifesto, aimed as much at her as at France. It seems to her, as to us, dangerous to introduce a new participant into the affairs of Morocco. She has proposed to France, in answer to the Emperor's gesture, to strengthen, by a new demonstration, the solidity of the Franco-British *entente* and to send, in the first fortnight of July, a large squadron to visit some French port such as Brest, after which a French squadron would enter British waters. Delcassé is already making preparations for these occasions.'

On 1 April Paléologue recorded the 'very great emotion' caused by this event in Paris. All eyes were on Delcassé. When Paléologue visited him he found him extremely calm and resolute. 'On the whole,' said Delcassé, 'I do not regret this brassy manifestation of William at Tangier. Nothing could produce a more salutary effect on the English people... Supposing William had manifested his ill humour in a piece of blustering at Metz or Strasbourg; the English would have taken no notice. But for a German ship to come and fly the flag of the Hohenzollerns on the coast of Morocco... Oh! Oh! The English would not stand for that! You may be sure that many of them today will be looking towards France.'

A week after the Kaiser's conversation with the Sultan, Sir Francis Knollys, Edward's principal Private Secretary, wrote to the marquis de Soveral: 'The German Emperor talked at Tangier in the most arrogant way, and quite in the strain of the first Napoleon... His falseness in *everything* is almost beyond belief.'

At the same time Edward wrote to Lansdowne: 'The Tangier Incident was the most mischievous and uncalled for event which the German Emperor has ever been engaged in since he came to the throne. He is no more nor less than a political *enfant terrible* and one can have no faith in any of his assurances.' On 4 April Edward wrote to President Loubet: 'The way my nephew behaves defies description. He neither knows what he is doing or what he is after.'

On 15 April Paul Cambon noted that the German government had declared the agreements of the *Entente* to be null and void. Pressure was brought to bear on Spain to retreat from her share in the agreement. Delcassé undertook to talk with Berlin about the situation. But the Germans played a clever hand. They avoided any conversations themselves and ordered Radolin to do the same. This gave Delcassé's enemies in the Chamber – Jaurès, Clemenceau and others – a chance to mount a campaign against him for refusing to talk with Germany. Radolin supported them by stating that the Foreign Minister only talked about the weather.

On 19 April the French Chamber debated the Morocco question. Delcassé came under heavy fire from Jaurès and the socialists. Delcassé was feeling overwhelmed and offered his resignation. President Loubet begged him to withdraw it, stating 'under the present circumstances this resignation would only serve the enemies of France.' Edward went so far as to send a personal message in his own name to Delcassé urging him to stay at his post. This was regarded by Lansdowne as 'a very unusual step'. He told Sir Thomas Sanderson, permanent Under-Secretary of State, that Delcassé's retirement would be a calamity for Europe. Delcassé, however, withdrew his resignation and Edward sent another telegram to congratulate him.

Paléologue, together with Georges Louis and Barrère, were alone in their optimism, which depended on the belief that the Kaiser was bluffing. But even at the highest level there were politicians who could not accept the belief in bluff and were almost hysterical in their fear of imminent war. On Saturday, 22 April Delcassé asked Paléologue to go straight off to Berlin and to put the French Ambassador in the picture. Next day he took the train for Berlin. At six o'clock that evening he arrived at the station of Potsdam. Bihourd was on the platform to meet him. His first words were: 'Do you bring me the order to yield? If we continue the policy of Delcassé it is war! Yes – war! and then we are lost!' Paléologue was dumbfounded. All this was said on the platform in front of some three hundred people to whom the tricolor cockade worn by Bihourd's valet betrayed his nationality if not his status.

On the journey from the station Bihourd continued his pitiful refrain. 'His fingers were trembling, his breathing quick, his speech gasping, the constant flickering of his eyelids, the anxious expression on his face' – all betokened a man beside himself with fear. Arrived at the Embassy, Paléologue tried to calm him. 'The best way to avoid war,' he said, 'is to appear not to be afraid of it.'

All this was observed by Paul Cambon in London with increasing concern. 'I am pretty pessimistic at the moment,' he wrote on 29 April and went on to make the same complaint which Lord Salisbury had made when he was in office, of the rapidity with which France changed her governments. 'It is this which makes the role of a Foreign Minister so difficult. In order to bring some matter to a satisfactory solution one must have both continuity and secrecy. Now, our perpetual changes in the personnel of government present an insurmountable obstacle to the following through of a project and our passion for chit-chat makes us incapable of any discretion.'

The agreement between Britain and France had been only an *Entente* and not an alliance, but the events of 1905 were pushing Britain to move in the latter direction. In the first place Russia had suffered a humiliating defeat in the war against Japan and was facing a threat of revolution at home. If need arose, France could not look for much help from her official ally.

'The weakening of Russia,' commented Cambon, 'had destroyed what might have been a useful counterweight,' but even so he was confident that the Kaiser 'would not have crossed our path if our own politicians, Socialists and others, had not given him the hope of being able, with their collaboration, to annul the results of our politics over the last few years. It is certain that with our understandings with Italy, England and Spain . . . the status of France has been considerably enhanced. Not for a long time has she inspired so much confidence and respect.' This enhanced status had been the achievement of Théophile Delcassé. This last bastion of her national pride the politicians of France now set out to destroy.

236

On 29 April Edward, after a cruise in the Mediterranean, stopped off in Paris and had a private talk with Loubet. After a large dinner at the Elysée, Sir Francis Bertie wrote to Lansdowne, the King had a long talk with Radolin. 'All eyes were fixed on the two and I have no doubt that much more than probably passed was and will be credited to this conversation. His Majesty told me this morning that Radolin was very sensible and regretted the misunderstanding, but argued that Germany had all along felt sore at being left out of account by England and France and Spain. His Majesty's impression is that the storm will now blow over.'

Cambon was not so sanguine. 'The game looks promising if we keep cool and collected and if we know how to play it,' he wrote on 4 May. 'But our newspapers, our Deputies, our Ministers seem to have lost their heads; we have no worse enemies than ourselves.'

The next day the King had lunch with the marquis de Breteuil. Delcassé was present and Edward was able to have a long private talk with him. The staff at the Quai d'Orsay found that he was much calmer after his conversation with the King. 'During these few days,' writes Brook-Shepherd, 'Delcassé seemed to be closer to this foreign monarch than to his own colleagues. He was behaving almost as though he were one of King Edward's own Ministers.'

On 11 May Lansdowne wrote to Knollys: 'The King's Mediterranean tour left matters in excellent shape so far as we are concerned.' It was, however, the sort of calm which precedes a storm.

On Monday, 8 May 1905 Prince Henckel von Donnersmarck had arrived in Paris. He was, though unofficially, representing the Kaiser. His mission was to bring about the fall of Delcassé. On his arrival he gave a luncheon to a number of leading politicians, including the Prime Minister, Maurice Rouvier, and a former Prime Minister, Jean Dupuy, the journalist, Francis Charmes and Eugène Etienne, Secretary of the Colonial Group. It was Dupuy who informed Combarieu of Donnersmarck's mission. The Kaiser had no views on Morocco and did not seek to obstruct the action of France. All they wanted was to set up certain warehouses and factories. His Majesty felt that Germany and

237

France ought to draw nearer to one another, sincerely, cordially and united by their common interest in the peace of the world.

The Kaiser, however, made certain conditions. He could not accept the politics of Delcassé and demanded that he should be sacrificed. He insisted that he himself should be received by France like other sovereigns had been. (Elsewhere Wilhelm expressed vehement disapproval of such sovereigns being received by republican France because it lent respectability to 'revolutionary' republicanism.) He wanted the Grand Cordon de la Légion d'Honneur. He demanded the withdrawal of the French Ambassador Bihourd from Berlin. One can just imagine how the Kaiser would have reacted if France or England had had the impertinence to demand the removal of his Foreign Secretary.

'And what', asked Combarieu, 'did he offer in exchange for these concessions?' Dupuy answered that he was not aware that he had formulated any precise propositions.

Maurice Rouvier and Eugène Etienne, both of whom had recently promised to vote for the Anglo-French *entente* 'with both their hands', now agreed to oust Delcassé. The spectre of 1870 haunted them. Delcassé had been responsible for the 'isolation' of Germany. He would not be able to accept the new regime. He must go.

The next day Paléologue learnt that Donnersmarck was intending to call on him. He went at once to the Quai d'Orsay. He has left one of the most vivid accounts of the fall of Delcassé, which he makes more immediate by the use of the historic present.

Delcassé receives me in a jovial manner which contrasts strangely with his frayed look and the distortion of his features. He affects an absolute confidence in the imminent success of the plan which he has outlined; he repeats several times 'the manoeuvring of Germany goes from fault to fault and from folly to folly.'

I bring in Francis Charmes so that he could interrogate him about his interview; he declines: 'I know exactly what that old spy of Bismarck's has come to Paris to do. He has come to look for collaborators. And he has found them. I even know of some who offered themselves. What a disgrace! What abjection!'

I now discern the basis of his thoughts – all the bitterness, all the righteous anger which are fermenting in his soul. Too agitated to remain still, he gets up and walks about. In a voice which he can no longer control he gives vent to his rage in a furious indictment of the President of the Council: 'this Rouvier . . . this traitor who dared to say to the German Ambassador, "*je m'en f. . . . de l'Alsace et de la Lorraine. Voulez-vous que je vous sacrifie Delcassé?*" It will soon become evident to you that these two miserable wretches are plotting against me.'

At last he finishes – exhausted.

At half past three Francis Charmes arrives. 'Yesterday,' he told me, 'the Prince von Donnersmarck, whom I have known for a long time, spoke to me in his usual free and easy manner. We talked for an hour and a half.'

This is what Francis Charmes gathered from the Prince:

The question of Morocco, considered in itself, could be resolved in five minutes, for there is in Morocco no incompatibility between the projects of France and those of Germany . . . But the present dissension goes a lot deeper than Morocco. What is at stake is the general relationship between France and Germany. We have had enough of being treated by you as if we did not exist. You talk intimately with all the Powers: you never want to talk with us. You receive in Paris all the foreign Sovereigns: you exclude only Wilhelm. In all the great capitals you are represented by very distinguished Ambassadors: at Berlin you have as your representative a vacant puppet with whom all conversation is impossible . . . Well! This has got to stop. And we want to have with you not only relaxed relations but intimacy . . . Yes, *intimacy*. Because if we do not bind ourselves *intimately* you will make an alliance with the English. Now! not at any price – you understand me? *Not at any price* will we allow a Franco-British alliance.'

239

He added that the Prince von Donnersmarck had also mentioned that he had just seen Rouvier and exclaimed: 'Now there is a real statesman! He has a clear judgement of affairs.'

Francis Charmes confessed that he was bowled over by this. 'We cannot go on disregarding Germany; we must get nearer to her; Delcassé in power is a danger to the nation. Ponder well these words of Donnersmarck; for myself I would resumé them in the formula; *L'intimité ou la guerre*. For God's sake get Delcassé to volunteer his resignation.'

The next day Paléologue reported this conversation to Delcassé. 'Francis Charmes has summed up very accurately what Donnersmarck said: "the Emperor offers us *l'intimité ou la guerre*." But what intimacy do you want between France and Germany while the trench of Alsace-Lorraine separates the two countries? At the very least there is no intimacy possible except on the one condition that the French nation comes and says to the people of Germany, like M. le Président du Conseil to His Excellency the Prince Radolin: "I could not care less about Alsace and Lorraine! Let us forget about the past! Let us embrace one another!" Well – France has not yet sunk as low as that. William is deceiving himself.'

On 12 May President Loubet wrote, in answer to a letter from Combarieu: 'What you tell me of our situation grieves me deeply. How could one think of accepting the proposal made by the Emperor? To break off the *Entente* with England without any qualms? This is just a dream. For myself I could not preside over such a development . . . I put too high a price, for the sake of my country, on the political achievements of Delcassé to be able to associate myself with his dismissal.

'I am disturbed by the attacks of the Press aimed at Delcassé and myself. Not that I am sensitive so far as I am concerned, but I fear that this campaign might be a sign of the cowardliness and the demoralization of our political world as well as the manifestation of personal hatred and emotions. It all makes me long for the arrival of February 18th, 1906.' That was the date at which he was due to retire.

On Monday, 15 May Paléologue reported that Lord Lansdowne was seeking a closer relationship with France 'to guard against any eventualities'. The matter was discussed the next day at the Elysée by Loubet, Rouvier, Delcassé, Barrère (Ambassador in Rome) and Paul Cambon. After a short debate Rouvier pronounced categorically against opening any such relations. He repeated several times to Cambon: 'For God's sake do not go any further with this matter. If the Germans came to hear of it they would attack us immediately.' 'Barrère, furious and disgusted, said to me, and rightly, "this funking by Rouvier will cost France dear! Every policy has its drawbacks, but I know of none so dangerous as the policy of fear."' Barrère was indignant at the 'crazy pessimism which he saw on all sides, even among some who appeared to be the wisest and the most solid – like Francis Charmes.' He himself saw nothing tragic in the situation. 'The arrogance of William II,' he declared, 'was nothing but bluff. The Germans, stupid as they are, are not so much so as to fall out with France over an issue which matters so little to them as the Morocco affair.'

The Germans, it must be said, were not as stupid as Barrère implies. On 12 May an article in the *Hamburger Nachtrichten*, a former organ of Bismarck's, spells out precisely what Barrère was saying. 'According to our Government, we ought to obtain at any price a success in Morocco. If not, the prestige of the Emperor would be seriously compromised; for, on the first occasion since Bismarck that Germany has shown her teeth, she would have met a humiliating check. That would mean that we would have to launch Germany into a war in order to repair the faults of our diplomacy.' The German government, however, did not represent popular opinion.

'The people of Germany do not share this opinion; we consider that the question of Morocco is not of sufficient importance to justify a war which will be a great disaster whatever the outcome. The Government has forgotten that in every diplomatic move, if one has no intention of finally drawing the sword, one must avoid placing oneself in the dilemma between backing out of it and mobilizing an army. Therefore, since it is impossible to go to war over Morocco, it would have been better to avoid committing ourselves fully, by the Kaiser's visit to Tangier, and to confine ourselves to diplomatic negotiations.'

On Saturday, 13 May 1905 Paul Cambon wrote:

I am more and more saddened and even ashamed of the servility of my compatriots; the slightest rumour makes them lose their heads. The Emperor William talks big deliberately. He has taken note of the general dismay and he knows that one can get anything out of us with a tuppenny cracker. We block our ears as if a cannon had been fired.

We have, nevertheless, many trumps in our hand – the assistance of England, the *entente* with Italy and Spain, the alliance with Russia which, although useless at this moment from a military point of view, is none the less a diplomatic support. All the Powers, except Austria, have distanced themselves from the idea of a conference . . .

We have been betrayed by our nerves, by the inadequacy of Bihourd, by the weakness of our Prime Minister Rouvier. He had the feebleness to enter in person, behind Delcassé's back, into conversations with Radolin . . . and he has made pronouncements that are irreparable – saying, for instance, that France had no interests in Morocco, that the Alsace-Lorraine issue was a thing of the past, that we would do whatever Germany wanted in Morocco . . . It is enough to make one cry.

But Cambon was big enough to concede that there were faults on both sides.

I admit that Delcassé has not had, in his dealings with the Germans, all the skill which he needed; it was necessary to humour the Potentate who has a million bayonets at his disposal; I recognize also that he has not taken either the Parlement or the Press seriously enough. He pursued his great schemes; he shut himself up at home to work; he saw very few people; he was not well served by his immediate associates. He believed that he was popular with both Chambers, whereas they were beginning to feel that he had been too long at the Quai d'Orsay and covetous eyes were cast on his portfolio. All that is true and all that explains, but does not justify the attitudes of men who sacrifice all the interests of France for their own pettty, private spites.

Meanwhile the British government was moving towards an even closer alliance between the two countries. On Saturday, 20 May Paléologue noted in his diary:

Dinner with the marquis de Breteuil, with Sir Francis Bertie, the British Ambassador, Lady Feodorovna Bertie, the Duchess of Manchester and others. In the smoking room Sir Francis Bertie, jovial and impulsive as ever, said suddenly to Courcel and myself: 'it is not enough to have arrived at an *Entente Cordiale*; we must give it muscles; we must give it the means of showing its strength. We will never save the peace unless these brawlers and fidgets are afraid of us.'

Later, I took our host aside to question him about the recent conversation between the King and Delcassé. For more than twenty-five years now the British Sovereign and the marquis de Breteuil have kept up an intimate relationship. When they were young they were companions in pleasure. Since then there has been much more serious-mindedness in their friendship. In fact I know it on good authority that Edward holds his French friend in the highest esteem because he recognizes in him all the qualities of courage, of honour, of conscience, of *sang-froid*, of tact and of natural nobility which make up, in his eyes, the model of the perfect gentleman. I do not doubt, therefore, that he repeated to him, at least in outline, his conversation with Delcassé.

Breteuil confirmed this.

The King confided to me the general sense of what he had said to your Minister, adding 'I authorize you to make very discreet use of it, if you feel it necessary' . . . You are, my dear Paléologue, the first person, and you will be the only one, to whom I will repeat the words of Edward VII, because it is important that you should be able, should need arise, to define more accurately the recollections of M. Delcassé . . . In conclusion the King said to him: 'Your policy over Morocco is beyond reproach from the point of view of international rights. Continue it resolutely, as you have begun it. But at the same time employ all your skill in relaxing your relationship with Germany; my Government will help you all it can . . . Otherwise France could find herself in serious difficulties.' These conclusions of the King seemed to me to be wisdom itself. Is not that your opinion?

'Certainly,' replied Paléologue; 'but did the King not say in addition what would be the reaction of England if, as the result of any provocation by Germany, France was obliged to take up arms? Delcassé seems to me to have taken away from his conversation with Edward VII the conviction that in those circumstances Britain would bring all its forces to our rescue?'

'That that was the private opinion of King Edward,' answered Breteuil, 'I am morally sure; but I find it difficult to believe that, with his customary correctness and prudence, he would have said anything that only his Ministers have the right to say. I have always found him very particular not to go beyond his constitutional role.'

On 18 May 1905 Lansdowne had an important meeting with Cambon, as a result of which Cambon reported back, inviting his government 'to take the road to a general understanding which would in reality constitute an alliance.' Lansdowne had not gone so far as that. What was new about his position was that it was now clearly directed against Germany. This was in response to German intervention in Morocco and the growing threat of Germany to Britain's naval superiority.

On Wednesday, 31 May Paul Cambon received a letter from Lord Lansdowne inviting the French government 'to discuss in advance with the British Government the various complications which are to be feared during the rather disquieting time which we are going through. I am not sure that I succeeded in making quite clear to you,' Lansdowne added, 'that there should be a full and confidential discussion between the two Governments, not so much in consequence of some act of unprovoked aggression on the part of another Power, as in anticipation of any complications to be apprehended during the somewhat anxious period through which we are at present passing.'

'The terms of the letter,' wrote Cambon, 'were carefully thought out; it had certainly been sent to me with the approval of the Prime Minister and possibly the King.'

Delcassé replied immediately to Cambon: 'Say to Lord Lansdowne that I am of the opinion that the two Governments ought more than ever to give evidence to each other of an entire confidence and that I am ready to examine with him all the aspects of a situation which is not without being a little disquieting.'

Events, however, were moving fast. On 2 June, writes Brook-Shepherd, 'Bülow played his trump card, or rather persuaded Morocco to put it on the table for him.' The Sultan of Morocco, acting under German influence, rejected the French scheme for internal reform and followed this up with an invitation to the Powers to join a conference on the future of his country. The future of Morocco was to be decided by an international conference. Paléologue comments: 'The Chérif, the Viziers and the notables here have become the instruments of Germany.'

On 4 June Paléologue received a telegram from Rome. It stated that the German Ambassador there had made a declaration to the Minister of Foreign Affairs, Titoni, that Germany 'had reason to believe that M. Saint-René Taillandier [Chargé d'Affaires in Fez] had threatened the Sultan with military occupation of certain places in Morocco in order to oblige him to reject the demands of Germany. If French troops cross the frontier of Morocco, following this threat, German troops would immediately cross the French frontier.'

Delcassé dismissed this oblique message as absurd. 'I never sent a word to the Sultan and Taillandier is not a man to take such an initiative upon

245

himself. Germany is going mad because she is feeling lost.' No doubt this was an attempt to frighten Italy out of her alliance with France and an indirect way of increasing the panic among French politicians.

The deliberately false alarm, however, was all that was needed. Rouvier went straight to the Elysée and gave his ultimatum to the President. 'Delcassé is leading us into war. Tomorrow I will oblige the Council of Ministers to choose between his policy and mine. Tomorrow one or other of us will be out of office.'

Just to make quite sure, Bülow sent an emissary to Rouvier to tell him that 'the German Chancellery knows, from an indubitable source, that Delcassé is negotiating with the British Government a military and naval alliance. If this alliance is concluded, Germany will immediately declare war on France. Before the British fleet could cause us any serious damage we will have broken up the French army and the route to Paris will be wide open to us.'

At the same time Rouvier received from Miquel, the First Secretary to the German Embassy, a list of Bülow's complaints, ending with the sentence: 'The Chancellor of the German Empire wishes to have no more dealings with M. Delcassé.' Delcassé was delighted. 'There, my dear Paléologue, is a phrase to have engraved upon my tomb. I could wish for no finer epitaph.'

Tuesday, 6 June was the fatal day. Paléologue records it in words of the utmost simplicity. 'This morning, at the end of the Council of Ministers, Delcassé handed in his resignation, which was accepted by the President.'

During his last speech, Delcassé sums up his position.

Germany threatens us. To me, this is just bluff. Therefore we should resist it. Now, here is England offering us an alliance with her; I think we should accept immediately. If it is just bluff, then it will be more difficult for Germany to keep up if she saw England ready to defend France. If Germany really did want war, she would have to reckon with the British Navy.

Ponder well the decision you are about to make. Today England strongly supports our cause. But tomorrow, if she sees us faltering, trembling before the insolent bragging of William, she will no longer place any reliance on us and, turning her batteries round, she will soon negotiate a reconciliation with Berlin and our colonial Empire will foot the bill.

Rouvier could only answer: 'Are we in a position to sustain a war against Germany? No! No! Even with the co-operation of the English fleet we would face a disaster worse than that of 1870 . . . We would be criminals to launch into such a venture. France would never recover from it.'

Delcassé knew that his fate was sealed and he spoke as if the verdict had already been pronounced.

What you have decided in this hour is not the fate of a man; it is the fate of a policy. It is a question of knowing whether France, thirty years after 1870, is yet her own mistress and can follow the policy which suits her, or whether she is reduced to being a dependent and subject State. It is a question of knowing whether France, whose possessions lie near Morocco, who has behind her the assent of England, Spain and Italy . . . can exercise her peaceful and civilizing influence over this troubled country; or whether France must bow before Germany's interference and demands when Germany's nearest territory is several thousand miles away from Morocco, and when, until fifteen years ago, not a single German subject had crossed the Moroccan frontier. If you give way to Germany today you will be forced to give way to her tomorrow; you will be forced to give way to her always, and you don't know whether you will always have, as you have today, the almost unanimous support of the whole world.

Rouvier's reply was as feeble as it was astonishing. 'You have been too successful in the policy you have pursued against Germany. You have detached Spain from her; you have stirred up England against her; a Franco-British alliance would mean war and defeat. My hand would dry up rather than sign such an alliance.' As a sort of parthian shot he added 'and you have debauched Italy'.

The debate, however, was a waste of time, for the result was a foregone conclusion. The motion was put to the vote. They voted unanimously against Delcassé. It is a serious condemnation of the personnel of the French government that not a single member of it was either intelligent enough or courageous enough to see the truth and the force of Delcassé's position. But it did at least give him his opportunity to provide posterity with an *apologia pro vita sua*.

That afternon Paléologue went round to Delcassé's office for the last time to collect some papers.

He did not conceal from me his emotion, which, moreover, had brought tears to his eyes. But no complaint; no recrimination; no invective; no bitter, wounding words; only a grave and noble sadness. In this outpouring of grief, the most intimate depths of his nature became apparent to me . . . It is not in his pride nor in his ambition that he suffers: it is in his patriotism, which is his whole religion.

I was also deeply moved myself, for during these last seven years I have been in daily intimacy with this Minister, whom History will certainly count among the great servants of France, and to whom I owe the finest hours of my career.

The impact of the news of Delcassé's fall is described by Stéphane Lauzanne, a journalist who wrote for *Le Matin*. 'I was on the train returning from Toulon when I got the Paris newspapers announcing the dismissal of the Minister for Foreign Affairs . . . There was not a man to take up Delcassé's defence! There was not a man who even had a word for him! The men who had burned incense before his shrine most ardently in the days of his power, who were the most instant in asking favours of him, were the first to toll M. Delcassé's political death knell.'

Lauzanne eagerly espoused this lost cause. 'There is no more keen delight for a writer than to fight a good cause alone.' He was indeed a lone voice.

His article appeared in *Le Matin* the next morning.

M. Delcassé has rendered his country great services, for which perhaps we may be grateful later on, when someone does not want his job or his scalp. He has signed treaties which, considered from any standpoint, have changed the political orientation of Europe. In every instance he has represented France with dignity . . . M. Delcassé has suffered a misfortune, that of annoying the German foreign policy. It is perfectly conceivable that certain people will reproach him for this, for there are citizens who would go so far as to say that they would rather be Germans than Frenchmen!

A few days later he went to visit Delcassé in his apartment on the Boulevard Clichy.

I found him very self-possessed, almost reserved. Not a bitter word came from his lips when I alluded to his present disgrace. He only seemed to show emotion when I spoke of his policy, which threatened to share in his downfall. Then he grew vehement . . . He described his policy to me.

They misunderstand the German policy in a strange manner when they think that it will be contented when they have satisfied it in one instance. Germany is not a country that can be appeased by concessions. Stretch out your little finger to her and she grabs your hand, then your arm and soon your entire body passes into her grip. It does not do to satisfy Germany's pride – she is not that sort of country. Germany is a country activated by principles of power and self-interest.

The question that is brought up at this time is a question of France's entire Foreign Policy and of the very future of France. It is a question of making up our minds whether or not we shall break off the national friendships which we have acquired in order to become the allies of Germany. That is what they want. That, in brutal frankness, is the point of what they are saying to us: a point all their diplomatic artifices conceal badly. Now I would never have consented to that. A French alliance with Germany would mean the ratification by France of her dismemberment and of the loss of her provinces.

Delcassé had been speaking to deaf ears. In view of the unanimous vote Delcassé had no choice but to resign. He took leave of the President and of most of his former colleagues. One of them said to him: 'Perhaps the future will prove that you were right.' Loubet had no option but to accept the verdict.

On Saturday, 17 February 1906 the day of his retirement to which he had so looked forward, President Loubet moved out of the Elysée. That evening, when Loubet had finished sorting his papers, he and Combarieu had their last chat together in his study. It was a time for reminiscence. Loubet had no regrets about leaving. 'The President,' wrote Combarieu, 'is truly happy to become once more a simple citizen of Montélimar and a rural landowner. He will very much miss being deprived from now on of the ceaseless information, telegrams and reports which enable him day by day to follow the politics of his country and of Europe. But as to honours, public ceremonies and decorations – no man ever had, for the ceremonial side of public life, an indifference more natural and even an aversion more sincere. A man of meditation and of study, the President's way of life is of the simplest; he is, by his bourgeois origins and his rustic tastes as far removed as it would be possible to be from official ceremonial, show, meetings with other Heads of State. But he accepts the boredom of them when these obligations are the duties of his position.'

Combarieu reminded him of the increase in the number of receptions of Heads of State during his presidency. 'I was only seeking,' he replied, 'to raise up friends and allies for France in order the better to

defend her interests and to increase her influence. I never felt any
hostility to Germany, let alone any intention to have a rupture with
her.

'Knowing that these people have insatiable appetites and that the
Sovereign is more or less mad and that he rules over subjects who submit
to obey him without discussion and without understanding, I supported
a policy which left us a free hand and protected us from aggression. It
was with this continually in mind that Delcassé and I wanted to
strengthen the Alliance and to establish relations of confidence and
friendship with England, Italy and Spain.'

The mention of Delcassé gave Combarieu his cue to raise his only
criticism – an event, he admitted, 'for which I am still in mourning.'

Loubet replied, with some feeling: 'do you think that I parted with
him with no sadness and no regret? I had a long talk with him and with
Rouvier . . . It was beyond my power to reconcile their respective points
of view about accepting the Conference [Algéciras]. At the next
meeting of the Council Delcassé had the unanimous vote of the
Ministers against him.'

'And why?' interrupted Combarieu: 'as the result of their intrigues?'

'I don't want to know,' answered Loubet; 'what seemed to me, after
long deliberation with my conscience, to be necessary, is that the
President of the Republic, after having defined his position, is obliged
to accept the decision of the Council, manifestly supported by the
majority in Parliament and by a clear undercurrent of popular opinion
. . . You will understand that I saw that it was my first duty to remain a
constitutional President, in order to place the authority which I exercise above party divisions; it should be, in case of a national emergency,
the place of sanctuary in which all Frenchmen could find their place and
find their unity.' It was not far from Edward's conception of constitutional monarchy. Combarieu averred that 'no-one is more confident
than I am in the judgement of Posterity on your period of office.'

On hearing of the Foreign Minister's fall, Mr Balfour wrote to the
King that 'Delcassé's dismissal, or resignation under pressure from the

German Government, displayed a weakness on the part of France which indicated that she could not at present be counted on as an effective force in international politics. She could no longer be trusted not to yield to threats at the critical moment of negotiation.' The status of the *Entente* was now at risk.

'Delcassé's resignation,' wrote Lansdowne to Sir Francis Bertie, 'has produced a very painful impression here. What people say is that if one of our Ministers had had a dead set made at him by a foreign Power, the country and the Government would have not only stood firmly by him, but probably supported him more vigorously than ever, whereas France has apparently thrown Delcassé overboard in panic. Of course the result is that the *Entente* is quoted at a much lower price than it was a fortnight ago.'

For Paul Cambon it was a bitter blow. On the same evening he wrote to Delcassé: 'I am profoundly affected by your loss, because, in addition to the feelings of affectionate attachment which you have inspired in me, I have experienced a deep satisfaction in marching with you. The friendship remains, the collaboration is no more than a dream, and I foresee, here above all, plenty of difficulties when you are no longer there. I have not seen anyone yet. This evening there is a dinner at Buckingham Palace for the King of Spain. I am expecting to be attacked on the subject of your resignation. What can I say that could be understood by the English? How can I account for a change of direction in the middle of the battle? It is heartbreaking.'

The politicians who had ousted Delcassé now found that they had no-one to put in his place. Rouvier himself took over the Quai d'Orsay. Cambon, in a letter to his son dated 15 June, is fairly scathing about the situation. 'We need at the Quai d'Orsay someone of great authority to restore the country from the ridiculous emotionalism we have been passing through, and I can see no-one to put in that position.'

But there was no time for dawdling. The day after the fall of Delcassé Prince Radolin set before Rouvier the Kaiser's demand for an international conference on the affairs of Morocco. Cambon, having discussed the situation with Lansdowne, returned to Paris and went to see Rouvier. He found him distraught. His problem was how to escape the dilemma: 'If I say No to the idea of a conference it means war with Germany. If I say Yes it means rupture with England.' That was the position into which they had got themselves. He said Yes, but it did not lead to rupture with England. Plans for the conference, which was to be held at Algéciras on the south coast of Spain, went ahead.

The first notes of discord, writes André Tardieu, had been sounded in February 1905 by the German Chargé d'Affaires in Tangier, Richard von Külmann. He said to his opposite number, the comte de Chérisey: 'we have noticed that we are being systematically brushed aside. We have formulated our position accordingly. I have been obliged to ask my Government for formal instructions. Count von Bülow informed me that the Imperial Government knew nothing of any agreements brought in on the subject of Morocco and does not admit itself to be in any way bound regarding this question.' This was untrue: they knew all about it.

On 5 October 1905 Bülow wrote in *Le Temps*: 'There are distinct matters to be considered. Morocco is the first, general politics the second. In Morocco we have important commercial interests. We have stuck to that and will continue to stick to it. On the more general question we have been obliged to respond to a policy which tended to "isolate" us and which, with this avowed intention, took on a character of open hostility.' He accused France of 'affecting to ignore Germany and dispensing with her'. In France's dealings with the Franco-Italian *rapprochement*, or that with England, she had managed to import 'an anti-German' aspect.

'In a few weeks' time the Conference will meet . . . I consider that this assembly, far from dividing us, should contribute to our *rapprochement* — a *rapprochement* on one necessary condition: that the French people make no mistake that the policy which tended to isolate Germany is a thing of the past; that this direction of yesterday is abandoned today with no return.'

Whether this feeling in Germany of marginalization was a figment of their own hyper-sensitive imagination or intended as a deliberate insult is a difficult question. The motives from which men act are not often open to scrutiny. It is not easy, on the face of it, to understand why an agreement between two other countries should be any concern of Germany's. But the fact is that Germany was feeling marginalized. The appeal to a European conference, however, was a tactical error. If Germany had hoped to dominate it, she was mistaken. On 20 September 1905 Paul Cambon noted: 'it is clear that the Germans, having dragged us into the conference, are now apprehensive of finding themselves in the minority . . . and fear that our position of preponderance, ratified by international agreement, may become unassailable. Since they have promised to support the Sultan and have represented the conference as the shield and buckler against the claims of France, they could be most embarrassed by an outcome so contrary to their promises. Their game is now to wreck the conference and put the responsibility for the failure on our shoulders.'

On 16 January 1906 the conference on the position of Morocco was opened at Algéciras. Great Britain and France stood firmly by each other. Edward, whose personal representative at the conference was Sir Donald Mackenzie Wallace, assured Cambon of our co-operation. 'Tell us what you wish on each point and we will support you without restriction or reserves.' The German envoy, Count Tattenbach, observed that 'the British were more French than the French.'

On 25 February Wallace reported that Russia was pressing Germany for concessions in the interests of peace. Edward commented: 'This letter (like all of his) is most interesting. Germany forced the conference on France and has never once attempted to conciliate or meet her in the views which she was bound to put forward. The gist of the letter was in the last two paragraphs – Germany's interest in France's humiliation and loss.'

Towards the end of the year 1905 the Kaiser had written to Bülow saying that he did not want a war until he had concluded a formal alliance with Turkey: and this must be brought about at all costs. We must strive to ally ourselves with all Arabian and Moorish rulers . . . We could not begin a war until some kind of pact with them had been sealed; neither could we conduct a war with France and England single-handed, *at least not on the sea* [these words had been heavily underscored] and, besides, the year 1906 would be particularly unfavourable for war since we would be renewing our artillery . . . But the greatest obstacle to a war is that we could not take a single man out of the country because of the Socialist menace – Shoot down the Socialists first, behead them, put them out of action, if necessary massacre the lot – and then war abroad! But not before.' Bülow did not record his reaction to this expression of opinion, but shortly before he had written: 'Alas! His Majesty's moods are more variable than April weather or the chameleon. Few monarchs have had more need of a level-headed, prudent, but above all courageous adviser.'

The German public seems to have been nearly as fickle as its ruler. Bülow himself had no illusions about the considerable difficulties that stood before them at Algéciras.

I was well aware that German public opinion would be dissatisfied even with a relatively favourable result. Our public opinion swayed impulsively between noisy imperialist demands and a vague and sentimental pacifism.

If, in spite of all this, I went to Algéciras it was because I considered it useful to show some proof that even then so complicated, grave and dangerous a conflict as Morocco could undoubtedly be settled without war, in friendly discussion across the conference table. Nine years later, in that disastrous summer of 1914, if the diplomats of all the Powers had kept their heads – the Germans, alas, lost theirs even worse than the others – if, in that fateful second half of July, a conference of the Powers had been summoned to settle the Serbian-Austrian conflict, the most terrible catastrophe the world has seen for centuries could have been averted.

Count Metternich, the German Ambassador to Britain since 1902, made the interesting observation:

> I have noticed how, as soon as in Germany people tend to become less anti-English, England rejects their advances and *vice versa*. The instruments are never simultaneously in key with one another; the harmony of the one is answered by the other's discord. England and Germany have not the same sounding boards.
>
> I told Mr Haldane [Secretary for War] that I was sorry to see from a speech by Sir Edward Grey [Foreign Secretary], whose views on foreign affairs carry special weight with the Liberal Party, that he too had made a *rapprochement* with Germany conditional on our swallowing France's policy in Morocco without protest. We urgently wished, I said, to be peaceful and friendly with the French, but we could not allow our rights to be trampled on.

Metternich could not have been unaware of Bülow's words to the Reichstag on 13 April 1904, a week after the signing of the *Entente*. 'It seems to be an attempt to eliminate the points of difference between France and Great Britain by means of an amicable understanding. From the point of view of German interests we have nothing to complain of.'

Gilbert Murray, in his study of *The Foreign Policy of Sir Edward Grey*, asks the same question: 'What had changed in the state of Europe between the time when Germany was friendly and indifferent to Morocco and the time when she suddenly burst out into threats? There is only one possible answer – France's only ally, Russia, had been heavily defeated by Japan and was for the time being powerless in Europe. France was alone, and Germany could not wait to take advantage.'

12

'Uncle of Europe'

On 4 December 1905 the Conservative Prime Minister, Arthur Balfour resigned. It looked like the long awaited chance for the Liberals. The King asked Sir Henry Campbell-Bannerman to form a cabinet.

Campbell-Bannerman was a great lover of the French, a fluent speaker of their language and a great reader of their novels. Edward had had an important meeting with him at Marienbad at the end of June at the table of Lord Carrington. Before departing, Edward said: 'I like Campbell-Bannerman immensely; I think he is quite sound on foreign policy.' That was clearly his priority. Carrington replied that, if the Liberals got in, 'Sir Henry will make Your Majesty a first-rate Prime Minister and will furnish you with a good Government.' He noted in his diary that he was 'very glad to get the chance of bringing the two together.'

Edward, as usual, observed the etiquette of not making any suggestions about the appointment of Ministers, among whom the Foreign Secretary ranked highest. Campbell-Bannerman wanted Lord Cromer, who would have been most acceptable to the King, but Cromer declined on the grounds of ill health. In the end Sir Edward Grey was offered and accepted the post. From the point of view of the *Entente* this was important. Grey was also a francophile.

He was also the King's godson, his father having been one of Edward's first equerries. More significantly, he had been Under Secretary of State in Gladstone's government.

It had been an instructive, if somewhat gruelling, apprenticeship. 'From 1886 up to the making of the Anglo-French Agreement,' Grey wrote in his *Memoirs*, 'we had been through a very disagreeable experience; our diplomatic position had been one of increasing weakness and discomfort. England had been on the brink of war with France or Russia or both and was diplomatically dependent on German good will.' In 1928, looking back over those years, he recalled that 'the relief felt at the conclusion of the Anglo-French Agreement was very present in my mind. I was quite determined not to slip back into the old quaking bog, but to keep on what seemed to me to be the sounder, more wholesome ground.' Grey was to continue where Lansdowne had left off.

But Grey was soon to find that the ground under his feet was not as wholesome as he had felt it was. The chapter in which he describes the scene is entitled 'The Atmosphere of Suspicion'. He admits his own shortness of sight. 'I did not realize the efforts that might be made to induce France to suppose that we would not act up to our obligations, nor how sensitive the French might be on this point and how easily confidence might be shaken.'

Grey may have been a francophile, but only in the political sense of the word. He had no personal experience of France or the French – '*gentil pays de la méfiance*'. Indeed, he had never been abroad. 'I was soon to be enlightened as to the difficulty of avoiding distrust in France,' he wrote. 'In diplomacy confidence has very shallow roots and the *Entente* with France was still young and untried.'

The next few years were to be a testing time for the strength of Anglo-French relationship. It was to come out the stronger for it. Fortunately Grey had a staunch ally in Paul Cambon, who was still at the French Embassy in London. It was well that he had such support, for, as he says himself, 'the critical moment came very suddenly.'

During the conference at Algéciras the Germans persuaded Austria to propose that Casablanca should be excluded from the arrangements. 'The French,' wrote Sir Edward Grey, 'considered the matter vital; the German delegates were equally firm in insistence. Our diplomatic support was pledged and was being given. At this crucial moment, when the tension was at its highest, there suddenly was circulated a report that we were going to abandon the French point of view . . . The first bomb fell on me in the form of a telegram from Bertie [still British Ambassador in Paris]. It was to the effect that M. Etienne, a member of the French cabinet, had said to him "So – you are going to abandon us."'

There was absolutely no truth in this assertion, which was categorically denied by Grey. But the episode somewhat undermined his confidence in France. In the course of a long letter Sir Francis Bertie set the record straight. 'It is unfortunate,' he concluded, 'that Frenchmen of education and position should be found ready to believe imputations about England of bad faith, but the hereditary distrust of our country, which has so long been characteristic of the French race, has been ably worked on by persons acting in the interests of Germany in order to create discord between France and England.'

These reports were attributed by Grey to German sources. 'The German manoeuvres,' he wrote, 'aroused in me neither surprise nor indignation. But if it were the German game to sow distrust between France and ourselves, it was equally clear that our game was to be loyal to each other, and I did resent the levity and ease with which France assumed that we would not play the game . . . How could any good take root in such shifting sands of suspicion and distrust?'

He did admit that 'diplomatically the French trusted us more, and not less, after the Algéciras conference than they had done before,' but he added: 'it seemed almost a miracle that the *Entente* survived.' There was, as he puts it, 'more delicate ground to be passed before this year ended. The wind of armed German pressure, though it had swept M. Delcassé out of the Foreign Office in 1905, had, in the long run, only caused France to draw the cloak of the *Entente* more closely about her. The sun of German cordiality was now to try what it could do.' The friendly demonstrations towards England to which this refers could, of course, be used in Paris to nurture mistrust.

Grey's personal relationship with Count von Metternich was always warm and frank. 'If the Germans would only let well alone,' Grey concluded, 'what is now well would continue to get still better.'

In all the official accounts and letters of this period, one of the most constantly repeated complaints was about the often nefarious influence of the press. 'The only thing of which the Germans complained for some time,' wrote Grey, 'had been the tone of the English Press. We have always answered this complaint by pointing out that the German Press was at least as bad.'

There had, in fact, been an almost spectacular increase, during the last years of the nineteenth century and the first years of the twentieth, in the growth, and therefore the potential power, of the press in England.

From about the year 1870 the leading type of newspaper was the penny morning paper. Owing to the difficulty of distribution, provincial papers were thriving. In London The *Daily Telegraph*, a conservative publication, the *Standard* which contained regular contributions by Lord Salisbury, and the liberal *Daily News* were still priced at one penny. In a class by itself was *The Times* which cost three pence. All these were perforce aimed at upper-middle-class and almost exclusively male readers. They were essentially political. The proceedings of Parliament and the speeches of the main ministers were faithfully recorded.

More important was the influence of the quarterly and monthly reviews, to which many distinguished politicians contributed. What R. C. K. Ensor has called the 'dignified phase' of English journalism lasted unchallenged until the early 1890s. It was to give way to an entirely new, less intellectual, less responsible, but far more influential type of paper. The pioneer of this movement, Alfred Harmsworth, was to become Lord Northcliffe, and his brother Harold Lord Rothermere.

Parallel with this movement was progress in the education of the people. In 1870 the Education Act had made schooling, albeit of a fairly rudimentary kind, accessible to all. But, if it taught children how to read, it did not necessarily tell them what to read. In 1902 came a further Education Act, devised by Sir Robert Morant. It is described by Ensor as 'one of the two greatest constructive measures of the 20th century'. The decline in illiteracy was matched nationwide by a steady rise in the sales of the well-established newspapers. The *Daily Mail*, launched in May 1896, soon attracted a daily sale of 202,000. Three years later the figure had risen to 543,000.

Lord Salisbury had described the press in his day as 'written by office boys for office boys'. Now, in the early years of the twentieth century, journalism was beginning to attract reporters of a far superior quality.

The journalist deals with the events of today which are to become the history of tomorrow. If the historian, writing with the benefit of perspective, can offer a more mature judgement, the journalist has the advantage of immediacy. Sometimes the eye-witness of events described, and often in personal contact with individuals whose decisions have directed the course of history, he can offer a chronicle of the period that makes good reading. Steed has the gift of making the reader feel that he is himself a spectator of historic events and even has a more than nodding acquaintance with some of the principal actors.

For twenty-seven years Wickham Steed was in the continuous service of *The Times* and the knowledge which he accumulated and the wisdom and insight which he gained made him the adviser of kings and rulers. Edward VII came to value him highly, consulted him on important matters and sometimes used him as an intermediary.

Political events were to lead Wickham Steed to concentrate on the complex politics of Austria-Hungary. He wrote an important book entitled *The Hapsburg Monarchy*. It got a favourable review from Professor Ottokar Weber in the *Frankfurter Zeitung*. 'Steed,' he writes, 'has observed keenly, has studied also the previous history of Austria, and, as a result of his studies, observations and research, he gives us this book which can be described as one of the wisest ever written on Austria. Without party or race prejudice he judges clearly the complicated conditions of our Fatherland.' The journalist had turned historian. He is particularly interesting on the subject of the Emperor Franz-Joseph.

In June that year, during the solemn procession with which the Austrians always observed the festival of Corpus Christi, there had been a sudden movement among the crowd of spectators. One of the newspapers had issued a single sheet announcing in large type the assassination of King Alexander of Serbia, together with his Queen Draga, his Prime Minister and a number of other high officials.

'In England,' wrote Steed, 'the Belgrade assassinations were looked on with horror. At the instance of King Edward diplomatic relations with Serbia were broken off, nor were they restored until the principal regicide officers had been removed from influential positions. This action was typical of the leadership which King Edward was rapidly gaining in Europe, to the annoyance of his nephew, the German Emperor.'

During the autumn of 1903 the King made a visit to the Emperor Franz-Joseph. Edward's visit to Vienna was quickly followed by that of the Kaiser and of the Tsar. The difference between the manner of reception of the three Sovereigns was highly significant and clearly underlined by the Viennese newspaper *Die Zeit*. 'The Tsar of All the Russias stepped hastily and timidly from a carefully disguised saloon carriage and drove between thousands of soldiers and policemen, who hardly left room for a thin line of spectators, to Schönbrunn . . . Then away again, between sabres, rifles and bayonets, to another railway station, away to the hunting district of Mürsteg, where gendarmes and detectives waited with quaking hearts for the arrival of one of the richest and mightiest rulers of this world, whose life is so hard to protect.'

In striking contrast to this was the complete absence of security at the reception given to Edward. 'The masses streamed to the railway station to see the interesting guest. Through a thick crowd of human beings waving welcome, a crowd which was not squeezed against the wall by soldiers, the King drove through our city to the Hofburg. He went everywhere freely and fearlessly; he even allowed himself visits to the Jockey Club, not included in the programme, and suited his acts to his mood as though he were an ordinary mortal.' *Die Zeit* summed up the position. 'The Englishman is free and without fear of his King, and the King is free and without fear of his people. Therefore King Edward was not afraid of the Viennese.' On 4 September Edward wrote to Lansdowne: 'My visit to Vienna went off admirably, and I hope to have an opportunity of seeing you and telling you my conversation with the Emperor, and also with the King of the Hellenes at Marienbad.' Sir Francis Plunkett, the British Ambassador in Vienna, informed Lord Lansdowne that 'nothing could have passed off better'.

After Edward came the Emperor Wilhelm. 'Vienna greeted him also heartily in her streets. He also drove in an open carriage through the whole City, and the soldiers who kept the route were more a festive spectacle for a military-minded Kaiser than a protection . . . The Emperor William loves military pomp, but he does not fear his foes. When he enters a crowd, the crowd must know who is coming. Guns must thunder, bayonets glitter and chargers prance. His desire is not to be protected but to be greeted by soldiers when he arrives. Three receptions, three systems. A ruler enjoys the freedom and lives the life which he bestows upon his people.'

During the visit of the King to Vienna Wickham Steed was presented to him. Edward was most impressed by the speed with which he got his news out and desired that in future it should bypass the Ambassador and be sent straight to him. It was most important that the King should be informed with the utmost rapidity. Sir Stanley Clarke, Chief Equerry while the King was at Marienbad, was henceforward to receive Steed's information direct and not via the Embassy. When Edward returned to England, Steed received a telegram from the royal yacht at Flushing thanking him and congratulating him that his news had always arrived thirty-six hours before that from the Foreign Office.

263

Marienbad, a little-known spa in Bohemia, just across the Austrian frontier, had become the meeting place where Edward could discuss, in a relaxed way, the problems of Europe with the leaders of Europe. He combined business with pleasure, but he was doing his job.

In August 1905 Wickham Steed made one of his rather rare visits to England. He was somewhat taken aback.

Despite the German Emperor's visit to Tangier in March, despite the removal of M. Delcassé from the French Foreign Office at German dictation in June, I found the English public as light-hearted and careless as if the world were a garden party. The lessons of the South African war seemed to have been entirely forgotten, and doubts – which German agents carefully encouraged – were freely expressed whether the policy of agreement with France were not a serious mistake . . . But in France, where I spent a fortnight before returning to Vienna, I found an entirely new spirit. After the panic to which M. Delcassé had been sacrificed, France had determined no longer to be made afraid by any German threat. Her people were convinced that death in battle would be better than suicide through fear. So strong was my impression that a new France had arisen, or was arising, that I described it in a public letter to the Editor of The Times on September 6th and exhorted Englishmen also to face the facts and the dangers of the international situation while there might yet be time. Luckily, German insistence upon an international conference on the Morocco question gave an opportunity to England to stand by France; and by the time the Conference met at Algéciras early in 1906, England, France, and Italy had drawn closely together.

In August 1906 Wickham Steed was again at Marienbad while Edward was doing his 'cure'. 'The King,' he writes, 'discussed with me more than once the future of Austria-Hungary and her position in Europe.' It was a great compliment to a journalist and to his profession.

'The King thanked me for having kept him informed in 1904 of events in the Far East, scolded me for having gone to England in 1905 instead of coming to Marienbad, and asked me to report regularly to him upon current news during his stay. Then he began an animated conversation on Austrian and European affairs and told me, in general terms, of his talks with the German Emperor at Friedrichshof, near Homburg, on the way to Marienbad.' In the course of a long conversation Steed disagreed with Edward on one point. 'Quite right,' concluded Edward, 'never mind contradicting me if you think I am wrong.'

In the course of this conversation, Wickham Steed continues: 'Of the Emperor Francis-Joseph the King spoke with affection. One bond between the two sovereigns was their joint distrust of the German Emperor. Of him they talked as often as they met. But in other respects the King of England and the Emperor of Austria had little in common. True, they both desired peace – King Edward because he loved it for its own sake; Francis-Joseph because he feared war. But the one was jovial, confident, open-hearted, big-minded; the other sceptical, irascible and disappointed. Though he was by no means ill-natured and could be courteous with the polished courtesy of the *grand seigneur* of the old school, Francis-Joseph had not the courtesy of the heart. His political character was an enigma.'

Wickham Steed quotes Count Khuen-Héderváry, who had served the Emperor for thirty years. 'I have probably had more experience of him,' he wrote, 'than any other Minister in Austria or Hungary, but I do not, and never shall, feel that I know him . . . An invisible veil has always fallen between him and me, insulating him, as it were, from any current of human sympathy. Behind the veil would be, not a man, but a monarch, persuaded of his own Divine Right and of his own responsibility to none save the Deity.'

On 26 October 1906, Cambon noted, the resignation of M. Sarrien caused a ministerial crisis. It brought Georges Clemenceau to the Presidency of the Council. Cambon welcomed the appointment. 'The arrival of Clemenceau,' he informed his son, 'to the head of the

Government will not change our foreign policy; he is a great partisan of the *Entente Cordiale* with England and will put it into practice more overtly than his two predecessors.' But Cambon was still profoundly pessimistic about the state of his country.

On New Year's Day 1907 he wrote to M. Boppe, French Consul General in Jerusalem. He was chiefly concerned to express disenchantment with the current atmosphere in Paris.

Le *'je m'en fichisme'* est *l'ordre du jour* [the 'couldn't care less' attitude is the order of the day] . . . But they cannot help it, and having blustered against the people, against everything and against themselves, they are resigned to anything. I can see no remedy to a situation the gravity of which our country will not understand until it has reached its full development, that is to say when the ruin of our influence is complete . . . Our Governments don't know what it is all about and never will. They witness, without turning a hair, the downfall of all our achievements over the past fifty years.

Unfortunately there have been all too many similar occasions in our history; we take pleasure in demolishing with our own hands, three or four times in every century, all that we have built up. I hope that France is worth more than Paris, but I find Paris heart-breaking. It does not raise sympathetic vibrations in hearts and minds; it makes me think of the last days of Rome or of Byzantium. The ignoble panic last June revealed the stature of the personalities of the year 1906. I would not swear that a frown on the face of the Kaiser would not be the signal for a new outbreak of panic. It is extremely rare these days to meet, in any social class, anyone who cares for the interests and dignity of the country.

Paul Cambon, perhaps because he was so much in England at the time, did not see the gleam of hope which Wickham Steed had glimpsed in Paris as early as August 1905.

On 26 August 1908 Georges Clemenceau lunched with Edward at

Marienbad. Shortly before this Clemenceau had an interview with Wickham Steed, and Sir Edward Goschen, the British Ambassador in Vienna, asked Steed to produce some notes with which to prime the King.

It turned out to be a very important conversation. Steed had supposed that his notes were intended to prime Goschen who would then relay the gist of the matter to Edward. Goschen, in fact, merely passed Steed's notes directly to the King. Steed was afraid that he had been too outspoken, but Edward told him that Clemenceau had more or less repeated all that was said in Steed's notes. 'They were excellent,' Edward assured him; 'I have sent them on to Hardinge.'

Clemenceau's words were very hard-hitting. 'We must remember,' said Steed, 'that Clemenceau's reputation as an Anglophile is so strongly established that he feels he can talk to us with the utmost frankness; and what Clemenceau says aloud today is what most Frenchmen whisper to themselves – and what they will all shout if a European crisis comes and we are slow to understand its purpose.'

The French Premier did not pull his punches. 'He spoke with the force and velocity of an express train. For nearly two hours he "let himself go". I defended England to the best of my ability and tried to give him as good as he sent. The hotter the fight, the more Clemenceau seemed to enjoy it; and we parted on the best of terms.'

Wickham Steed prints most of these notes in his autobiography.

M. Clemenceau was already aware of the not entirely satisfactory outcome of the discussions on the subject of Anglo-German naval armaments. He spoke with considerable apprehension of the international outlook and appeared to think a conflict probable. 'I believe,' he said, 'that the conflict will be brought about by *some imprudence on the part of English public men* or some untimely movement of English public opinion. In England the exposed position of France is very imperfectly understood. Though there is much talk of invasion by Germany, no one seriously believes it to be possible, and confidence in the power of the British fleet to destroy the German fleet in case of need has not been seriously impaired. But, for France, the danger of invasion is very real. We know that on the morrow of the outbreak of war between Germany and England, the German armies will invade France by way of Belgium. What can England do to help us? Destroy the German fleet? In 1870 there was no German fleet, but the Prussians entered Paris all the same.'

This confidence in the power of the English fleet was beginning to look inadequate. In early 1908 Germany's determination to rival Britain on the seas was becoming serious. The Liberals, however, were clearly desiring to reduce expenditure on our fighting forces in order to increase their budget for social reform. Edward was not happy about this. He believed in having a strong navy and he had a firm faith in the competence of the First Sea Lord, Admiral Sir John Fisher. Perhaps the highest compliment could be said to have come from Lord Esher, who wrote to *The Times* on 6 February 1908: 'There is not a man in Germany, from the Emperor downwards, who would not welcome the fall of Sir John Fisher.'

The Kaiser responded in a letter to Lord Tweedmouth, describing Esher's letter as 'unmitigated balderdash which has created an immense merriment in the circles of "those who know" here . . . This perpetual quoting of "the German danger" is utterly unworthy of the great British nation with its world-wide Empire and its mighty Navy . . . Once more – the German Naval Bill is not aimed at England and is not "a challenge to British Supremacy of the Sea."'

Lord Rosebery made what was probably the most interesting summary of the situation. Speaking in Parliament, he said: 'My only apprehension is that we are making ourselves quite ridiculous by the fuss which has been made. We have seen a whole world of absolutely insane inferences drawn. There is a section of the Press in both countries which seeks to create bad blood. Those sections take up every trivial incident – and this is a trivial incident – to excite morbid suspicions between the two nations which is gradually developing into a danger to European peace.'

On 20 December 1908 Edward commented on a report from Asquith. 'As the increase in naval expenditure is so great I can well understand that there was a considerable difference of opinion between members of the Cabinet. As long as Germany persists in her present programme of shipbuilding we have no alternative but to build double.'

Wickham Steed had discussed all this with Clemenceau who had told him: 'When I asked Sir E. Grey what England would do if the Germans entered and overran Belgium, he replied, 'It would make a great stir in England.' What France would require would not only be a stir but help. One hundred thousand men in Belgium would not be much good, but 250,000 or 500,000 would change the course of the war. As it is, England could not send even 100,000 without the greatest difficulty. Your Territorial Army is a plaything. I am convinced that our position will continue to be one of extreme danger until England has a national army worthy of its name.'

This army was still far from having been made, and even if the men were forthcoming, there did not exist the weapons or the ammunition for them to use. 'These things,' continued Clemenceau, 'cannot be improvised. I know you Englishmen do not want to be entangled in a Continental war, but I ask you, as I have asked Campbell-Bannerman, Haldane and Grey, whether your policy is today what it was a century ago – to prevent the domination of Europe by any one Power? If it is, then you ought to look things in the face.

'If war comes and we are smashed for want of timely and efficient help from you, you will afterwards be obliged to incur obligations vastly greater than any now requisite – or you will have to bow your necks to the victor. I have preached this in season and out of season, and recently in the *Temps* during the visit of President Fallières to London. But it is hard to get Englishmen to look at things from our point of view, or to understand the exigencies of our situation. *Some of your public men are appallingly ignorant.* The fact is that England cannot maintain her position in Europe and in the world, nor can her friendship with France be secure against surprises, unless she has an adequate army.'

Wickham Steed maintains that Clemenceau was wrong 'about the ultimate value of the British Territorial Army, though it was not in 1908 what – thanks largely to Mr Haldane – it had become by 1915. Pregnant, too, are his remarks about the non-existence of the weapons or ammunition for the use of a British national army. That 'these things cannot be improvised' is a truth which we were to learn at the cost of tens of thousands of splendid lives.'

By the end of 1909 Wickham Steed was beginning to get the measure of Edward.

Towards King Edward VII I felt dutiful loyalty as an Englishman; but as a journalist my mind was open. He was the recognized leader of Europe. Whither was he leading her? To some, the turn he had given to European affairs since his accession seemed statesmanship of the first order. To others, including not a few public men in England, he appeared to be an amateur diplomatist, the more dangerous because he wore the British crown. Which was the true view? As I reflected on my first talk with him and analyzed my impressions rather than his actual words, the reasons for his leadership and for the disquietude it had aroused became clearer. He was strongly magnetic – an essential quality in a leader – but his mind moved with a swiftness that could hardly fail to disconcert the slow-thinking among his advisers, who would be likely to find his frankness startling and his directness of purpose uncomfortable. Moreover he accepted and even appeared to welcome contradiction – a rare trait in a sovereign. In any case – an uncommon man and a big man.

Later my experience convinced me that the chief secret of his power really lay in his goodness of heart and honesty of intention. He wished well to the world. While loving England with the encompassing affection that only those can feel who have looked upon England from without and know what she has meant and may mean

270

to foreign peoples, he held her noble among the nations and desired never to forget that *noblesse oblige*.

There was in him no antecedent enmity towards any foreign country, though he could feel fierce resentment against persons who deliberately misrepresented him or sought perversely to thwart him. His purpose was to keep the peace. From it he never swerved. The notion that he wished to 'hem Germany in', to surround her with a ring of hostile states, was either ignorant or malicious, but he knew from long and intimate experience, how devious were German paths and what pitfalls might await those that trod them guilelessly.

The true test of the statesman, as distinct from the mere diplomat or politician, according to Wickham Steed:

lies not only in his ability to overcome difficulties as they arise, but also and especially in his power to put himself in the place of foreign statesmen, to see their problems from their angles of vision, and so to frame his own policy that it may be attractive to them in the light of their own country's interests. The supremely able statesman will not use his power for the immediate profit of his own country alone, or for the ultimate harm of foreign countries, but will strive so to guide events that, in the long run and on balance, the world may recognize his work as having been generally beneficent.

Steed clearly considered that Edward possessed these qualities.

The political conversations which I had with King Edward in August, 1909, made upon me an abiding impression. His grasp of the fundamentals of European politics was greater than that of any contemporary statesman whom I have met. His care for Europe was almost paternal. It sprang from knowledge acquired chiefly by personal experience and observation and from an ever present sense that, though England was the heart and the head of the British

271

LINKS OF FRIENDSHIP
by Linley Sambourne *Punch*, 20 April 1902 and 1903

* Edward VII dances a quadrille with France and Italy. In the background, Portugal.

Empire, she was, and must increasingly be, an essential part of Europe.

Had anyone called Edward a philosopher, he would have smiled; but no public man, certainly no monarch of recent times, has surpassed him in the practical philosophy of statecraft. Many Ministers and Monarchs were 'cleverer' than he. He was not clever, but able. In point of shrewdness King Leopold of Belgium was doubtless his superior, and Ferdinand of Bulgaria might have been more than a match for him in a mere contest of wits. But neither of them had King Edward's essential quality – the sympathetic insight that is born of good will.

In August, 1909, he was perturbed. He seemed to see, in the long run, no way out of the situation which the annexation policy [of Austria] had created or revealed. He felt, rather than saw, that the Emperor Francis-Joseph was not master of his own house and that it would be useless to count on Austria-Hungary as an element of stability. He was not despondent, because despondency was alien to his temperament; and though his health was obviously precarious – there were anxious moments even during his stay at Marienbad – his doubts came rather from a premonition that the task of preserving peace, to which he had utterly devoted himself, would grow harder and harder as time went on.

13

The Death of King Edward

In the course of the year 1909 the King's health was giving increasing grounds for uneasiness. Sir James Reid, now personal physician to Edward, was in fairly continual attendance. On 8 February he accompanied Edward and Alexandra on a state visit to the Kaiser. Relations between the two countries had been marginally better of late and it was hoped that this demonstration might improve them further.

The Controller of the Kaiser's household, Count Trützschler, noted that 'the King of England is so stout that he completely loses his breath when he has to climb upstairs. The Emperor told us that at the first family dinner he fell asleep.' At the lunch at the British Embassy he was 'indisposed for a few minutes, but he eats and drinks and smokes enormously.'

Wilhelm remembered the good services which Reid had rendered him during the last days of Queen Victoria and bestowed upon him the First Class Grand Cordon of the Crown, the ribbon of which was 'very pretty, like the Garter'. He wore it proudly at the Gala Dinner. This was a very sumptuous affair, more impressive in Reid's eyes than any he had experienced at Windsor. 'I was *very* careful with my eating,' he claimed, 'but I *had* to taste various wines that one has a chance of only once or so in a lifetime!' The Kaiser was extremely friendly and gave him a telegraphic code to be used as private cypher in case of emergencies. Thus 'Radium cures can be reckoned with' meant 'please come at once'.

The King was, in Reid's phrase, 'fairly well but not *quite* the thing.' On one occasion he choked and fainted, but this was attributed to the tight collar of his Prussian uniform.

Those closest to the King began to have misgivings. 'For some years before his death,' writes Lord Redesdale, 'his health – though this was not generally known – had caused no little anxiety to his doctors. He was subject to violent fits of spasmodic coughing, from which it sometimes seemed as if he could scarcely recover. The exertion was terrifying to those who witnessed it, and occasionally he appeared to be choking. This was the reason for his annual visit to Biarritz . . . These journeys, which have been ungenerously attributed to the love of pleasure, were really a matter of necessity; they furnished in a mild degree that oxygen which in a pure state is administered to the dying in order to relieve the pain of breathing – the pain from which he so often suffered.'

On 7 March Edward went to Biarritz. The night before, according to Redesdale: 'he gave a great dinner-party – only men. He was in excellent spirits and after dinner went the round of his guests, as was his wont, and chatted gaily with each of them. As he was leaving the room he stopped for a moment to talk to me, and spoke with all his natural cheerfulness, like a boy before a holiday, of his journey which was to take place on the morrow.' By the time he arrived at Biarritz he was 'very unwell'. His old friend the marquis de Soveral was with him and, of course, Mrs Keppel, who was 'much alarmed' at his condition.

The tale of Edward's *amours* would be out of place in this book, but something must be said about Alice Keppel. Sir Charles Hardinge wrote 'a private note' on what he described as 'a delicate matter upon which I am in a position to speak with authority.' He dealt with it delicately. 'Everybody knew about the friendship that existed between King Edward and Mrs George Keppel, which is intelligible in view of the lady's good looks, vivacity and cleverness . . . I would like to pay here a tribute to her wonderful discretion, and to the excellent influence which she always exercised upon the King. She never utilized her knowledge to her own advantage, or to that of her friends; and I never heard her repeat an unkind word to anybody. There were one or two occasions when the King was in disagreement with the Foreign Office, and I was able, through her, to advise the King with a view to the policy of the Government being accepted. She was very loyal to the King and patriotic at the same time. It would have been very difficult to find any other lady who would have filled the part of friend to King Edward with the same loyalty and discretion.'

Back in Biarritz the King's state of health was causing Reid increasing anxiety. 'For a week,' writes Lord Redesdale, 'he seemed to be wrestling with Death: that time he conquered, but the victory was ephemeral. On April 27th he came home. He was well enough, or imprudent enough, to go to the opera, which he never willingly missed. He was devoted to music; it was the poetry that called to his soul. I happened to be sitting in a stall near his omnibus box. I noticed that he was looking very tired and worn. He sat through one act, all alone. Then he got up and I heard him give a great sigh. He opened the door of the box, lingered for a little in the doorway with a very sad expression on his face – so unlike himself – took a last look at the house, as if to say farewell, and then went out. I never saw him again.'

On Monday, 2 May Reid was summoned to the palace at 11.15 p.m. Early next morning, when he got home, he said to his wife Susan: 'the King might recover, as he did at Biarritz, but if not he will be dead in three days.'

On Tuesday Edward got up as usual and set to work, seeing Lord Roberts, who was surprised to note that he was not smoking, and the American Ambassador, Whitelaw Reid. 'Our talk,' the latter observed, 'was interrupted by spasms of coughing and I found he was suffering from a good many symptoms of which I had had such painful experience myself . . . Still he is a man of tremendous vigour of constitution and of extraordinarily energetic habits. The general public think of him as being in perfect health; but I am impressed with the notion that in the inner circles there is more anxiety about him than I have observed at any time before.'

On the next two days, Wednesday and Thursday, he got up but was advised not to talk much. In spite of this he continued to receive in formal audience representatives from the Dominions. On one occasion he had a terrible coughing fit and was urged to rest. But he refused, saying: 'I shall not give in. I shall work to the end.'

On Thursday, 5 May, according to Sir Almeric Fitzroy, Edward declared: 'I am feeling better: I am going to fight this.' That evening, however, a bulletin was issued, signed by Sir James Reid and Sir Francis Laking, which stated that the King was 'suffering from bronchitis and his condition causes some anxiety'.

On Friday Reid reported that Edward was worse. He had had a bad night with much dyspnoea and some cyanosis. Edward was calm and collected. He tried to smoke a cigar, but could not enjoy it. He admitted that he felt 'miserably ill'.

It so happened that the King's horse Witch of the Air was to run that afternoon at Kempton Park in the Spring Two-Year-Old Plate. To everyone's delight and astonishment she won. The news reached Edward just in time.

At six that evening the next bulletin was issued. It described the King's condition as 'critical'. He had sat in his chair all day and when Mrs Keppel called at 5 p.m. 'he barely recognized her'. Alexandra, in what Giles St Aubyn describes as 'a gesture of heroic magnanimity', had invited her to come. At 11 that evening Edward was lifted into bed, quite unconscious, and at 11.45 he died. The Archbishop of Canterbury, Randall Davidson, was present at the end. 'I have,' he said, 'seldom or never seen a quieter passing of the river.'

Lord Grey was spending the weekend at his cottage on the Test. He was not expecting that anything was imminent. But Lord Hardinge sent him a private message to say that he had received very bad news from Buckingham Palace. Grey returned immediately to London, where he was joined by his brother at his house in Queen Anne's Gate, and they sat up together.

'Late at night, all was quiet about us. Presently the silence of the deserted street was broken; something was being cried; we leant out of the window and heard the newsvendors calling "Death of the King!" It is not till a thing has actually happened,' he reflected, 'that we know the full import of it. Prepare for it as we may, try all we may, we cannot beforehand realize all that it will mean to us. I felt that something irreparable, like a landslide, had happened.'

Those who described the impact of Edward's death upon them were naturally led to reflect upon the features of his character and reign. Having recorded his emotions, Lord Grey then proceeded to write his own obituary of the King. There were few more qualified to do so, for of all the wide area of his responsibility, foreign affairs were closest to Edward's heart and of all his ministers the Foreign Secretary was perhaps the closest to him. Lord Grey deserves to be quoted at some length.

To explain what King Edward was it is necessary first to get rid of some misconceptions about him, which have obtained abroad rather than in his own country. A legend arose in his lifetime, which perhaps was believed more widely afterwards, that British foreign policy was due to his initiative, instigation and control. This was not so in my experience. He not only accepted the constitutional practice that policy must be that of his Ministers, but he preferred that it should be so. He read all the important papers, and now and then a despatch would come back with some short marginal comment approving of something contained in it; but comment of any sort was rare, and I do not remember criticism or suggestion.

In conversation he would always show that he was aware of all that was being done and had followed it, but his comments would be on some point immediately in hand. He did not care for long and sustained discussion about large aspects of policy, though he brought strong common sense and good judgement to bear on any concrete matter of the moment. It would be a mistake to infer from this that he was indifferent to the general trend of our foreign policy. It must be remembered that the course for this had been set before I went to the Foreign Office in 1905. I was continuing a policy with which he was already familiar and in sympathy.

He took an active interest in high diplomatic appointments, such as those of Ambassadors, but it was from the point of view of their personal qualities, not from that of policy. He wished us to be represented abroad with dignity and personal prestige.

What, then, were the qualities that made him so important to the country? They are not easy to describe because they were the intangible qualities of a personality peculiar to himself. Let the more commonplace be considered first. He had in a very high degree the gift, proper and valuable in a Sovereign, for ceremonial. No one knew so well as he how ceremony should be arranged, ordered and carried through in the manner most effective and impressive. By his own person, and by the part which he took in it, he added dignity to it. In all this he performed to perfection the function that only the Sovereign can perform for the British Empire . . .

King Edward had a rare, if not unique, power of combining *bonhomie* and dignity. The *bonhomie* was warm and spontaneous, but it never impaired the dignity. His bearing was a perfect example of tact, ease and dignity, and to these were added good sense and judgement that not only avoided mistakes, but perceived the things that should be said to suit the occasion or please an individual. There was, however, something more that gave a spirit and an aspect to it all, and this was due to his individual personality. Warm, human kindness was of the very substance of the man.

He had a capacity for enjoying life, which is always attractive, but which is peculiarly so when it is combined with a positive and strong desire that every one else should enjoy life too . . . I imagine that the humblest devotees of horse racing in a Derby-day crowd knew that King Edward was there to enjoy the national festival in precisely the same spirit as themselves, that their enjoyment was part of his own.

The effect was due, no doubt, to the genuineness of his own feeling; but when all has been said, something is required in the nature of genius to account for this remarkable power of projecting his personality over a crowd.

He became intensely and increasingly popular . . . Popularity such as this, centred in a constitutional Sovereign, was an immense advantage to the State. The position is one which cannot be combined with responsibility for policy. Any association, past or present, of the Sovereign with political controversy would be fatal to it. The manner in which it was filled by Edward, and his great popularity, made him a real asset of national stability . . . His death was felt as a national loss, especially by his Ministers.

Grey goes on to offer an *apologia* for monarchy.

The strength and endurance of the Monarchy has been due to its adaptability to new conditions. The United States and France have shown that Monarchy is not essential to modern states: the British Empire today demonstrates that even in the most democratic country there is a place for Monarchy . . . Certain conditions are necessary. The succession must be hereditary: no other method of choice will give a Sovereign that complete aloofness from rivalry and controversy which is essential to his peculiar position.

Lord Redesdale, one of the men who knew Edward best, gives an intimate picture of the King's character and achievements.

It is a difficult matter for anyone who knew King Edward to write an appreciation of him. The danger of lapsing into indiscretions is obvious. At the same time it is equally clear that those who did know him intimately can give a just estimate of his character; and to leave his portrait to be painted by those who did not know him, or only knew him slightly, however gifted they may be, must inevitably lead to misconceptions and misrepresentations, and that is still more dangerous.

The fact is that King Edward had as many sides to his character as a brilliant has facets . . . No diamond could be more purely clear and honest than King Edward, and it was that pellucid truthfulness which made him so powerful in his relations with foreign sovereigns and statesmen: they knew that when they were dealing with him they had to do with a King as honest as Nathaniel, a man in whom there is no guile.

It is well known that it was through conversation and the press that the Prince acquired that marvellous fund of information which enabled him to hold his own in any company. His memory was phenomenal: he seemed unable to forget. The business of kingcraft is not one that is easy to learn. It is impossible for a King to specialize in any one subject, but he must be sufficiently posted in the trades of all sorts and conditions of men to be able to listen intelligently when they address him upon their own subjects; and to listen intelligently implies knowledge of no mean order.

King Edward did this to perfection, and we must remember one thing, and that is that this power is not acquired all of a sudden, like a miracle conferred upon him by an ointment at his coronation; it was the result of long years of patient attention and enquiry – of those same long years which his detractors would have us believe were spent to exhaustion in the pursuit of frivolous occupations and in the selfish sacrifice of duty to pleasure. No more false charge was ever brought against a man in his exalted position.

He knew not fatigue. That was an immense help to him. In later life he allowed himself more rest, but as a young man he seemed to be almost independent of sleep.

Redesdale recalls an occasion when Edward invited him to Marlborough House after dinner.

We sat smoking and talking of old times for a couple of hours. Towards midnight he got up and said: 'Now I must bid you good night, for I must set to work', pointing to a huge pile of the familiar red boxes. 'Surely,' I said, 'your Majesty is not going to tackle all that work tonight!' His answer was: 'Yes! I must! Besides, it is all so interesting', and then he gave me one of his happy smiles and I left him.

So interesting – that was the frame of mind in which he faced his work – the man we are asked to believe could not be brought to attend to business!

I have no desire to speak unfairly of the article in the 'National Dictionary' [article by Sir Sidney Lee]. In many passages it lavishly praises some of the great qualities of the King, and yet the general impression conveyed is unfortunate. The reader of the future – and it is for the future far more than for the present that such an estimate is important – will rise from the study of this biography with an altogether false impression of its subject. He will see in it the portrait of a man with many lovable characteristics indeed, but with little conception of the high functions to which he was called; he will see a prince self-indulgent, impatient of duty, 'with little political acumen' – these are the actual words used – 'even in those matters of foreign policy in which he took the highest interest, giving little concern to home affairs, unremitting in his devotion to social pleasures, showing aloofness from the working of politics and a certain disinclination hastily to adapt his private plans to political emergencies'. I hope to show that it is in his more favourable comments that Sir Sidney Lee is right, though unfortunately in his hands the beam inclines too much to the debit side.

It is to be hoped that some day a life of the King may be written in which more stress is laid upon the noble features of his nature, and not such exaggerated weight given to those transient foibles which mark the first escape of an ardent youth from pedagogic thraldom.

(It is only fair to add that Sir Sidney Lee ultimately produced a two-volume biography of Edward which goes a long way towards meeting Redesdale's criticisms. Redesdale was writing in 1915. Lee's biography came out twelve years later.)

The King's body remained in his room for nearly a week and Alexandra invited some of his best friends to come and take a last look. Among them was Lord Esher. 'The Queen sent for me,' he wrote in his Memoirs, 'and there she was in a simple black dress, moving gently about his room as if he were a child asleep. The King was lying on the bed in which he always slept. His head was inclined gently to one side. No appearance of pain or death. There was even a glow on his face and the usual happy smile of the dead who die peacefully. The Queen talked for half an hour, just as she always talked to me, with only a slight diminution of her natural gaiety, but with a tenderness which betrayed all the love in her soul.'

Meanwhile the authorities had made the decision that 'the remains of his late Majesty King Edward VII, of blessed memory, should lie in State from 17–20 May.' This had never happened before but it turned out to be fully justified. As Lord Grey said, 'the unprecedented, long-drawn-out procession to pass the bier of state in Westminster Hall was a manifestation of genuine and personal sorrow as well as of national mourning.' The crowd was said to have extended for six miles at one period, Sir Sidney Lee noted, 'and it was estimated that some 250,000 people passed through Westminster Hall during the three days of the lying-in-state.'

The King's coffin was carried down the Mall to Westminster Abbey on a gun carriage drawn by eight black horses, while bells tolled and batteries of guns in Hyde Park fired a farewell salute. As the procession left Buckingham Palace the Royal Standard was hoisted once more, visibly asserting the dictum: 'The King is dead: Long live the King!'

A particularly interesting and moving account of the procession comes from the bandmaster of the Coldstream Guards, Mackenzie-Rogan, who was responsible for the choice and direction of the music. 'It had always been part of my musical faith,' he wrote,

> that the drum was an instrument of great potentialities when used not merely as a supplement to the rest of the orchestra, but as a separate and individual thing – an instrument which could, in its primitive and barbaric way, move the human heart even as the organ and the violin move it. As I heard it in my mind's ear, the music of the drums would open with a soft fluttering which would hardly be audible; gradually the whisper would rise to a tremendous thunder, then fade away into a delicate murmur and finally die away altogether.
>
> It was at the funeral of King Edward that it had its highest emotional and, if I may say so, poetic effect. That was by far the most sorrowful State funeral which I have known. I wanted the drums to tell a story of their own, to reach the very deepest chords of the mourning crowds.
>
> On May 17, 1910, at 10.45 a.m. the massed bands assembled outside the main gates of the Palace . . . The march began. The prelude of the drums started with that faint, far-off beating . . . That the effect was what I had striven for I could see from the very first bars. The people had been talking quietly and reverently, but, as the soft waves of eerie sound fell upon their ears, and as the reverberations swelled and fell and rose again, I could see a great change come over them all. Whispers and movement ceased; men seemed turned to stone; tremulous women were in tears. The drums were carrying their awe-inspiring message into the hearts of all of us . . . They did their work that day almost terribly.

He ends on a very different but deeply touching note.

> At the later procession on May 20, when the body of His Majesty was taken to Paddington Station . . . a great farewell to a great King.

285

As a simple and homely contrast to the Imperial splendour, there were the dead King's charger and his terrier Caesar, led by a gillie, following their master to the last. I doubt if one eye was dry at the pathetic sight of that little white dog paying his last tribute among all those Kings and rulers of the world . . . I can see now the terrier straining at the lead as the train disappeared – striving to follow the master that he loved.

The incident was depicted in the *Illustrated London News*.

The gun carriage was followed by a glittering cavalcade which included nine crowned heads of Europe, all of them related to Edward. They were followed by a procession of twelve carriages for other members of the royal family, together with Theodore Roosevelt and the French Foreign Secretary, Stephan Pichon. Roosevelt had intimated his decision that he would ride on horseback 'dressed in khaki and boots with a Buffalo Bill hat, a sabre and pistols'. Paul Cambon, still Ambassador in London, was now Dean of the Diplomatic Corps and found himself once more concerned with the organization of a royal funeral. At least this time he had his previous experience to guide him. He managed to get Roosevelt into a coach.

'In the twelfth coach,' writes Giles St Aubyn, 'sat a sorrowful figure whom few spectators recognized and whose humble place concealed his real importance.' It was Lord Knollys. Since 1870 he had been Private Secretary and Comptroller and Treasurer to Edward. Lord Rosebery was among the first to think of him. 'After the Family, I think most of you. It is half your life gone; but you can look back to forty years of unstinted and absolute devotion such as I think has rarely been given from man to man. That must be some comfort to you.' Lord Esher added his own appreciation. 'The world-wide tributes of the past week have been very wonderful, and you must have got some little consolation out of them. To me they appear, if you will let me say so, in some measure a recognition of your life's work. Perhaps no-one will ever know quite what you were to the King, but I think I have guessed.' Lord Charles

Beresford was even more personal. 'My dear Francis,' he wrote, 'no-one in the Empire will feel the terrible loss that has been sustained more than yourself . . . You may derive some small consolation from the knowledge that all your friends can never forget your splendid and affectionate devotion to our poor, dead King.'

On Wednesday, 11 May Addresses of Condolence were pronounced in both Houses of Parliament by those most qualified to do so. Clearly this could be no occasion for making remarks of the slightest deprecatory nature, but the speakers were honest and responsible men who would not have stooped to praise where praise was not due.

In the House of Lords the Earl of Crewe, Lord Privy Seal and Secretary of State for the Colonies, moved the Humble Address to the new monarch.

We look back at these last nine years with feelings of thankfulness and of pride. I think we all recognized at the time of the late King's Accession that the task before His Majesty was one of exceptional difficulty. He succeeded at a comparatively advanced age to the great Queen who had become in her lifetime almost a legendary figure, and whose person seemed to be, as it were, part of the British Constitution itself. Whatever King Edward's reign might be, it could not be the same as Queen Victoria's; and now, as we cast our thoughts backwards, we are able sincerely to declare that, though different, the late reign does not suffer by comparison.

His comments on Edward's contribution to the welfare of the Empire do not concern us here, but what he says about the impact of his foreign policy is of great interest.

British Sovereigns do not engage in the direct negotiations and transactions of diplomacy; but His Majesty's influence was none the less real and potent. His close knowledge of the continent of Europe, his freedom from insular prejudice, his absolute straightforwardness

287

– these, added to his position as an elder and beloved relative in so many Sovereign and Princely Houses, all gave him frequent opportunities which he used, needless to say, always for the benefit of this country, and with a perpetual and engrossing desire for the preservation of peace.

The Earl of Crewe was followed by the Marquess of Lansdowne, Edward's partner in the creation of the *Entente Cordiale*. He drew attention to the great number and wide variety of people who found themselves united in mourning. 'We all stand shoulder to shoulder in our desire to express, however imperfectly, our grief and consternation at the common misfortune which has come upon us.' He then passed on to the subject of foreign policy.

I am sure your Lordships must have listened with approbation to the sketch which the noble Earl gave us of the part played by His late Majesty in connection with the foreign affairs of this country. His Majesty has established with the chiefs and with the public men of other States, relations which enabled him to bear, unostentatiously and strictly within the limits of the Constitution, a distinguished and useful part in international affairs, and, to my mind, amongst the many remarkable attributes of the late King, none was more remarkable than his power of creating what I can only describe as an atmosphere of international goodwill and good feeling . . . At this moment I am convinced that there is not a Chancellery in Europe which does not recognize that with the death of Edward VII a great international force has been removed.

Lansdowne sums up with a penetrating appreciation of Edward's particular gifts.

It was not due to any deliberate pursuit of popularity for the sake of popularity, but to his spontaneous, instinctive, I would almost say irrepressible kindliness, and to the tact and good temper which were a second nature to him and which never forsook him throughout his life. It was the possession of these qualities which enabled him to feel as his people felt, to share our emotions, our joys and our sorrows, to take part in our aspirations and hopes, to rejoice with us in our achievements, if anything was achieved and well done; it was the possession of these qualities which led the people of this country to regard His late Majesty, not only as a ruler, but as a friend, and to reverence in him, not only the Sovereign, but the man.

The Prime Minister, Mr Asquith, naturally introduced the subject to the House of Commons.

I speak with the privilege of close experience when I say that wherever he was, whatever may have been his apparent preoccupations, in the transactions of the business of the State there were never any arrears, there was never any trace of confusion, there was never any moment of avoidable delay . . . He had in its highest and best development the genius of common sense.

Here, at home, he was, though no politician, a keen Social Reformer. Already, as Prince of Wales, he had entered with zeal into the work of two Royal Commissions – one on the housing of the Working Classes, the other on the problems connected with the Aged Poor. His magnificent service to our hospitals, both before and after his accession, will never be forgotten.

Asquith might have thought to include in this last statement the name of Queen Alexandra who greatly helped with this work and continued with it after Edward's death.

The last to speak was Mr Enoch Edwards. He spoke not on behalf of the elite but for the masses. He was well qualified to do so. Born in April 1852, he had started working in the coal mines at the age of ten and continued until he was twenty-five. In 1904 he became President of the

Miners' Federation and became a member of the Royal Commission on Mines. In 1906 he was elected Labour Member for Handley.

I do not know that it is necessary that anyone should arise from these benches to assure this House and the country of the sympathy – the earnest and sincere sympathy – of the great masses of the working classes of this country in the loss which the nation has sustained. I do so, however, with a very intimate knowledge of large sections of the industrial community. I assure this House that no loss has been more felt and will affect so much the lives of the great masses of the people as that which we have sustained during the last few days . . . The greatest eulogy that could be paid to anyone will be that which will come from the lowest strata of society – the great and enormous masses of men, women and children who have learned to love and respect King Edward . . . and in thousands of cottage homes will go up in their rare sincerity the honest prayers of honest men and women that the Queen may be sustained in her sad and serious loss.

The newspapers of Europe gave considerable cover to the death of the King. The *Frankfurter Zeitung* for 7 and 8 May tends to see Edward in terms of his connections and relations with Germany. It goes into his German antecedents at some length and is a little grudging in its assessment of his foreign policy. 'In recent years,' it states, 'relations between England and Germany have much improved, for which the King carries much of the credit. The King's death fell in a period of a systematic and dangerous isolation from Germany. Perhaps if the reign of Edward VII had lasted longer he might have come to the conclusion that it would have been better for world peace and for England if the two Germanic Empires had gone about their business in friendship rather than in enervating animosity.'

The next day the same theme was taken up again. 'In Foreign Affairs England moved away from the one-time much valued isolationism by forming a number of alliances. In the initiation of the most important of these relationships, the *Entente* with France, the King played an important part . . . The ultimate value of his whole French policy remains uncertain. It is open to question if it might not have been better, for England as well, to soften the opposition of Germany.'

The Russian paper *Rotch* describes the death of Edward as a great loss 'not only for his own people but for the cause of peace in Europe.' The paper stresses his brilliant diplomatic talent and enormous political successes, some of which were achieved at Russia's expense. 'King Edward was, all in all, the opposite of Wilhelm II. Unassuming, he rejected the pomp of sabre-rattling kingship. He was a thoroughly modern, constitutional King who knew his people and the limits of his God-given office.'

In France *Le Temps* devoted a predictably generous amount of space to the subject. The leading article on 9 May claimed that: 'For us, who knew him as a young man, the eminent role which he has played since he came to the throne has been no surprise. For he has been all along a man of action . . . with common sense translated into action; he managed to be impressive by sheer simplicity . . . He had a deep knowledge of men and was himself profoundly human . . . History will say that he was a great King; we mourn a very staunch friend.'

The Editor added a paragraph on the impact of Edward upon France.

It is, in fact, impossible not to be struck by the emotion with which the news of the King's illness was received in France and its swift and cruel ending. The despatches which I am receiving from all sides show clearly that this reaction has not been less vivid or less profound in the provinces than in Paris. It is really a deeply personal and yet universal feeling which identifies France with the mourning of a friend and a neighbour. In fact, King Edward, as everyone knows, enjoyed a genuine popularity with us, even among the masses . . . He was considered naturally as a friend of France.

It is no less true that the *Entente Cordiale*, twice broken off in the course of the last century, was only resumed thanks to the royal diplomacy. The day after the agreement of 1904, Sir Michael Hicks-Beach [Lord St Aldwyn] paid tribute at Bristol to the personal part played by the Sovereign.

Fifteen days after the death of Edward *Outlook* published an article that was more of an *In Memoriam* than an obituary. Having lain in State in the Great Hall at Westminster, the mortal remains of the King had been transferred to the last resting place of English sovereigns. 'The intervening fortnight,' declared the article, 'his subjects had spontaneously given themselves up to the respectful demonstration of their loyalty, affection and sorrow.' The coffin was, of course, surrounded by 'the massed emblems of regal splendour and historic tradition. But what struck the observer was that it was not Edward *Rex et Imperator*, but Edward *the Englishman* to whom we have paid our last respects.'

14

Epilogue: Europe Goes to War

The death of Edward hastened the catastrophe of 1914. The war might have been postponed: it is doubtful if it could have been finally averted. But Europe had lost its leader.

On 28 June 1914 the Archduke Franz Ferdinand, the heir to the throne of Austria, was shot by a fanatic, Gavrilo Princip, at Sarajevo. Edward Grey was at first sympathetic to Austria. 'But when it began to be presumed,' he wrote, 'that the Serbian Government was itself responsible for the crime, sympathy paused. The theory did not seem to be probable; it was even improbable; a conclusion that could not be accepted without evidence.'

It was the beginning of a period of ever increasing tension between Grey and Cambon. Grey sincerely and passionately wanted peace – but not at any price. He deeply desired to maintain the most friendly relations with France – but not necessarily if that posed a threat to peace. Cambon, like so many Frenchmen of his time, was haunted by the spectre of 1870. Then, they had had no allies in Europe. Now they had an *Entente* with England which had stood the test of the Algéciras crisis, and an alliance with Russia. Russia was in a bellicose mood and might have provoked a war in which France was bound to support her. England, however, was under no formal obligation to support France

293

in these circumstances. The *Entente Cordiale* was facing its severest test.

This is perhaps the place in which to recapitulate the successive stages of the *Entente* and to draw together the main threads.

The movement may be said to have had its genesis in the meeting at Chatsworth at which the Duke of Devonshire, Joseph Chamberlain and the Baron von Eckardstein agreed that the days of 'glorious isolation' were over. As a policy it was not without merit. Lord Salisbury, replying to the approaches of Germany, had said: 'my answer was always that England never gives assurances of unconditional support, unless under existing treaties. Our conduct in any future war will depend largely on the *casus belli*; as that cannot be foreseen , so neither can our attitude be foreseen.'

At a deeper level, however, isolation is dangerous. It is only a short step from insularity. The English tend to lack understanding of foreigners. This is sometimes from a sense of superiority which may have been the offspring of imperialism. This lack of undertstanding is also partly due to linguistic reasons: the Englishman's traditional difficulties with the gallic tongue is notorious.

As Wickham Steed points out: 'those who are not known cannot be loved; and in the latter decades of Queen Victoria's reign, England was not known abroad. King Edward translated her to the continent and gained for her respect and, in some quarters, affection. Whether he talked in English, in French or in German, he always spoke 'European.' It is in this context that his contribution to the *Entente* with France must be seen.

This abandoning of isolation at least opened up the possibility of alliances with other countries. But the first alliance envisaged was between Great Britain and Germany. Chamberlain was in favour of it; Lansdowne was in favour of it. Almost his first move on taking over the Foreign Office was to write to Sir Francis Lascelles, British Ambassador in Berlin: 'we should use every effort to maintain and, if we can, strengthen the good relations which at present exist between the Queen's Government and that of the Emperor.'

In May 1901 a Draft Convention was actually drawn up by the Foreign Office, but, as Lord Newton says: 'the great objection was that neither we nor the Germans were competent to make the suggested promises.'

In August Sir Valentine Chirol, a distinguished member of the staff of *The Times* and author of *Fifty Years in a Changing World*, chronicled the repeated but unsuccessful attempts of the two countries to come to an agreement. In spite of the affection of the Kaiser, manifested on the occasion of Victoria's funeral, in spite of the fact that Chamberlain had asserted that Germany was Britain's natural ally, Bülow had expressed his disapproval and on one occasion provoked a violent outbreak of anglophobia.

Meanwhile the situation in France was beginning to improve. This had been to a large extent due to the work of Thomas Barclay.

Edward's triumph on the occasion of his first visit to President Loubet has already been described. His exact role in the approach to the *Entente* has been variously interpreted. Brook-Shepherd goes so far as to say that during these negotiations Edward 'was behaving as if he was one of his own Ministers'. Ponsonby had said as much. 'The visit to Paris seemed to strain the limitations of a constitutional Monarch to breaking point.'

It is a little difficult not to regard this as an exaggeration. It would perhaps have been advisable on the occasion of the State Visit to Paris for Edward to have taken Lansdowne with him rather than Hardinge. Hardinge had all the makings of a diplomat, but he was not in office at the time. But there was no great outcry and the matter passed off easily. It had been Edward's expressed intention to be a constitutional monarch *in the strictest sense of the term*, and Edward was a man of his word.

The evidence against Brook-Shepherd and Ponsonby is of two sorts, one positive and the other negative. On the positive side is a statement made by Balfour in a letter to Lansdowne dated 11 January 1915. It concerned the publication of a book by Holland Rose entitled *The*

Origins of the War. Balfour writes: 'I was much surprised to see that he quite confidently attributes the policy of the *Entente* to Edward VII – a foolish piece of gossip which prevailed at the time of Edward's death . . . Now, so far as I can remember, during the years when you and I were his Ministers, he never made an important suggestion of any sort on large questions of policy.' Lord Newton endorses this affirmation. 'A study of the correspondence relating to the Anglo-French agreement cannot fail to convince anyone that it was the result of long and laborious work on the part of his Ministers.' The chief credit for the successful negotiation of the *Entente* he gives to Lord Lansdowne himself.

The other evidence is negative. Both the Foreign Secretaries concerned, Lansdowne and Grey, state categorically that Edward did not trespass beyond the boundaries of his position, but that he had achieved a position with the authorities of other countries 'which enabled him to bear', as Lansdowne puts it, 'unostentatiously and strictly within the limits of the Constitution, a distinguished and useful part in international affairs.' Grey endorsed this opinion, adding that the King 'preferred that it should be so'. He goes on to insist that Edward's influence was due to 'intangible qualities of personality peculiar to himself'.

Such charisma defies definition. Wickham Steed, who probably knew more about Edward's reputation abroad than anyone, credits him with 'a sympathetic insight that is born of good will . . . Stay-at-home Englishmen hardly understood what Edward's name and personality meant to continental people. Under him British policy had become calculable and tangible. 'Splendid isolation' had ceased. Isolation on the part of one country is apt to produce in others the same feelings of estrangement or of positive dislike that men cherish towards individuals who keep them at arm's length.'

Edward's strength was that he knew and loved the French. The French like to be known and loved. They respond to those who have taken the trouble to learn and to appreciate their beautiful language and to value their distinguished contributions to the visual arts and to literature. Edward's naughty escapades in Paris as a young man did not incur the censure of Parisian opinion. His later, serious-minded under-standing of international politics gave him a more solid position.

It must be remembered, however, that it was by no means only in France that he exerted this influence. Another occasion on which Edward created this *rapport* was three months after his return from Paris when he made a visit to Ireland. Relations between England and Ireland have nearly always been problematic, but Edward's visit was an unqualified success. George Wyndham, the Secretary for Ireland, describes the outburst of joy with which the King was received – 'an interminable lane of frenzied enthusiasm . . . the King, perfectly calm among dancing dervishes and horses mad with fear and excitement, bowing and smiling and waving his hands to the ragamuffins in the branches.'

Balfour stressed the political advantages of this. 'The popularity among all classes which Your Majesty so deservedly obtained must ever be a powerful element for good in all future developments.' Lansdowne, a man not given to exaggeration, wrote on the same occasion: 'It is impossible to exaggerate the effect produced on the simple people of this glen [Derreen, which he owned] by the kindness of Your Majesty's demeanour; they refer to it constantly and always in terms of good will and admiration.' When Edward died there was no one who could step into his shoes.

By 1914 the picture of Europe had changed, and changed for the worse. Everywhere one looked there seemed to be potential trouble. As regards Russia, Grey felt that 'more allowance should have been made for the inherent instability in Russian Government; for the possibility that, in a moment of great crisis and excitement, the Tsar might be rushed into some imprudent act. It needs more than good will to pre-serve peace in a crisis; it needs steadiness and strength. The Tsar was not strong and the Kaiser was not steady, and in each country there was a militant element.'

Unfortunately England was divided. Neither in the Cabinet, nor in

Parliament and certainly not in the country at large was there any sign of that solidarity and united determination without which a war could not be contemplated.

Grey was in a very difficult position. He makes it clear in his own writings.

The question of whether we went to war would depend on how the war came about. No British Government could go to war unless backed by public opinion. Public opinion would not support any aggressive war for a *revanche*. [The word at this time and in this context always refers to France's desire to recover possession of Alsace and Lorraine.] If, however, Germany was led by her great, I might say unprecedented, strength to attempt to crush France, I did not think we should stand back and look on but should do all we could to prevent France from being crushed . . . Germany had shown a desire for some agreement with us to ensure that we would under no circumstances take part against her if she was at war. But we had decided to keep our hands free. If Germany dominated the policy of the Continent it would be disagreeable for us as well as for others, for we should be isolated. We did not realize how inveterate and deep-rooted at Berlin was the habit of attributing a sinister and concerted motive to any proposal from another country. Nor was it understood, as it would be now, how certainly competition in armaments led to war.

France presented one of the most delicate of the problems which confronted Grey. 'To understand the great and most embarassing difficulty in which the whole Government was placed in answering the French request for a promise of help, it is necessary to review the state of opinion inside and outside the Government. This was very divided up to the last moment; and when there is a division on such an issue as peace and war, it cannot be bridged by formulas.'

Grey had a clear vision of the horrors and of the horrific scale of a modern war. 'I felt that, if the country went in for such a war, it must do so wholeheartedly, with feeling and conviction so strong as to compel practical unanimity. It was clear to me that no authority would be obtained from the Cabinet to give the pledge for which France pressed more and more urgently, and that to press the Cabinet for a pledge would be fatal; it would result in the resignation of one group or the other and the consequent break up of the Cabinet altogether.' Seen from the French angle this constant refusal by Grey to commit Britain to supporting her was agonizing.

At this point an important intervention was made by an article in *The Times*. On Tuesday, 21 July Wickham Steed was lunching with Count Albert Mensdorff, the Austro-Hungarian Ambassador in London and his Commercial Attaché, Baron von Frankenstein. Mensdorff said: 'I appeal to you, as a friend of Austria, to use your influence with the British Press to make the position of Austria-Hungary understood. It is impossible for us longer to tolerate Serbian provocation. Serbia must be punished. But if *The Times* will give the lead, the rest of the press will follow, British public opinion will remain friendly to us and the conflict localized.' Wickham Steed answered: 'I am a friend of Austria and have proved it by warning your people that your policy has been fatally wrong . . . I am too great a friend of Austria to help her commit suicide.'

'Suicide?' answered Mensdorff, 'do you think that we, a country of fifty million people, are so weak as not to be able to deal with a little people of three or four millions like the Serbs?' Steed had his answer ready. 'At the first shot Russia will cry "Hands off!", Germany will summon Russia not to intervene and Russia will refuse . . . Germany will then mobilize and bolt through Belgium into France, and when England sees German troops in Belgium she will intervene against Germany and against you.' It was as good a summary of the situation as could have been made in advance.

While the Foreign Office continued to agonize over the difficulty confronting them, Steed went straight to the office of *The Times* and persuaded Northcliffe 'to speak carefully and cautiously, but very firmly' to the nation. On 22 July a leading article appeared entitled 'A danger to Europe'. 'This article,' claims Steed, 'made a profound impression in England and abroad . . . When the crisis reached its height at the end of July, the British people knew broadly what was at stake and were, in some measure, prepared for the fateful choice awaiting them. In accordance with its best traditions, *The Times* led the country.'

On 28 July Austria sent an ultimatum to Serbia, the wording of which was such that no self-respecting country could have accepted it. Grey described it as 'unexpectedly severe; harsher in tone and more humiliating in its terms than any communication of which we had any recollection addressed by one independent country to another. The Austrian ultimatum was not supported by any evidence of the complicity of the Serbian authorities in the murder.' Austria, secure in the knowledge of Germany's support, was spoiling for a row. It brought the world to the brink of war.

'All this,' continues Grey, 'gave rise to a strong feeling that Serbia was being dealt with more harshly than was just . . . The Austrian ultimatum had gone even further than we had feared in the way of peremptory severity. The Serbian answer went further than we had ventured to hope in the way of submission. Yet Austria treated that reply as if it made no difference, no amelioration. From that moment things went from bad to worse.'

The next day Cambon requested a statement on British intentions. To Grey it was purely a matter of Austrian or Russian supremacy in the Balkans. As he said at the time: 'that one or other of these two powers obtains pre-eminence matters little to us.' But he went so far as to say that 'if Germany aided Austria against Russia and if France was involved, it would be a question of European equilibrium and England would have to consider whether she ought to intervene.'

Cambon then wrote to René Viviani, the French Premier and Foreign Secretary: 'We await from one hour to the next for Germany to demand that we remain neutral while she attacks Russia. Such assurance we cannot give her. We are obliged to aid Russia.' To Cambon there was the danger of another 1870, writes Eubank: 'Germany would overrun France and become the arbiter of Europe while Grey pondered legal technicalities. Cambon regarded the problem from a strategic standpoint, Grey from a legal one.'

On 1 August Germany sent an ultimatum to Russia demanding that she should put an end to mobilization. In Paris, continues Eubank: 'Viviani had informed the German Ambassador that "France will act in accordance with her interests". By 3.45 p.m. the same afternoon the French Government ordered mobilization of the armed forces. At 5 p.m. the Imperial German Government ordered mobilization and by 6 p.m. had declared war on Russia.' Early in the morning on 2 August Cambon received a telegram announcing that Germany had invaded Luxembourg.

At this juncture it so happened that Wickham Steed looked in on the French Embassy in London. Cambon showed him the text of the treaty of 1867 which guaranteed the neutrality of Luxembourg. 'There is the signature of England!' he cried, 'I have asked Grey whether England means to respect it.' Steed asked what reply he had given. 'Nothing! Nothing!' came the answer, 'I don't even know whether this evening the word "honour" will not have to be struck out of the British vocabulary!' Cambon described 2 August as 'the day through which I passed the darkest moments of my life.' It seemed as if the *Entente Cordiale* had come to the end of the road.

During the night of 1–2 August, however, a meeting took place in Chamberlain's house at which the leaders of the Opposition in both Houses of Parliament, Andrew Bonar Law and Lord Lansdowne, agreed to support France. On 2 August Bonar Law wrote to Asquith: 'Lord Lansdowne and I feel it our duty to inform you that in our opinion, as well as that of all the colleagues whom we have been able to consult, that it would be fatal to the honour and security of the United Kingdom to hesitate in supporting France and Russia at the present juncture and we offer our unhesitating support to the Government in any measures they may consider necessary for that object.' This was all that Grey needed.

The evening of 3 August was the crucial one. Cambon sent a telegram to the Quai d'Orsay to say that Grey had carried the day in Parliament with his request to enforce the treaty guaranteeing the neutrality of Belgium. An ultimatum would be sent to Germany. On 4 August Grey informed Cambon that this ultimatum had been sent and that, if no satisfactory reply was received by 11 p.m., the British Government would 'take steps necessary to uphold the treaty'. Cambon asked what would happen if no satisfactory reply were received. Grey replied: 'War.'

Eubank completes the picture. 'Cambon returned to the Embassy around 10.30 p.m. on August 4th, after seeing Grey and obtaining the latest information on the ultimatum to Germany. Before he went to bed after a tiring day, he stopped to talk with some of the secretaries. As the clock struck 11, all fell silent. "Gentlemen," Cambon remarked quietly, "England has declared war." The *Entente Cordiale* had become a fighting force.'

Bibliography & Sources

Amery, Julian & Garvin, J. L., *Life of Joseph Chamberlain* (Macmillan, 1951)

Andrew, Christopher, *Theophile Delcassé and the making of the Entente Cordiale: A reappraisal of French Foreign Policy 1898–1905* (Macmillan, 1968)

Balfour, Michael, *The Kaiser and His Times* (Norton & Company, 1964)

Balfour, Lady Frances, *Life of George, 4th Earl of Aberdeen* (Hodder & Stoughton, 1922)

Barclay, Sir T., *30 Years of French Reminiscences* (Houghton Miflin, 1914)

Bell, P. M. H., *France and Britain, 1900–1940: Entente and Estrangement* (Addison-Wesley Publishing Company, 1996)

Bompard, L.M., *Mon Ambassade en Russie* (Librairie Plon, 1937)

Breteuil, Henri, Marquis de, *La Haute Société, Journal Secret, 1886–1889* (M Jullian, 1979)

Breteuil, Henri-Francois de, *Un Château pour tous cinque siecles de souvenir d'une famille Europeenne* (Philippe Gentil, 1975)

Brook-Shepherd, Gordon, *Uncle of Europe* (Collins, 1975)

Buchan, J., *Memory Hold the Door* (Hodder & Stoughton, 1944)

Bullen, R. J., *Palmerston, Guizot and the Collapse of the Entente Cordiale* (Athlone Press, 1974)

Bulow, Prince von, *Memoirs Volume 2* (Little Brown & Co., 1931)

Cambon, P., *Correspondence Vol 2* (1940)

Chamberlain, Professor M., *The Character of the Foreign Policy of the Earl of Aberdeen* (1960)

Clark, Christopher, *Kaiser Wilhelm II* (Pearson Addison Wesley, 2000)

Combarieu, A., *Sept Ans a l'Elysee avec le President Emile Loubet, de l'affaire Dreyfuss a la Conference d'Algesiras* (Hachette, 1932)

Delcassé, T. *Ou allous nous?* (1882)

Duhamel, Jean. *Louis-Philippe et la Premiere Entente Cordiale* (Pierre Horay-Flore, 1951)

Eckardstein, Hermann, Baron von, *Ten Years at the Court of St James, 1895–1905* (Paul List, 1921)

Esher, Viscount, *The Influence of King Edward and essays on other subjects* (John Murray, 1915)

Eubank, K. *Paul Cambon* (University of Oklahoma Press, 1960)

Fitzroy, Sir A.W., *Memoirs* (Hutchinson & Company, 1925)

Fraser, P., *Joseph Chamberlain: Radicalism and Empire, 1868–1914* (Cassell, 1966)

Grenville, J., *Lord Salisbury and Foreign Policy: The Close of the Nineteenth Century* (Athlone Press, 1964)

Grey, Viscount, *Twenty-five Years 1892–1916* (Hodder & Stoughton, 1925)

Guizot, F., *Embassy to the Court of St James* (Richard Bentley, 1862)

Hanotaux, Gabriel, *Contemporary France* (Archibold Constable & Company, 1903)

Hanotaux, Gabriel, *Histoire de l'Entente Cordiale* (1912)

Hardinge, Lord, *Old Diplomacy* (John Murray, 1947)

Hibbert, Christopher, *Edward VII, a portrait* (Allen Lane, 1976)

Holland, S., *The Duke of Devonshire* (Longmans, 1911)

Holland, S., Lord Knutsford, *In Black and White* (Edward Arnold, 1926)

Jackson, Patrick, *The Last of the Whigs: Political Biography of Lord Hartington, later 8th Duke of Wellington (1833–1908)* (Fairleigh Dickinson University Press, 1994)

Jones-Parry, E., 'Relations between Guizot & Lord Aberdeen', *History Today* (1938)

Lanessan, J. L. de, *Histoire de l' Entente Cordiale* (1916)

Lauzanne, S., *Great Men & Great Days* (D. Appleton and Company, 1921)

Lee, Sir Sidney, *King Edward VII* (2VOLS) (Macmillan Co., 1925)

Lewis, David, L., *Prisoners of Honour: the Dreyfuss Affair* (Cassell, 1975)

Lyttleton, Sarah, Lady, *Correspondence of Sarah Spencer, Lady Lyttleton* (1912)

Mauvois, A., *King Edward VII and his Times* (1933)

Neton, Alberic, *Delcasse (1852–1923)* (Academie Diplomatique Internationale, 1952)

Newton, T., Lord, *Lord Landsdowne* (1929)

Paleologue, M., *Journal de l'affaire Dreyfuss* (Librairie Plon, 1955)

Paleologue, Maurice, *Un Grand Tournant de la Politique Mondiale* (Librairie Plon, 1934)

Ponsonby, Sir Frederick, *Recollections of Three Reigns* (Eyre & Spottiswoode Ltd, 1957)

Porter, Charles Wesley, *Career of Theophile Delcassé* (University of Pennsylvania Press, 1936)

Redesdale, Lord, *King Edward VII: A Memory* (Hutchinson & Co., 1915)

Reid, Michaela, Lady, *Ask Sir James* (Hodder & Stoughton, 1987)

Roberts, Andrew, *Salisbury:Victorian Titan* (Weidenfeld & Nicolson, 1999)

Saint-Rene Taillandier, *Ce Monde Disparu* (Librairie Plon, 1947)

Steed, Wickham, H., *Through Thirty Years* (William Heinemann Ltd, 1924)

Tardieu, A., *La Conference d'Algesiras* (P. Alcan, 1909)

Trevelyan, G., *Grey of Fallodon* (Longman's London, 1937)

Wallace, D. M., *Our Russian Ally* (Macmillan, 1914)

Whittle, Tyler, *The Last Kaiser: A Biography of Wilhelm II, German Emperor & King of Prussia* (Heinemann, 1977)

William II, *My Memoirs, 1878–1918* (Cassell & Co., 1922)

Wilson, P., *The Greville Diary. 2vols* (Doubleday, Page & Co., 1927)

Woodward, E. L., *The Age of Reform 1815–1870* (Clarendon Press, 1938)

Index

Aberdeen, Earl of; Foreign Secretary 9,
    14, 15, 18, 19, 21
Albert, Prince Consort, *Treuer Coburger*
    27, 28, 29
  religion 31
  letter to Edward 37, 38
  death of 38
Alexander II, Tsar 55
Alexandra of Denmark, Princess
  engaged to Edward 36
  and death of Edward 278, 284
Algéciras, international conference 254
Alix, Princess of Hesse 93
Asquith, Herbert; Prime Minister 289
Asquith, Margot 176
Athlone, countess of 76, 79
Aumale, duc d' 49
  collection at Chantilly 68
Austria
  and Serbia 293, 299–300

Balfour, Arthur; Prime Minister 175,
    251

Barclay, Sir Thomas; President of
    Chamber of Commerce in Paris
    150, 178
  impact of Kruger telegram on France
    127
  Marchand at Fashoda 136
  Anglo-French relations 144,
    150
  Combined Chambers of
    Commerce meeting 152
  on Boer war 155
  on French reaction to death of
    Victoria 177
  on British monarchy 178
  contribution to *Entente* 226
  goes to Germany 226
  Franco-German relations 227
Beckett, Ernest; later Lord Grimthorpe
    226
Benckendorf, Count von; Russian
    Ambassador 194
Beresford, Lord Charles 286, 287
Berry, duc de 17

307

Bertie, Sir Francis; Ambassador in Rome
201
and *Entente* 206
French distrust of English 229,
230
Bihourd, Georges; Ambassador in Berlin
235, 236, 238
Birch, Henry; tutor 30, 31, 32
Bismarck, Herbert 75
Bismarck, Prince
meets Lord Salisbury 48
meets Victoria 48
proclaims German Empire 55
on France 48, 63
Wilhelm's opinion of 70
Death of 99
Bompard, Maurice; Ambassador in
Russia 195
Bonaparte, Louis, Prince Imperial 69
Bordeaux, duc de 17
Bradlaugh, Charles 61
Bresson, comte de; French Ambassador
in Berlin 16
Breteuil, marquis de
friend of Edward 58, 59, 70, 71, 72
meets Salisbury 77
Bruce, Robert; Governor 33, 34
Buchan, John 127, 128
Bullen, Roger 20
Bülow, Count; German Chancellor
179
professes to support Britain 180
accepts *Entente* 217
and Morocco 232, 233
objects to isolation of Germany 253,
255
Bulwer, Sir Henry; Ambassador in Spain
19, 20

Cambon, Jules; Ambassador to USA
111
Cambon, Paul; French Ambassador in
London 112, 113, 115, 161
invited to Windsor 113, 230
on Egypt 120
on the innocence of Dreyfus 135
at funeral of Victoria 177
talks with Lansdowne 193
and state visits 206, 213–14
signs *Entente* 218–20
and Morocco 229, 236, 242, 252–4
and Russia 236
on France 242, 265
on Delcassé 236, 237. 242. 245.
252–3
at Algéciras conference 254
on Clemenceau 265
as Dean of Diplomatic Corps 286
tension with Grey 293, 300–1
and Germany 242, 245, 300–2
'England has declared war' 302
Campbell-Bannerman, Sir Henry
leader of Opposition 188
Liberal Prime Minister 257
Caprivi, Leo General; Chancellor 182
Carlos I, King of Portugal 196
Carrington, Charles; Lord Lincolnshire
and Edward 29, 257
special envoy 186
cartoons 62, 100, 105, 114, 115, 117,
132, 140, 141, 152, 174–5, 208,
272
Cecil, Lady Gwendoline 53, 65
Chamberlain, Joseph
receives Edward in Birmingham 61–2
Foreign Secretary 121
and Delcassé 138

and isolationism 140, 173, 293
and *Entente* 213
and War 301
Chambord, comte de 1, 56, 67
Charles X, King of France 1
Charmes, Francis; journalist 239
Chatsworth, conference at 171
Chirol, Sir Valentine; *The Times*
   correspondent 179, 295
Churchill, Lord Randolph 95
Churchill, Winston 122
Clarendon, Earl of 28
Clemenceau, Georges 54
   publishes *J'accuse* 129
   denounces condemnation of Dreyfus
   131
   becomes Premier 265
   as an anglophile 266–7
   pleads for British re-armament 268
Clifden, Nellie 36
Cobden, Richard 46
Combarieu, Abel; Secretary to Loubet
   101, 250
Coombe, Sir George; phrenologist 30
Courcel, baron de; Ambassador in
   Berlin 218
Crewe, Earl of; Lord Privy Seal 287–8
Crispi, Francesco; Italian Premier 89
Cromer, Lord; Consul General in Egypt
   214

Davidson, Randall; Bishop of
   Winchester
   at death of Victoria 163
   on death of Edward 278
Decases, duc de; Foreign Secretary 72
Delcassé, Théophile 85–6, 96–7, 98, 220
   writes 'ou allons nous?' 87

on Triple Alliance 87, 90, 95
Franco-Italian relations 87, 109,
   111
and Anglo-French relations 88, 95,
   111–12, 210
Franco-Russian alliance 91, 95,
   101–2, 108
on danger of Germany 89, 234, 235,
   237
and Colonial France 97, 98
becomes Foreign Secretary 98–101
and the USA 110, 111
and Morocco 111
and Sudan 121
on Fashoda 138–9
and the *Entente* 213–18, 225
extreme fatigue 230–1
and talks with Edward 236
the Kaiser and the fall of 234–40,
   246, 249–50
Devonshire, Duchess of 171
Devonshire, Duke of
   political career 172–5
   cartoon of 174–5
   end of 'glorious insolation' 294
Dilke, Sir Charles
   attacks Monarchy 61, 64
   defeated in Commons 64
   friend of Gambetta 57
   dinner with Churchill & Edward
   58
Disraeli, Benjamin 82
Dogger Bank episode 106–8
Donnersmarck, Prince Henckel von
   237–8, 239, 240
Duff Cooper, Alfred 3, 156
Dufferin, Lord; Ambassador in Paris 143
Dreyfus, Alfred 129, 131

Eckardstein, Baron von; acting
    Ambassador in London 112, 113,
    171, 181
  on Jameson Raid 122–3
  on Kruger telegram 126
  on Caprivi 181
  desires rapprochement 206
  end of 'glorious isolation' 294
Edward, Prince of Wales
  birth 27
  childhood 25, 29
  Education 32–3, 35
  Travel 34
  relationship with Nellie Clifden 36, 37
  marriage to Alexandra 38
  becomes Duke of Cornwall 39–40
  visit to Paris 44
  visit to Germany 46
  Spanish revolution 49
  gets typhoid 62–3
  death of Prince Imperial 69
  acceptance of French Republicanism
    70, 73, 79–80, 81, 96, 195
  and European Conference 82–3
  Russian sinking of British vessel
    106–7
  outrage at French cartoons 115
  visits Suez Canal 119
  the Kruger telegram 125
  death of Victoria 165
  becomes King 167–71, 185, 187, 191,
    192
  a devout Anglican 190
  interest in Russia 194
  cruise in Mediterranean 194, 196–204
  signing of Entente Cordiale 218
  and Kaiser 225, 232, 234
  private talks with Loubet 237

  meets Delcassé 237
  and Campbell-Bannerman 257
  visit to Emperor Franz-Joseph 262–3,
    265
  and the English fleet 268
  as a European statesman 271, 272–3,
    287–91
  failing health 275, 276, 277–9
  visits Kaiser 275
  visits Biarritz 276, 277
  and Mrs Keppel 276–7
  death, to lie in state 279, 284–7, 290,
    291, 292
  character 280–3
Edwards, Enoch; MP 289, 290
Enghien, duc d' 1
Entente Cordiale
  proposed by Louis-Philippe 19
  rejected by Lord Palmerston 23
  Entente Cordiale Society 147, 148
  rapprochement and state visits 201–12
  Delecassé and Lansdowne
    negotiations 213–17
  signing of 218
  reactions to signing of 218–28
  ratification of 228
  and Germany 217, 224–8
  resignation of Delacassé 252–3
  conference at Algéciras 254, 259–60
  and Grey 257
  and Clemenceau 265–6
  death of Edward 288, 290–1
  tension within 293–6
  becomes a fighting force 298–302
Entente Cordiale Society 147, 148
Esher, Lord 284, 286
Esterhazy, Prince Paul; Austrian
    Ambassador 5

Eugénie, Empress
   visit to London 43
   learns of defeat at Metz 51
   escapes to England 52
Exhibition in Paris, 1876 79

Ferdinand VII, King of Spain 19
Fisher, Admiral Sir John 268
Fitzroy, Almeric 175–6, 278
Franco–Scottish Society 144, 146
Frankenstein, Baron; Commercial
   attaché 299
Franz-Ferdinand, Archduke of Austria
   murdered at Sarajevo 293
Franz-Joseph, Emperor of Austria 262,
   265
Frederick, Crown Prince 75, 77

Gambetta, Léon
   escapes in a balloon 55
   and Edward 57, 58, 60
   death of 59
Gladstone, William Henry 29
Gladstone, William; Prime Minister
   on Egypt 120
   education of Edward 168
Grammont, duc de; Foreign Secretary
   declares war on Germany 49
Granville, Earl of; Ambassador in Paris
   Foreign Secretary 7
   visits Thiers 68
   Edward dines with 80
Greville, Charles 3, 22
Grey, Sir Edward; Foreign Secretary 257
   crisis at Algéciras 254
   relations with Metternich 255
   and Edward's death 278–81
   apologia for Monarchy 281

and Cambon 293, 301
and war 298–9, 300–2
Guizot, G. 7–8, 9, 10, 11, 18, 19

Haldane, Richard; later Viscount
   secretary for war 256
   creation of Territorial army 270
Halsbury, Lord; Lord Chancellor 189–90
Hamilton, Lord Ernest 159
Hanotaux, Gabriel; journalist and
   historian 86, 147
Harcourt, comte Bernard de;
   Ambassador 72
Hardinge, Sir Charles; Ambassador to
   Russia 107
   Edward's accession 187
   accompanies Edward on tour 196
Hatzfeld, Count von; Ambassador in
   London 122–3, 183
Hintzpeter, Georg; tutor to Wilhelm
   74
Holland, Sydney; later Lord Knutsford
   191
Holstein, Baron von 182

Japan
   Mikado declares war on Russia 106
   new fleet destroyed 108
Jameson Raid 121
Joinville, Prince de 13,15–16

Kaisers, Year of the Three 77
Keppel, Mrs George; Edward's last
   mistress 276, 278
Kingsley, Charles; Edward's tutor at
   Cambridge 35
Kitchener, Field Marshal
   at Fashoda 137

Knollys, Sir Francis; private secretary to
    Edward 161, 234
  in funeral procession 286
Kruger, Paul; President 123–4
  visit to Paris 155–6

Lansdowne, 5th Marquess; Foreign
    Secretary 158–61
  talks with Kaiser 179
  and Germany 180
  'marcher d'accord' with France
    193
  talks with Delcassé 209–10, 213
  signing of Entente 217, 218–21
  talks with Cambon 244–5
  on resignation of Delcassé 252
  on death of Edward 288–9
Lauzanne, Stéphane; journalist 248
Lee, Sir Sydney; biographer 283
Leo XIII, Pope
  receives Edward 200
Leopold of Saxe-Coburg 4
Liddell, Dean of Christchurch 33
Lieven, Princess 8
Loubet, Emile; President of France
  at Rambouillet 101
  visits Rome 198
  and Edward's visit to Paris 198, 202
  visit to London 207
  supports Delcassé 240
Louise, Queen of Belgium 12
Louis-Philippe, King of France
  offered the throne 1
  entertains Victoria 12–13
  return visit to England 18
  Order of the Garter 19
  proposes Entente 19
  abdicates 24

Lyons, Lord; Ambassador in Paris 51,
    57, 81
Lyttleton, Lady; governess 28

Macmahon, Maréchal
  defeated at Worth 51
Marchand, Captain
  At Fashoda 116, 121
Marienbad; spa in Bohemia 264, 267
Marschall, Baron von; Foreign Secretary
  and Kruger telegram 126
  'étranger aux affaires' 183
Mary, Queen of Scots 146
May, Princess of Teck 167
Melbourne, Viscount 29
Mensdorff, Count Albert; Austro-
    Hungarian Ambassador 299
Metternich, Count; German
    Ambassador 256
Millenium Exhibition, Paris 150
  Edward chairs British Commission
    152
Milner, Viscount 122, 128
Milner, Viscountess 124, 129
Monson, Sir Edmund; Ambassador in
    Paris
  on French cartoons 114
  demands withdrawal of Marchand 137
  British distrust of French 150
Morocco
  importance to France 213–15
  abandoned by Britain 219
  German interest in 228
Mouravief, Count; Foreign Minister 101

Napoleon Bonaparte
  on Egypt 119
  ashes returned to France 25

Napoleon III; Emperor 41
   visit to London 42
   visit of Victoria to Paris 44
   commands French army 50
   defeated 51
Napoleon, Louis; Prince Imperial 69
Newton, Lord
   on Lansdowne 160, 221
   on Royal tour 196
Nicholas II, Tsar
   accession and coronation 93
   belief in Divine Right 93
   war with Japan 106
   visit toVienna 262
Nicolson, Sir Arthur; Under Secretary
   at Foreign Office 115

Ollivier, Emile 47
Orléans, duc d' 15
Orléans Hélène, duchesse d' 14

Paléologue, Maurice; Ambassador in
   Russia 91, 92
   on Dogger Bank 106, 107
   on Holstein 181–2
   on the Entente 217, 219
   German opinion hostile to Entente
   227, 228
   Russia–Japan relations 230
   the fall of Delacasse and 230, 231,
   232
   Kaiser welcomed in Tangier 233
   diplomatic mission to Berlin 235–6
   meets Donnersmarck 238
   closer Anglo–French relations
   243–4
Palmerston, Lord; Foreign Secretary 5,
   8, 9

disliked by Louis-Philippe 22
   rejects Entente 23
   no longer Foreign secretary 42
Paris, comte de 70
Parkinson, Sir Roper; Founder of
   Entente Cordiale Society 147
Peel, Sir Robert 14
Pelouse, Mme 145, 146
Ponsonby, Sir Henry; Private Secretary
   to Queen
   Victoria against French alliance 72
   on death of Victoria 164, 176
   on Edward 188
   and Royal tour 197, 199, 206
Press, British
   increasing influence of 160
   European appreciations of Edward
   290
   on Edward as King 292

Radolin, Count von; Ambassador to
   France
   'plays down' Edward's visit 202
   German acceptance of Entente 217
   talks with Edward 237
Redesdale, Lord
   on Edward at Eton 29
   Edward as host 168
   Edward a devout Anglican 190
   account of coronation 192
   fears for Edward's health 276
   Edward's stag party 276
   on death of Edward 281–3
Reid, Lady 161
Reid, Sir James
   medical attendant to Victoria 161–5
   accompanies Edward to Berlin 275
   Edward's last days 277–9

Renals, Sir Joseph; Lord Mayor of
London 147
Rhodes, Cecil 121
orders Jameson Raid 121
Rochfoucauld-Bissacia, duc de la;
Ambassador 73
Rodd, Sir Rennel; Councillor in Rome
200
Roosevelt, Theodore, President
at funeral 286
Rosebery, Lord; Foreign Secretary 170
forwards dispatches to Edward 170
predicts war 228
on suspicions of Germany 268
comforts Knollys 286
Rouvier, Maurice; ex-Premier
against Delcassé 238, 246
opposes relations with England 241
Foreign Minister 252
Russia
sends new fleet to Japan 106
Dogger Bank crisis 106–8

Saint-Cloud, château 45
Salisbury, Marquess of
meets Bismarck 48
pro-French 53, 66
anti-German 54
parliamentary career 64, 65
on French Revolution 67, 151
congratulates Edward in speech 81
on French cartoons 115
on Egypt 121
on Jameson Raid 121
and Dreyfus case 134
and Fashoda case 137
advises Edward 151
retires from Foreign Office 157

gives Edward access to documents 170
on death of Victoria 171
Smuts Jan Christian 122, 123, 127
Soveral, Marquis de; Foreign Minister in
Portugal 196
Spanish Throne 19, 20
Spuller, Eugène; editor 86
Foreign Secretary 109
Steed, Henry Wickham
reporter to The Times 212
expert on Austria 261
presented to Edward 263
talks with Edward 265
talks with Clemenceau 267
character of Edward 270–1, 296
talks with Mensdorff 299

Talleyrand, Prince de; Ambasador in
London 3, 4
Temple, Frederick; Archbishop of
Canterbury
at first Privy Council 187
crowns Edward 192
The Times
details of Entente 222–4, 225
on Serbia 300
Thiers, Louis-Adolphe; President 56
Tirpitz, Alfred von; admiral 184
Treves, Sir Frederick
operates on Edward 191

Vaughan, Cardinal 189
Victoria, Princess (Vicky)
marries Wilhelm II 74–5
Victoria, Queen
and Louis-Philippe 12, 21
seeks rapprochement 16
in Coburg 21

birth of Edward 27
as a mother 28
Edward not in love with Alexandra
36
blames Edward for death of Albert 39
refuses Edward training 168
first English sovereign to go to Paris
45
writes letter to her people 63
Golden Jubilee 71
receives Cambon at Windsor 113
disgusted by Wilhelm II 124
deplores Kruger telegram 124
declining health 161–5
death of 165, 176
symbol of an age 167

Wilhelm II, Kaiser
birth 74
childhood 74, 75–7
memoirs 78
Divine Right 102
'Yellow Peril' cartoon 102
Dogger Bank 106
claims 'Weltreich' 123
telegram to Kruger 123
on death of Victoria 165
visit to Tangier 233
demands dismissal of Delcassé 239
demands international conference
252
visit to Vienna 262
Germany's supremacy at sea 268